Richard Henry Wilde

His Life and Selected Poems

RICHARD HENRY WILDE

By J. Eastman Johnson. Reproduced as an engraving by J. Sartain
in Rufus Griswold, *Prose Writers of America* (1847)

Richard Henry Wilde

His Life and Selected Poems

By

EDWARD L. TUCKER

UNIVERSITY OF GEORGIA PRESS

ATHENS

To the Memory of

MY MOTHER AND FATHER

PS 3316
. T8

GL Storage

Copyright © 1966
University of Georgia Press

Library of Congress Catalog Card Number: 66-16984

Printed in the United States
by Printing Department, University of Georgia

Contents

Preface

THE combination of politician and pioneer in Italian scholarship is unusual in American literature, especially in Southern literature. And yet Richard Henry Wilde, who derived his income almost entirely from the practice of law and from his duties as a member of the national House of Representatives, spent over five years in Italy writing biographies of Tasso and Dante and translating numerous Italian poems.

This combination of interests, however, did not escape criticism. Rufus Griswold, who included Wilde in both of his anthologies on poets and prose writers of America, stated: "His miscellanies, in several magazines . . . are elegant and scholarly, and make us regret that his whole attention has not been given to letters."* On the other hand, Stephen Miller, who appreciated his skill as a lawyer, believed that Wilde's finding "many a shining particle of Italian lore, about as interesting to the bulk of mankind as the *agonies* of a naturalist over the geometrical skill and gossamer fabrics of a very wise but unpopular insect" was really "a sacrifice of himself much regretted by many of his partial countrymen."**

There is no satisfactory long account of Wilde's life; his original poems have never been collected; only two or three of his translations, exclusive of those from the works of Tasso, have been published; and his prose works remain almost entirely in manuscript. This work attempts to correct some of these deficiencies.

Some of the people who have helped me by sending information about Wilde are the following: Mrs. Lewis Chase of Washington; Mr. Jefferson Davis of Tucson, Arizona; Mr. J. I. Giraud of San Antonio, Texas; Mr. Vyvyan Holland

---

Prose Writers of America (1847), p. 268.
**Bench and Bar of Georgia* (1855), II, 360-367.

of London; Mrs. Arthur Loving of New Orleans; Professor Thomas O. Mabbott of New York City; Mrs. Penland Mayson of Augusta, Georgia; Dr. George Raffalovich of New Orleans; Mr. Joseph Cumming of Augusta; and the Reverend Arthur Weltzer of Augusta.

The following people and institutions have given me permission to quote from manuscript material in their collections: Mrs. Virginia Giraud Crockett of Los Angeles; Miss Nannie H. Rice of State College, Mississippi; Mr. David Richardson of Washington; Mr. Aubrey H. Starke of Washington; Mrs. Kathleen Wilde Viscarra of Los Angeles; Mrs. Emily P. White of Augusta; Boston Public Library; Library of Congress; Duke University; Harvard University; Historical Society of Pennsylvania; Henry E. Huntington Library; Longfellow House, Cambridge; New York Historical Society; New York Public Library; University of Georgia; University of North Carolina; University of Virginia; and New York State Library.

I have especially enjoyed correspondence about Wilde with two other English teachers: Miss Nathalia Wright of the University of Tennessee, who sent me numerous sources and copies of manuscript letters; and Ralph Graber of Muhlenberg College, who wrote a University of Pennsylvania dissertation entitled *The Fugitive Poems of Richard Henry Wilde with an Introduction* and who helped in determining correct readings of many of the poems in manuscript. Professors William Ritter, Thomas MacAdoo, Roy Ellis, and Tench Tilghman aided in various linguistic problems. This work was first suggested by Professor Edd W. Parks of the University of Georgia, who has remained a courteous guide and a close friend. It was submitted to the publisher several years ago but had to be returned when Mrs. Crockett sent me, for temporary use, several boxes of Wilde manuscripts. These manuscripts may in future years be housed in the Library of Congress.

I have been aided by the staffs of the various libraries that I visited, especially the Library of Congress and Mr. David C. Mearns, Chief of the Manuscript Division. At the Longfellow House in Cambridge, the curator, Mr. Thomas H. de Valcourt, was gracious and hospitable. I certainly cannot overlook the assistance of Mr. John W. Bonner and Mrs.

William Tate of the University of Georgia Library, who were diligent in their attempts to find for me Wilde material. At Virginia Polytechnic Institute, Miss Gladys Johnson, Miss Lucy Lee Lancaster, Mrs. Thomas Wright, Miss Agnes Davis, and Mrs. Hazel Hubbard helped me to secure important information. Financial grants from the Alumni Foundation of the University of Georgia and the University Center in Virginia helped to bring the work to completion.

Of all those who have aided me, I am most deeply grateful to two fine people: Mr. Aubrey H. Starke, who, after working several years on a book about Wilde, turned over to me in the summer of 1955 all the material he had collected; and Mrs. Virginia Giraud Crockett (Mrs. John Crockett), the great-granddaughter of Richard Henry Wilde and the owner of the literary property rights to all Richard Henry Wilde manuscripts.

EDWARD L. TUCKER

English Department
Virginia Polytechnic Institute

PORTRAIT OF WILDE BY AN UNKNOWN ARTIST
Owned by the Augusta Museum

Part One
LIFE

WILDE'S HOME IN AUGUSTA
Now owned by Mr. Craig Cranston

I

Dublin and Baltimore, 1789-1802

WHILE Richard Henry Wilde was in Florence, Italy, searching through the family trees of Dante and various other authors, he decided to see whether he could find out anything about his own background on his father's side, but he had little success. He already knew that his father was named Richard and that his grandfather was called Michael. In addition he learned that the name Nicholas appeared frequently here and there in the family tree. He believed the De Wildes were originally Dutch, but just when the De Wildes or Wildes arrived in Ireland, he could never determine. Though the family name Wilde was an uncommon one, he had the feeling that at some time or other it would "make a noise in the World."[1]

Richard Henry Wilde, the son of Richard Wilde and Mary Newett Wilde, was born in Dublin, Ireland, September 24, 1789. The Newitt (or Newett or Newet) family was a prominent one in Dublin of that day, the occupations of two members being linen weaver and dyer. Since the Newitts belonged to the Irish branch of the Anglican Church, they could hold public office; one Newitt ran for a political position in 1767. Mary Newitt was the daughter of Jonathan Newitt, a strong Royalist, and her mother's maiden name was probably Mary Gorman, for a marriage license was issued to a Jonathan Newett and a Mary Gorman in the Dublin Diocesan Consistory Court in 1760. Mary Newitt's brother, John Newitt, who owned some flour mills in America, sold them at the beginning of the Revolutionary War and returned to Ireland.[2]

An ironmonger and hardware merchant at 12 High Street, Dublin, in 1784-1785, and later at 73 Thomas Street from 1786-1795, Richard Wilde became a partner in the firm of

Wilde and McCready, Button Manufacturers and Hardware Merchants, 73 Thomas Street, and remained there from 1796 until 1800. He married Mary Newitt on July 20, 1783, and they had twelve children—Michael, Mary, John, James, Ann, Richard, Elizabeth, James, Catherine, Ann, John, and Ann. Four of the children died as infants while Richard and Mary Wilde were still in Dublin. Ten of the children were born in Dublin; the last two were born in Baltimore, Maryland.[3]

Although Richard Wilde decided to come to America, he did not sell all his belongings in Dublin, for he was afraid that he might not like the new country and would want to return home. When he loaded a vessel owned by Captain Richard Lemon, he had a definite understanding with the latter gentleman that when the ship arrived in America it would be sold, with the profits to be divided between them. The ship left England in the summer of 1796, and shortly afterwards Lemon and Wilde formed a partnership in America. But Lemon died soon after arrival in America. A notice in a Baltimore paper in the fall of 1796 stated that Richard Wilde, who was the "surviving partner" of the firm of Lemon and Wilde, was opening a store at 165 Market Street, Baltimore, and had for sale various kinds of clothes such as "superfine and refine cloths of the most fashionable kind" and "Barcelona and Bandana handkerchiefs." In addition the store sold a wide assortment of hardware and "ironmongery." All the goods had been "selected and laid in a few months since by Richard Wilde, when in England."[4]

Richard Wilde returned to Ireland; and in December, 1796, he, his wife Mary, and their six surviving children—Michael, Mary, Richard, James, Catherine, and Ann—left for America. The ship also carried additional merchandise, for when it arrived in Baltimore, Maryland, in January, 1797, Mr. G. Prestman seized both the ship and cargo, stating that everything belonged to the estate of Captain Lemon. After an expensive law suit, Richard Wilde managed to recover his share.[5]

Some members of the Wilde family had belonged to the Church of Ireland while in Dublin; but, after arrival in America, they became Catholics. Richard Henry Wilde remained a Catholic throughout his life, though not an ardent one.[6]

[2]

The bitter rebellion of 1798 broke out in Ireland, and Richard Wilde regretfully learned that all his property in Dublin had been confiscated and that his partner McCready had been convicted of high treason. With the loss of his property there, Richard Wilde had to depend solely on his business in Baltimore. In 1799 he struggled as ironmonger at 130 Baltimore Street and in 1800-1801 as a hardware merchant at 159 Baltimore Street.[7]

When one child, Ann, died soon after arrival in Baltimore, the parents, who were fond of the name, gave it to another daughter born in the United States. On July 20, 1802, Richard Wilde's oldest girl Mary, just slightly over seventeen, was married by a Roman Catholic priest to Thomas Pasley of Baltimore County.[8]

When Richard Henry Wilde was very young, he suffered a great deal from bad health; in fact, he was for a while not expected to live. Throughout his life he was never very strong and often complained of illness.[9]

The future poet, who was eight years old when the family moved from Dublin to Baltimore, had very little formal education. He spoke of this lack years later:

Never in my life having had the advantage of instruction in a school or from a tutor, more than a year altogether, and at distant intervals, I was wholly uneducated, except the fruits of my own acquirement, an imperfect knowledge of French, Spanish and Italian, a still slighter smattering of Latin, and such superficial acquaintance with the times, laws and history I was about to investigate, as might be gathered from a single perusal of a few modern histories.[10]

For a brief period he had a tutor in Baltimore, who taught him writing and Latin grammar; and he may have attended an academy for a short while. Most of his education that was not self-taught, however, came from his mother, who wrote some works "remarkable for their vigor of thought and beauty of versification"; in fact, some of these works survived at least until 1855. In addition, Richard Henry Wilde's poor health caused him to be naturally retiring, and he spent all of his leisure time reading. All his life he was a student. In 1842, just five years before he died, he wrote to one of his sons:

The very little Latin I had, was of the greatest importance to me, and I felt so sensibly the want of much more, that even now at 52 I am reading Latin more or less every day to try and make up my deficiency, which I have often bitterly regretted (tho' it was not my fault) and after I get on a little farther with my German, have serious thoughts of attacking the Greek![11]

Wilde, in his long poem *Hesperia*, spoke intimately of Baltimore, which to him was the "nurse of [his] infant days" and the "scene of [his] boyish dangers, griefs, and plays." He loved its hills, woods, and streams.[12]

Wilde's first sweetheart—the first of many—was an "innocent and lovely girl" named Agnes, who was about his own age, not quite thirteen. He, she, and her brother formed a happy group. Once he told her of his affection but was forced to add that they could never marry, for he had no fortune. She, in her innocence, said that the attachment was mutual, and she was confident that there would really be no financial problem, for her father was rich and certainly there would be enough money for all. But the sweethearts soon separated; when Wilde saw her as a married woman later on, she had completely forgotten him.[13]

Richard Wilde was unable to make much profit from his business, a condition which his son called simply "the embarrassments of my father"; consequently, Richard Henry Wilde in his eleventh year started to work in the store so that none of the tiny hoard of money would trickle into the hands of those outside the family.[14]

Finally Richard Wilde died on October 13, 1802, still a young man of thirty-eight years; he was buried in the city to which he had come only six years before. Wilde spoke of Baltimore as containing the "grave of [his] sire!"[15]

The father died without leaving a will, and on October 20, 1802, Mrs. Mary Wilde and two friends, John Crawford and Laurence Sylvester Thelan, bound themselves to the State of Maryland for the sum of ten thousand dollars. This bond would become void after Mrs. Wilde had faithfully performed the duties required of her by law as administratrix of the estate of her husband.[16]

On December 8, 1802, she presented an inventory of her husband's possessions. The list, which had a total value of

$2412.13, included a very large number of hides and skins, some locks and hinges, buckles and buttons, dry goods, and such other items that the merchant of a general store might have on hand; in addition, it had a number of articles of household furniture as well as other items such as two cows, two horses, one hog, and one Negro boy six and a half years old, the latter valued at fifty dollars.[17]

Some means of support had to be found for a widow with several dependent children; therefore, Richard Henry Wilde set out for Augusta, Georgia, in 1802 to find work.

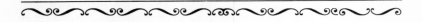

II

Georgia: 1802-1835

WILDE loved Augusta, his "more than place of birth," "the quiet village" where he spent his early days either in "humble grief or rustic mirth." Even though he traveled to many other places, he, nevertheless, hoped to die in this Georgia town. Augusta, "the spot where [his] hopes & affections first grew," was far more precious to him than Dublin, the city in which he had been born.[1]

Augusta was a popular town for Irish immigrants. Wilde's brother, Michael, five years older than the future poet, journeyed there from Baltimore and discovered that he was able to make a decent living. He suggested that his younger brother —only thirteen at the time—should also come to Augusta and try his fortune.

Wilde took the suggestion and was able to find employment in a store owned by an old Irish friend, Captain John Cormick. The latter had been born in Dublin, Ireland, in 1762 and throughout his life remained a devout Catholic. Cormick, to whom Wilde wrote a tender epistle, had fought for his homeland in the Irish Revolution; consequently, he "became a mark'd object of vengeance to British misrule in Ireland, and was compelled to leave his native country." After coming to America in 1799 with other Irish patriots, he lived in Augusta for the rest of his life.[2]

The store owned by Cormick, who had the title of Captain from an army unit that he belonged to, advertised many kinds of items, such as bacon; "Spanish Segars, of Superior Quality"; "one trunk of cotton and silk hosiery, with elegant embroidered clocks; . . . One cask of Baltimore Manufactured Chewing Tobacco, and one of Double Battle Gun-Powder"; and even a cider boiler and "stills of a superior quality." But young Wilde had his eye on certain books on the grocery

[6]

shelves—law books, such as "Peake on evidence, Chitty on bills, Burrow's reports, Graydon's digest, Blackstone"; "Bousaquet and Puller's reports, and McNally's rule of evidence."[3]

After both Michael and Richard Henry Wilde were firmly established, they persuaded their mother and the dependent children—Catherine, James, John, and Ann—to come to Augusta. They arrived in 1803. In less than two years, Mrs. Wilde, with a talent for business and a desire to make some necessary money, opened a store. Since she had to have help, her son Richard Henry left Cormick's employment and started to work for his mother. A typical advertisement of her wares is the following one which appeared in an Augusta newspaper in 1806:

Mrs. Wilde has received in addition to her former stock of millinery the following fashionable articles, viz: feathers & flowers—silk, silver . . . & cotton trimmings—pic[n]ic, silk . . . & leather gloves—crape, muslin, & lace caps & turbans—dress bonnets— . . . all kind[s] of silk & silver buttons & trimmings, cords & tassels . . . —plain & worked muslins, laces, veils, etc.

As a result of his work, Wilde learned many terms peculiar to ladies' fashions, for in a poem entitled "An Album" he speaks of such items as gores, gashes, and spatterdashes. The store did, however, venture into other fields; one notice, after mentioning all kinds of clothes for women, added at the bottom: "Likewise, Dry Goods. Also Sugar, Coffee, Rum, Iron, etc."[4]

The competition facing Mrs. Wilde in the operation of her store was keen, for several other ladies—Mrs. Hannah A. Dickinson, Mrs. Harriet Newton, Mrs. Chatfield—had similar stores. Augusta, which was next in population in Georgia to Savannah, the largest city, was really not large, since it had only 2,482 people, according to the census of 1810, of whom 1,161 were white and 1,321 were Negro. Although Mrs. Wilde and her children worked hard, they were always poor. Wilde, in a poem written later on in life, stated that he, "an early orphan . . . strove thro' all his youth with indigence."[5]

At the same time that he worked in the store owned by Cormick and later in the one owned by his mother, he read what he could and taught himself bookkeeping. He urged a friend, George Cary, to collaborate with him on a series of essays in 1805 or 1806, which they signed simply "Narrator"; these were Wilde's entry into the literary field. Cary in later years remembered fondly this early literary interest and received great delight from his "unbroken and undecayed friendship" with Wilde.[6]

The first two poems by Wilde that can definitely be dated were written in 1807, each being typical of his later work. The Romantic Age was flowering in England, and the interests of Romanticism were drifting to America. Wilde, following the trend, became an early Romantic poet in America. One poem entitled "On the Death of a Young Lady" has a melancholy subjective mood, for, as the poet thinks of the dead girl, he hopes that she will not be aware of the weeping and sighs of the people left behind; rather if she looks down from the "starry sky," he trusts that they will seem "happy as ever." In the other poem, beginning "Whilst busy Memory fondly strays," which has the affectation and pose that he often employed, Wilde through the power of Memory can recall the past with its "griefs and joys of other times." Only eighteen years old when he wrote the poem, Wilde describes himself as a person made wise by Time, spending much time alone, pondering about the future and forming "vain schemes of happiness."

These poems have a brooding quality not because Wilde was a sad, unhappy child, but because he was simply copying the literary fashion of the day. As a matter of fact, his surroundings were pleasant. His mother was kind, generous, and good. In later years, when he wrote to a certain Marchioness, who had just had a child, he stated: "The mere name of *mother* recalls the memory of mine, in whom I first perceived, what I am certain you experience, that if Earth has any thing like Heaven, it is a mother's love and a mother's care." His mother impressed upon the children that they should avoid yielding their "own reason, judgment, and sense of duty to the fear, opinion, or importunity of others." She had a little couplet that she recited to them:

> Better to stand alone in conscious pride
> Than conscious err with millions on your side.[7]

Mrs. Wilde was a slave owner, just as her son was to be later on. In 1805 she offered a reward of five dollars for the return of a slave named Perry, a mulatto boy, who was well known about Augusta and who was wearing a sailor's blue jacket and trousers when he ran away; in her advertisement she warned that anyone harboring Perry would be prosecuted. The boy was not of much value, for the lowest reward ever offered was five dollars while sometimes fifty dollars was offered for the return of a valuable slave.[8]

Since Mrs. Wilde's store apparently brought in no great amount of profit, she set off in 1806 for Ireland, hoping to recover some of the money once owned by her husband; but she had no success. Not wanting the trip to be a complete loss, she picked out some clothes for her store. In a newspaper advertisement of the early part of 1807, in which she stated that she had changed the location of her business, she added that she had "visited Europe herself last summer" and had purchased a number of "fancy articles" by means of which she would be able to supply "the ladies of Augusta and the country, with everything fashionable & elegant."[9]

Although Mrs. Wilde had a difficult time making a living for her children, help came from two unexpected sources. Joseph Cormick, also born in Dublin, who went into partnership with his brother John on August 1, 1806, died the same year; and in his will he stated that during his frequent periods of sickness he had received excellent attention from Mrs. Wilde and her family. "In consideration of which and the large family with which she [was] encumbered," he left her and her daughter Mrs. Mary Pasley all of his estate "except $500.00, [his] musical instruments, music, books, watch chain and seals." These latter items he left to his brother John.[10]

Furthermore, Mrs. Wilde profited from the land lottery. Certain lands obtained from the Creek Indians were laid off into numbered square tracts. Since there was an abundance of land, tickets were put in a lottery wheel, and there were some drawings. Mrs. Wilde, a widow with children under twenty-one, had two draws. According to an official announcement dated Louisville, Georgia, September 4, 1807, the list of "Fortunate Drawers in the Land Lottery" included "Richard, James, Catherine, John, & Ann Wilde (orphans)."[11]

Up until 1808 the only thing that Wilde could do was be a clerk in a store. The question was: What occupation or profession could he enter? After all, he was intelligent; and, though he had little money, he was burdened by a desire to become successful.

The large assortment of law books on the shelves of Captain Cormick's store had had its effect. Law, Wilde decided, would be his profession.

When he was about eighteen, he persuaded the lawyer Joseph Hutchinson that he should be allowed to read in his office. This gentleman, one of the most distinguished men of Augusta, had served as clerk of the various courts of Richmond County and even as intendant, the equivalent of mayor, of the City Council of Augusta. Hutchinson, a law partner in 1808 with Freeman Walker, the latter destined to become one of Wilde's best friends, was a kind man who, in addition to giving the young man advice, also lent him text books. But income was not ignored: Wilde continued working in his mother's store. And, fearing disappointment, he did not let many people know about his professional plans.[12]

In preparing for his law examinations, Wilde forced himself to read at least fifty pages and to make five pages of notes each day. Furthermore, since he wanted to improve his speech and correct a slight impediment, he helped to organize a dramatic group, known as the Thespian Society and Library Company of Augusta. This group, officially recognized by the state, also had as another charter member Wilde's younger brother, James.[13]

The budding organization, which as early as February 25, 1808, was performing a play entitled *Heir at Law*, rebuilt its theater, which fire had destroyed in the fall of 1808; and it continued in the same place until 1823. This society not only presented amateur plays but also helped to bring important actors, including Auguste Placide and the elder Booth, to Augusta. The reason given for the establishment of the theater was "truly laudable," for the Thespians wished, with their profits, to "establish a public library for the use of the citizens of Augusta." It was felt that the group certainly deserved "the countenance and support of every friend to literature and science" in the city.[14]

After studying law for a year and a half, mostly in secret, Wilde wished to be tested; but since he did not want his mother to hear of a possible failure, he went outside Richmond County, "pale and emaciated, feeble, and with a consumptive cough," to take his examination. He at the time was only nineteen. The judges of the court that he went to unfortunately had no power to admit him. But he met a friend who took him to Greene Superior Court, and there Judge Peter Early was presiding in the March Term of 1809. Known for his strictness, Judge Early, who wondered why a boy would leave his own territory to take a law examination, subjected Wilde, before a committee, to a rigorous test for three days. Yet the young man competently answered all questions "to the satisfaction and even admiration of the committee"; and Judge Early decided that Wilde could not have left his own circuit because he was unprepared. After his friend affirmed his strong moral character, Richard Henry Wilde was admitted, without a dissenting voice, to practice law. He also qualified for admission to the bar of South Carolina before he was twenty years old.[15]

Wilde joyfully returned to Augusta; and in the same year, 1809, Joseph Hutchinson chose him for a new law partner. A general notice of their partnership stated that they intended to practice in the counties of Columbia, Warren, Jefferson, Burke, Scriven, Washington, Richmond, Lincoln, Elbert, Wilkes, Greene, and Hancock, as well as in the Federal Circuit Court; furthermore, they agreed that one of the partners would be always present at the office while the other was practicing in the circuit court.[16]

An important honor came to Richard Henry Wilde in 1811. Governor David B. Mitchell was elected on Thursday, November 7, 1811; at twelve o'clock on the following day he as inaugurated; and on Saturday, November 9, 1811, some officers were elected to serve with him including "Richard H. Wilde, Esq. Attorney General *vice* John Forsyth, Esq. resigned." Wilde received the office automatically because he was solicitor general of the middle circuit of Georgia, the one in which Augusta was located; the solicitor general for that circuit also became attorney-general for the state. Though he served as attorney-general from 1811 until 1813, he made only one official statement in the Augusta *Chronicle*, and that was scarcely of earth-shaking proportion: he simply stated that the office of the attorney-general was going to move down the street and anyone who wanted to see him could find him at his new location.[17]

Eventually Wilde was persuaded to run as a representative to the Congress of the United States; after being elected, he served in the Fourteenth Congress. In 1817, just as his term was expiring, he received another honor when the following announcement was made: "Richard Henry Wilde, Esq. of Georgia, has been admitted at the present term, to practice in the Supreme Court of the United States."[18]

During this early period as a lawyer Wilde prepared a bill, approved by the legislature December 10, 1812, entitled "An Act More Effectually to Prevent the Crimes of Forgery and Counterfeiting," described as "one of the finest specimens of preventive legislation on record; for it enumerates everything connected with the uttering, fabrication, and attempts to pass false paper that human ingenuity could conceive." For his work the banks of Augusta presented Wilde five hundred dollars. The bill seems harsh today, for those people who counterfeited bank bills upon any bank such as the Bank of Augusta or the late Bank of the United States were to be adjudged felons and were to "suffer death by hanging, without the benefit of clergy." For a lesser crime such as using the bills, a person was to be fined several hundred dollars and to be whipped publicly with from ten to thirty-nine lashes.[19]

Later Wilde wrote an important pamphlet, which he designated as his entry into the political world. During the War of 1812 the General Assembly of Georgia passed the Stay Law, which had as its object the suspension of the collection of debts by process of law. This law was described as "preventing suits being commenced against those men who are on a tower [sic] of duty in the service of their country, and suspending executions for twelve months, on the defendant giving security for the debt, within ten days after judgement has been obtained." The act helped debtors but it "seriously impaired the obligation of contracts and hindered lawyers in the lucrative practice of their calling." Wilde, who seriously opposed the constitutionality of the law, published at his own expense a "small edition" of his arguments delivered in court.[20]

The profession of law was profitable even in a town as small as Augusta, which was flooded with lawyers. Wilde, interested in his work to a great extent because of the possible income, once refused to accept a certain law case, stating: "It is usual . . .to require an advance on account of the Costs and fees from plaintiffs who reside out of the county where the action is to be commenced." And in one of his best passages in *Hesperia* he praised gold, which earlier in life he had scorned:

> I do repent me of that early sin,
> The folly of my inconsiderate days;
> And now, however late, would fain begin
> To burn thee incense, and to hymn thy praise;
> If all who truly worship thee may win,
> I too would offer thee a Laureate's lays,—
> Haply for ears tuned to sweet chimes unfit,
> And yet not worse than have for GOLD been writ.[21]

Even though Wilde apparently was able to make a good income from law and was successful in his profession, and in spite of John Patterson Wilde's statement that Richard Henry Wilde had always had a liking for the Science of the Civil Law to which he "applied himself with zeal and industry to acquire a complete knowledge of its principles," there are reasons for believing Wilde was never especially happy with the profession. He wrote in an epistle of 1809:

> Or whether I shall waste my life
> 'Mid Courts and law and care and strife
> Still slowly plodding o'er and o'er
> The same dull round I've trod before
> Till youth and joy and fancy fly
> And hope and love and pleasure die.[22]

Furthermore, in his introduction to the arguments on the Stay Law, he spoke of "groping among the gloomy rubbish of law logic," and he believed that "fame even of a first rate barrister, is at best, but a pitiful object of ambition." He recognized that his presenting arguments about this particular law would be inadequate as a foundation for a fine career, for to him that man must be insane "who should build up hopes, even of a short and miserable notoriety, upon no better foundation, than a wretched argument had on a local question, in a remote village of the new world!"[23]

In addition to his income from law, after his first term in Congress Wilde did have another position. Plans were formulated in 1816 for the establishment of a branch bank at Augusta of the second Bank of the United States. Wilde, on the "simple ground of suitable qualifications in every respect, excepting only what is acquired by experience," was chosen from "several Candidates" to become cashier of this private bank. He had the usual duties: handling of money, securing of assistants, writing official letters.[24]

Wilde busied himself in a number of community projects. He was briefly a legal consultant for the Richmond Academy; at a meeting of the Board of Trustees of the school on December 27, 1815, B. W. Miller was appointed attorney of the board "in place of R. H. Wilde, Esquire, resigned." Wilde also became a member of a committee to help Savannah in 1814. An editorial stated that Augusta was removed from the "din of war," though its young men had been soldiers. But the city of Savannah was threatened; and since the people in that city had given all the money they could for defense, the City Council of Augusta, headed by Joseph Hutchinson, intendant, appointed a committee of Hugh Nesbitt, Thomas Cumming, and Richard H. Wilde to receive contributions. These three men, in making their appeal, passionately called on the citizens of Augusta "in the venerated name of our country to perform the sacred duties of patriotism and humanity towards those who are connected . . . by the dearest ties of kindred or of friendship."[25]

Mrs. Anne Newport Royall (1769-1854) saw Wilde in the House of Representatives during his first term and left a brief physical description: "Honorable Richard H. Wilde of Georgia is one of the most noble looking men in the House. A tall, manly figure, and very black hair. I could distinguish no more."[26]

Though he might look noble, he still suffered from poor health. In 1816 he wrote that his eyes, because of "late hours reading and want of exercise," were "occasionally very weak and painful." He asked a friend to send him "a good pair of green spectacles with double glasses of a very light green inclining to yellowish something of the grass color" to ease the pain. And in 1818 he was forced to ask for a leave of absence during the warm weather from his employers, the President and Board of Directors of the Office of Discount and Deposit of the Bank of the United States in Auugsta, because of ill health:

[14]

A recent billious attack at so unusual a season, succeeding a long series of ill health admonished me to respect the advice of my physicians, who told me to avoid, if possible, the effects of a Southern summer upon a constitution never strong and latterly very much enfeebled by the climate.

Newspaper editorials argued that the climate of Augusta was healthful in the summer. Though Wilde believed the town "to be one of the healthiest of the South, & more so than New York taking the year through," he stayed away as much as possible during the warm weather; the higher land surrounding Augusta offered relief from the heat.[27]

Three members of the Wilde family died during the period 1810-1815. A newspaper obituary of Michael Wilde, the oldest child of Richard and Mary Wilde, stated: "Died, Mr. Michael Wilde, late a resident of this city." At the time of his death in 1810, he was twenty-six years old; Richard Henry Wilde became the oldest male in the family.[28]

Wilde's younger brother James, who had been an officer in the United States Army and had fought against the Seminole Indians in Florida, was killed in a duel near Savannah on January 16, 1815; his death became the background for Wilde's most famous poem, "The Lament of the Captive." James, paymaster of the Eighth Regiment United States Infantry, owed a certain amount of money to the government at the time of his death. Richard Henry Wilde acted for his brother concerning the debt in a case that lasted for several years.[29]

About six months after the death of James Wilde, and to some extent as a result of the death of her son, Mrs. Mary Wilde died on July 21, 1815, in her fifty-sixth year. A resident of Augusta for the last thirteen years of her life, she left behind "a numerous and affectionate family to lament their irreparable loss." She was buried under the front part of St. Paul's Episcopal Church in Augusta, a church she had always loved.[30]

With the loss of his brothers and his mother, Richard Henry Wilde had remaining in the family in Augusta his sisters Catherine (or Kate), Ann, and his brother John; his older sister was also there most of the time. He loved them all, and the devotion was returned. They worried about him frequently, as for instance when he had to travel on a boat from Washington to Savannah. Wilde sent word that John, or

"Jackey," as Wilde affectionately called him, was to comfort the girls by saying that "no vessels are ever lost in May."[31]

During the period 1809-1819 (Wilde was twenty in 1809 and thirty in 1819), he began to receive his first recognition as a lawyer and politician. He also began to write original poetry including his most famous poem "The Lament of the Captive," beginning "My life is like the summer rose." Some poems were dedicated to friends, such as his epistles to Ignatius A. Few and George W. Crawford, both of Columbia County.[32]

Wilde was always attracted to the ladies. For example, according to one of his poems, as he looked at a certain "wanton maid," while she lay in a "voluptuous trance," he was forced to admit that "virtue slept and passion['s] soft infection crept . . . into [his] very inmost soul." One friend in particular was Rebecca Tiernan of Baltimore, who was able to play off "mischievously her whole artillery of witcheries" against him; he at the time was just a "poor, awkward, juvenile bachelor author" incapable of overcoming her "sprightly malice."[33]

Looking about for a suitable mate, he finally found her: Caroline S. Weyman, a widow with a ten-year-old child. For practically all of her life Caroline had been a part of the clothing world in one way or another. Her two brothers, Abner and William, kept a great clothing warehouse at 33 Maiden Lane, at the corner of Nassau Street, in New York City; and their children continued the business.[34]

On March 23, 1802, Caroline, still in her teens, married William Buckle, another resident of New York City. The two, anxious to make their fortune away from the city, migrated to Augusta, Georgia. There they lived, with no particular recognition, for several years. Buckle made the newspapers twice while in the Southern city. The first entry stated that a furious F. Phinizy was bringing a law suit as a result of a blind horse that the wily Buckle had sold to him. The second newspaper entry recorded his death in July of 1809.[35]

A girl named Caroline Jane was born to the couple shortly before William Buckle died. With a baby to support, Mrs. Caroline Buckle turned to the family profession—clothing. By 1811 she had a store in operation which in that year advertised "Gentlemen's Ready Made Clothes for Sale." Subsequent advertisements listed such diverse items for sale as lottery tickets for the Susquehanna Canal Lottery and "cheap Negro clothing . . . from five to seven dollars per suit."[36]

By 1816 Richard Henry Wilde had taken a long look in the direction of the attractive widow, even though she was a few years older than he. While in Washington, he wrote John Walker Wilde that he was sending the daily *National Intelligencer* home; it was the duty of the younger brother to give it to Mrs. Buckle just as it arrived. A courtship followed, and by November of 1818 the two made plans for a marriage; Mrs. Buckle, who had found a protector, announced to the citizens of Augusta that she was "intending to relinquish" her clothing business.[37]

On Saturday, February 6, 1819, the day before the marriage, the office of the Clerk of Ordinary, Richmond County, recorded a license bond. And on Sunday, February 7, 1819, the Reverend Dr. John Egan, who conducted an academy in Augusta, married Wilde and Mrs. Buckle. The witnesses were Dr. Alexander Cunningham, who became president of the Medical College of Georgia, and John Walker Wilde.[38]

Richard Henry and Caroline Wilde had three children, all born at Augusta and all sons. The first child, named Richard Henry Wilde, was born on December 30, 1820, and baptized on February 17, 1821, the two sponsors for the baptism being John Patterson and Miss Buckle. This son, who lived slightly more than one year, died in June of 1822. The following poem in honor of the child appeared shortly afterwards:

> Yes, _____, he is gone, that in
> The morning promised many years, but death
> Hath in a few hours made him as stiff, as all
> The winds and winter had thrown cold upon him
> And whispered him to marble.[39]

The baby was buried at the Wilde home, located in a suburb of Augusta called Sand Hills, later known as Summerville because many people built summer homes there; today this section is generally called "The Hill." The stone marking the grave of the child had a poetic inscription on it, probably by Richard Henry Wilde:

> Love, hope, and pride lament thee, lost too soon.
> Yet even our very grief with every breath
> Confesses length of days in misery, and the boon
> Heaven sends its favorites—an early death.

[17]

Later on both Richard Henry Wilde and his wife were buried near the grave of the child. When interested friends removed the body of Wilde to the cemetery in Augusta, the bodies of the child and Caroline remained behind. The stone for the child was taken down, and eventually the ground for the two remaining graves was levelled.[40]

The second child named William Cumming Wilde was born June 6, 1823. On June 29 the parents and Miss Caroline Buckle were sponsors at the baptism. The child received his name from one of Wilde's best friends, a man who, as a colonel during the War of 1812, had distinguished himself in several battles on the Canadian border.[41]

The third son, John Patterson Wilde, at his baptism on June 27, 1824, had as his sponsors William H. and Martha McMillan Jones. John Patterson, who had been a sponsor for the oldest child, was the brother of the famous Betsy Patterson of Baltimore, who married Jerome Bonaparte, the brother of Napoleon.[42]

Richard Henry Wilde's wife lived for only eight years after their marriage. In the early part of 1827 the following notice appeared about her death: "The friends and acquaintances of Richard H. Wilde, Esq. are respectfully invited to attend the Funeral of *Mrs. Wilde*, from his residence in Augusta, to the Sand-hills, *this morning* at 9 o'clock." She was buried on January 27 in the garden of the old home on the Hill. Later on, when the family of James Paul Verdery owned the property, they moved the old home to the back of the lot; and the little cemetery, which they levelled, became the yard and garden.[43]

Wilde wrote many of his original poems in the period from 1827 to 1829, and occasionally a passage, such as the following one, shows that he was probably thinking about his wife:

> Some few brief moments from repose I steal
> To pour for one much loved—now far away
> Some part of all I hope and think & feel
> And thus to hallow this her natal day.
>
> Blest be the day! and blest forever blest
> The purest gentlest being upon earth
> But Language has no words to speak the rest
> She knows what I had been but for her birth.

In the year of her death Wilde wrote to a friend: "I . . . feel deeply how deplorable has been the end of that domestic life on which I had ever fixed my fondest hopes, & in which I did suppose myself capable of giving & receiving happiness." During 1827 he "suffered much in body & mind" and desired "to escape for a time from all that [was] associated with bitter recollections." His consolation was his children: Will, a "fine stout fellow" and John "slender & called very beautiful" with his "long curly locks and girlish face." The latter, however, a "frail delicate little being" with a "most unconquerable spirit," thrashed his older brother on all occasions.[44]

Caroline Jane Buckle, the stepdaughter of Richard Henry Wilde, married James G. Ringgold of Baltimore on May 30, 1827, in St. Paul's Episcopal Church, Augusta. The marriage produced two children, Mary and Richard. But James died in May of 1831, and in 1832 Wilde was desperately involved in the complicated problem of trying to save Caroline something from the confusion of her husband's estate. On November 28, 1839, Caroline was married again, this time to Colonel George G. Mathews of Greensboro.[45]

Wilde's older sister, Mary Pasley, died on September 8, 1822, after a life "the greater part of which was embittered by sickness, sorrow and unmerited calamity." She was buried in the family vault in Magnolia Cemetery in Augusta. Catherine, another sister, remained single; and Ann, the youngest member of the family, married a physician, Dr. John M. Anthony, in 1835.[46]

Wilde's only surviving brother, John Walker Wilde, rose to prominence in Augusta and in Georgia. He too became a lawyer and eventually a judge of the City Court of Augusta from 1832 until 1851. At the same time he was cashier of the Augusta branch of the Georgia Railroad and Banking Company from 1836 until 1851. Of his numerous community activities perhaps the most important was his being president of the Board of Trustees of the Medical College of Georgia. Yet John Walker Wilde is of the most interest because he, like his brother, wrote poetry. Although his output was small, some of his works appeared in the *Southern Literary Messenger*.[47]

Typical problems of the day plagued Wilde. A Negro woman whom he owned named Hagar fled from him on July

[19]

7, 1821, and he advertised a ten-dollar reward to the person who would lodge her in the Augusta jail. Yet Wilde was sympathetic to some of his slaves. When Maria, a slave, was temporarily forced to abandon her quarters, he made certain that she had a place to stay. Wilde's sister Catherine liked Maria's child and wanted to keep her. Wilde was going to let Maria earn what she could; and, if he could remove some trifling renters from some small buildings, he planned to let Maria live in one.[48]

Also he offered a reward of fifty dollars for the return of a trunk which was lost or stolen behind the Savannah stage on December 31, 1825; it contained various articles of clothing belonging to him, and, in addition, papers having to do with his professional business in the Circuit Court of the United States, such as accounts, notes in suit, and briefs of arguments. Apparently the property was never recovered, for the notice appeared in the papers from January 3, 1826, until April 25 of the same year.[49]

An excellent physical description of Wilde during the period after his marriage exists:

He was an attractive specimen of physical and intellectual manhood. Six feet one inch in height, well-proportioned, graceful, with an expansive forehead, black flowing hair, an emotional mouth and bright eyes. Cheerful in his disposition, dignified and yet affable in his address, brimful of anecdote, eloquent in speech, impressive in action, and quick at repartee. He shone alike in legislative halls, at the bar, and in the social circle.

But his poor health remained. He had "continued indisposition" with the possibility that he was "going to hybernate in bed." At one time he spoke of a "rash attended with fever"; at another time, of his "rheumatiz." In 1832 he wrote to his brother: "My last year[']s enemy the Quinsy laid violent hands on my throat about ten days ago & has kept me to my bed ever since. This time however I was aware of the rascal's coming & contrived to loosen his grip somewhat earlier, tho' he has left the print of his fingers behind him. I am up at present and taking Quinine, so there is no danger." In September of the same year his "symptoms of Erysipelas & fever" had very much diminished and he had "strong hopes of getting through the autumn without an attack—the first escape for six years."[50]

Yet in spite of poor health, Wilde traveled a great deal; often he was "on a whirl of visits & invitations . . . so numerous as almost to amount to an infliction on one of [his] turn." Law cases and work as a Congressman carried him throughout Georgia and to Washington. During 1832 to get away from the cases of cholera in Washington he stayed at Everettsville, Virginia, and borrowed books in languages from the University of Virginia Library. Pleasure trips consumed his time also. There were delightful visits to his wife's family, the Weymans, in New York City. In 1828 he took an extensive trip through the northern part of the United States and parts of Canada. And in summers he went to resorts such as Indian Springs, Georgia, "a rather dull place after all as most watering places are." There "the men [made] love & the ladies silk guard chains—and both [played] the piano the fiddle or the fool as leisure[,] capacity & inclination [admitted]."[51]

Wilde continued his interest in community activities after his marriage. He was a director of the Branch Bank of Georgia and a member of the Board of Trustees of Richmond Academy beginning December 31, 1823. He endorsed a law school in Augusta to be run by Colonel W. T. Gould.[52]

Nicholas Ware stated in a newspaper notice that, during his absence from the state as United States senator, Richard Henry Wilde would take care of the business matters for Ware's clients in the Federal Courts. Furthermore, since Colonel Ware had been mayor of Augusta, Wilde was appointed in his place. He served as judge of the Mayor's Court from December 12, 1821, until April 10, 1822. At least one notice appeared signed by Wilde in his official position as mayor. It stated that members of the City Council of Augusta would be elected on April 8, 1822. After giving the names of the candidates in the various districts in Augusta, the article stated that "the Managers will keep the Polls open from 9 o'clock, A.M. until 2 P.M. and communicate to the undersigned the names of the persons elected. Richard H. Wilde, Mayor."[53]

Wilde also aided young men studying for the law. William H. Torrance, after serving as a merchant's clerk in Augusta and after suffering losses in an enterprise he attempted, began in 1819 to study law under Colonel Seaborn Jones. In 1820 he studied with the "gifted and generous man, Richard Henry

Wilde. Under his direction, young Torrance gave all his spare hours to miscellaneous reading and the sedulous study of the law." Another young man who studied law under Wilde was George W. Crawford, a native of Columbia County, who eventually became governor of the state.[54]

Wilde became a law and business partner of Joseph M. White (1781-1839). A native of Franklin County, Kentucky, White moved to Pensacola, Florida, in 1821. He authored several important acts and served in Congress from 1825 until 1837 as delegate from Florida. The friendship between Wilde and White began to thrive in 1827 and continued until the latter's death in 1839. They were law partners in one case presented before the Supreme Court: an argument concerning Colin Mitchell, F. M. Arredondo, and others against the United States.[55]

White's wife, Ellen Adair, was one of the most celebrated and beautiful women of her day. Born on June 5, 1801, she was the daughter of General John Adair (1757-1840), a rival of Andrew Jackson and also a member of Congress for ten terms. Since her husband was known as Florida White to distinguish him from another White in Congress, she received the name Mrs. Florida White. According to the *Adair History and Genealogy*, such men as Washington Irving, John Quincy Adams, and Thomas Moore praised her; furthermore, she met Coleridge, Lamb, Bulwer, and Queen Victoria. She wrote a work entitled *Souvenirs of Men and Women I Have Known* but never published it. A work of hers that did appear in print was a poem beginning "Farewell to thee, land of my birth," written at the time that she and her husband took a trip to Europe.[56]

Wilde often visited the Whites at their estate, Casa Bianca, near Monticello, Florida. A trip there in 1827 was especially delightful: ". . . a beautiful sand beach to bathe from, the sea breeze blowing in every day with delightful & refreshing coolness, guns, fishing tackle & books to amuse me, excellent claret my only drink, & gofer [*sic*] soup every day. My health good & my laziness increasing, & my project of establishing a plantation in conjunction with Col. White ripening apace."[57]

The plantation was an ambitious project. White and Wilde would share expenses, and the whole undertaking would be supervised by White's brother, Everett. In 1829 there were 150 acres in corn, 20 in cotton, and 31 in sugar cane. Of the latter crop, Wilde stated: "In many places I have seen the sugar cane growing very handsomely & I am persuaded the day is not distant when all the low country of the Southern states will cultivate the cane to a considerable extent." But expenses were tremendous: the steam engine and boilers cost from $15,000 to $20,000.[58]

Wilde was optimistic about plans for the sugar plantation. He felt that with good crops they could "calculate with certainty . . . on $125 to $150 per annum to the working hand." He managed to get some workers for the Florida plantation when a revenue officer of the United States captured a Spanish vessel with a number of African slaves on board because it was violating the slave acts of the United States. The Africans, looking "hearty and happy" in their new jobs, were "better fed[,] clothed and lodged than any slaves in the territory."[59]

Wilde and his sons also frequently visited the Adair home known as Whitehall at Harrodsburg, Kentucky. Sometimes the boys went by themselves, and so devoted were they to the place that Wilde called them "Kentuckians." Will called General Adair and his wife "Grand Pa and Grand Ma." And when John could find no other amuusement, he would "hang about his aunt Ellen and be petted." The leisurely life there, especially during the summer months, was ideal for Wilde himself: "Books[,] Music and Conversation, with a romp among the boys furnish me employment enough, and the contrast of my quiet and retired life, with the bustle and turmoil of the past, render it quite agreeable."[60]

Wilde was devoted to the Adair family, especially to Mrs. Ellen Adair White and to her sister, Mrs. Isabella M. Adair Pleasants, two of the daughters of General John Adair. To the former, "a fair lady the very hem of whose garment all the world of Washington [was] dying to kiss," he dedicated his long book-length poem *Hesperia*. A tradition has grown up that he was deeply in love with her; to be certain, he addressed her in adoring terms but he had a number of such lady friends with whom he flirted mildly in the same way. After the death of her husband in 1839, Wilde probably never considered for a moment marrying her. For one thing, though she was beautiful she always seemed to be in poor health: it was "very delicate"; she suffered greatly during damp weather; at one time she was even complaining of a sore thumb. In general, she was not a very cheerful soul; a letter from her to Wilde written in 1841 began: " My dear friend, . . . O! I have suffered in so many ways since we parted that I have learned to be humble under the sod—& look only for release beyond the grave. . . . I have been in bed some days."[61]

Of the two, Mrs. Pleasants' disposition was really more to Wilde's liking. She was the wife of Benjamin F. Pleasants, an employee of the Solicitor of the Treasury Department in Washington. Wilde saw her frequently in the city, especially at Miss Polk's boarding house, where they both took meals. In introducing I.M.P., as Wilde affectionately called Mrs. Pleasants, to John Walker Wilde, he described her as "a very particular friend of mine of great good humor and vivacity, and sister to my friend Mrs. White." Wilde later on teased John Walker Wilde about the charming woman, especially since Wilde acted as an intermediary for letters written between the two. She also took an interest in Wilde's sons, and Wilde wrote to his brother: "Mrs. P. says she has determined my boys *shall* come with her, so there's no denying it—I suppose, unless *you* will be chivalric enough to stand up against the wicked cross eyed fairy who is for stealing off the dear little children, a degree of heroism, of which judging by your letters & hers, I have some doubt."[62]

After knowing these two ladies for about four years, Wilde wrote to his brother concerning a rumor:

I am not married nor in imminent danger thereof, unless some fair or [b]rown unknown desperately bent upon mischief and matrimony should, instigated by the Devil on two sticks, with force & arms &c clap the padlock of wed-lock upon my fet-lok, with her own pretty hands, & in spite of all resistance—Hardly a supposable case—as I never knew a man married by violence except thro the interposition of fathers[,] brothers or other male animals whom I contemn and defy. But you need not contradict any thing you hear of me in that way except so as to have it believed more firmly. The reputation of being a marrying man, and just on the brink of ruin—felicity I mean—does a ci-devant jeune homme no harm. And I am so sick of all sorts of affectations as Sir Hugh calls them, that, unlike all those many who swear they are inconsolable, I am determined all appearances and reports to the contrary in any wise thereof notwithstanding to maintain the single wretchedness or blessedness and independence of this my *dissolute* condition, until I can find some one aimiable [*sic*] enough to induce me to hang myself, by a look. N. B. no such person as yet found.

Even if Ellen and Isabella Adair had been single or widows, Wilde would probably have made the same comments.[63]

During this period one of the most interesting events that Wilde was involved in, although indirectly, was a duel between his very good friend, Colonel William Cumming, and George McDuffie, who was born in Columbia County, Georgia, and for whom McDuffie County, Georgia, was named; later on McDuffie became Governor of South Carolina and eventually a senator of the United States.

In all the two men met four times. The *Democratic Press* of Philadelphia, edited by John Binns, on June 25, 1822, said that an original essay in a Georgia paper, which actually brought about the first encounter, was written by a "Mr. W. of Georgia," who was a married man and a friend of Colonel Cumming.

Since Richard Henry Wilde was the only person who fitted the description given in the *Democratic Press*, he furiously wrote about Binns and the person who had given the editor the information printed in the paper: "They have done me an injustice, and owe me reparation. I have a right[,] therefore, to demand of Mr. Binns and his informant, satisfactory assurances that I am not the individual, intended to be designated by them, as Mr. W. of Georgia."

In reply to the statements made by Wilde, John Binns said that there was no reason for believing that "Mr. W." was Wilde (though the editor of the Augusta *Chronicle* stated that no one else could have been meant). But, although Binns said that he had never heard of Wilde before and that so far as he knew Wilde was not meant, he would not name his informant. Wilde, believing that the latter was probably someone who wished to injure him, wanted the man's name or at least an assurance that the informant did not wish to harm him. If these assurances could not be given, Wilde would assume that an injury was meant.

Even though Binns finally apologized publicly and even though friends made attempts to reconcile the differences between the two men, Wilde was still upset three years later when he wrote Binns on February 25, 1825:

I merely seek the name of the person who gave you a statement unfounded in truth & injurious to me. You published it I doubt not upon what you deemed sufficient authority, & I am willing to admit upon your own declaration that you have since done me all the justice in your power;—except that of telling me who was the author of that calumny.

But Wilde apparently never learned the name of the informant; and, in his autobiography, Binns, for his part, avoided any mention of this highly embarrassing episode.[64]

Congress: 1815-1817, 1825-1835

Virtuously Wilde remarked that he could "pledge passive obedience and implicit faith to the future doctrines and discipline of no party whatever," for he had found none "which did not at times exact of its members, what no honest man ought and no gentleman" could do. And to his brother he confided concerning his political popularity after a victory: "I won it without ever deserting a friend or flattering an enemy & I will wear it on the same terms, or I will wear it no longer."[1]

In spite of such high-sounding ideals, Wilde supported, successively, the principles of three political factions or parties in Georgia: he followed the policies of George Michael Troup rather than those of John Clark; later he was a candidate for the State Rights Party, which opposed the Union Party; and finally he supported the Whigs rather than the Democrats. There was a consistency in his stand, for many Troup followers joined the State Rights Party in the 1830's, and then in the late 1830's and the 1840's they joined the Whig Party.

The chief problems of discussion that Wilde took part in when he was a representative from Georgia were the following: the removal of the Cherokee Indians, the protective tariff, nullification, internal improvements, and the financial state of the United States. He published separately his speeches on all these subjects.

The first public suggestion of Wilde as a candidate came near the latter part of 1813 when an announcement stated that he was a "proper person to fill the Vacancy in the House of Representatives of the United States, occasioned by the appointment of the Hon. Wm. W. Bibb to the Senate." The suggestion was without Wilde's permission, and one week later a notice appeared stating that Wilde had declined the honor. He could not accept the office because he was only twenty-four years old.[2]

But in the latter part of 1814 he did reach the legal age of twenty-five, and well-meaning friends persuaded him to run. One newspaper took great pleasure in reporting: "R. H. Wilde, Esq. will be a candidate at the ensuing election, to represent this state, in the House of Representatives of the 14th Congress of the U. States." In the political returns Wilde came in fourth out of a total number of nine candidates; the six top men became the representatives from Georgia to the Fourteenth Congress (March 4, 1815—March 3, 1817).[3]

This Fourteenth Congress was the one that Wilde was to exalt in 1832: "At that time I had the honor to be a member of this House. It was an honor then." Filled with the enthusiasm of youth, he described the House of Representatives, in a speech delivered on January 17, 1817, in the following way:

Mr. Wilde said, he never thought of that House without comparing it in his own mind to a vast, grand, magnifiicent, political amphitheatre, [in] which were exhibited specimens of intellectual gladiatorship, infinitely more wonderful, quite as interesting, and sometimes scarcely less dangerous (he would not say cruel), than those that contributed to the amusement of ancient Rome; or rather—for he wished to make no comparison which should not be expressive of his high respect for that body, and for every member of it—to a gay and gallant tournament, where the "keen encounter of wits" was substituted for that of weapons; where sarcasm and ridicule were the sword and the lance, authority and argument the casque and the shield.[4]

Political giants filled this House; in the tariff speech delivered on June 12, 1832, Wilde praised six of them in particular—William Lowndes, William Pinkney, John Randolph, John C. Calhoun, Henry Clay, and Daniel Webster.[5]

William Lowndes (1782-1822) of South Carolina, "the purest, the calmest, the most philosophical of our country's statesmen," Wilde also celebrated elsewhere when he said of Lowndes and William Crawford: "Mr. Crawford and Mr. Lowndes were the only two men of my day whom I ever ardently desired to see President of the United States."[6]

William Pinkney (1764-1822), praised in the tariff speech as "the first of his countrymen and contemporaries as a jurist and statesman, first as an orator," was the father of the poet Edward Coote Pinkney.

Wilde mentioned John Randolph (1773-1833) of Virginia,

[28]

"thoroughly imbued with the idiom of the English language—
... master of its strength, and beauty, and delicacy, . . . capable
of breathing thoughts of flame in words of magic and tones of
silver," in another place—a brief passage in *Hesperia* about
Richmond, Virginia:

> Chief of her cities! can I pass thee by,
> Richmond! without at least one grateful word
> To hail the pile that towers toward the sky,
> Thy Capitol,—where late I saw and heard
> Thy chosen sons in council grave and high,
> Marshall and Madison, and him who stirred
> Men's hearts with eagle gaze and thrilling voice,
> Randolph! the friend of Leigh and Tazewell's choice![7]

John C. Calhoun (1782-1850) of South Carolina, the author
of the nullification proclamation and at one time Vice-President of the United States, received the following description:

Engrossed with his subject—careless of his words—his loftiest
flights of eloquence were sometimes followed by colloquial or
provincial barbarisms. But, though often incorrect, he was always fascinating. Language with him was merely the scaffolding
of thought—employed to raise a dome, which, like Angelo's,
he suspended in the heavens.

Of the six men included in the tariff speech, only Henry
Clay (1777-1852) became a close personal friend. Wilde celebrated him in *Hesperia* in a passage mentioning his home at
Ashland, Kentucky:

> Ashland! far other thoughts thy glades awake,
> Far different strains thy patriot statesman asks;
> Though well I know my rhymes will never break
> The brief, bright leisure of his lofty tasks:
> And if I name him, 'tis but for the sake
> Of one he praised. His fame her worship masks,
> And she will laud, if she should see this lay,
> More eloquently far, the eloquence of CLAY![8]

When Wilde spoke of Daniel Webster (1782-1852) of
New Hampshire, he concentrated on his coldness:

Nor may I pass over in silence a representative from New
Hampshire, who has almost obliterated all memory of that distinction, by the superior fame he has attained as a Senator from
Massachusetts. Though then but in the bud of his political life,

[29]

and hardly conscious, perhaps, of his own extraordinary powers, he gave promise of the greatness he has since achieved. The same vigor of thought; the same force of expression; the short sentences; the calm, cold, collected manner; the air of solemn dignity; the deep, sepulchral, unimpassioned voice; all have been developed only, not changed, even to the intense bitterness of his frigid irony. The piercing coldness of his sarcasms was indeed peculiar to him; they seemed to be emanations from the spirit of the icy ocean. Nothing could be at once so novel and so powerful; it was frozen mercury becoming as caustic as red hot iron.

Elsewhere, Wilde wrote to his sister about this same characteristic of the man: "I forget who Mr. W. is you are talking about . . . in your letter? Is it Webster? I don't know whether he is married or a bachelor, but he is [a] cold stony icicle of a yankee who except party spirit has not a warm feeling in his whole system."[9]

From his very first term, Wilde spoke frequently, often in long speeches, in the House of Representatives. Generally he gave the impression of speaking with great humility as, for example, when he said that he preferred "the safety of silence to the hazards of debate"; but, as no one had presented his views on the subject, "he would venture to intrude them as briefly as he could, that at least they might not tire those whom they did not please." But this comment was followed by a speech of over four thousand words, which was not, by any means, one of his long speeches.[10]

During the period 1815-1817 Wilde was appointed to two committees. He was on the Committee on the Judiciary, one of the standing committees; in addition, he was appointed chairman of a committee formed to comply with a suggestion made in President James Madison's opening speech to Congress. The committee had the name On a National Seminary of Learning. A year later Wilde was reappointed chairman of the same committee, which had changed its name to On the National University. The House never seriously considered a long report that he prepared, and on March 3, 1817, he made a motion that the members postpone the consideration of a National University indefinitely. In speaking of his appointment, he felt "he had the misfortune . . . to be appointed the chairman of a select committee, to whom was referred a very small and a very unimportant portion of the President's message." Since the report of his committee did not come up for discussion, he believed that time was being wasted, for "he had long known that success was not even doubtful." The measure, if indeed it were a good one, had "fallen upon evil times." The only good resulting was that members of the House "would listen, a little less seriously, to those noble and captivating projects which others heretofore have had the merit of proposing, and that House the odium of rejecting."[11]

Wilde had perhaps a little too much optimism during this first term, and his defeat for the Fifteenth Congress was the result of his believing that a compensation bill, which proposed to increase the salaries of Congressmen, would not disturb Georgians. But Wilde made a basic mistake, for the people opposed an increase or change of any kind. A Compensation Act was passed, with the approval of the senators from Georgia and the disapproval of the members of the House of Representatives. But Wilde, with others, had not denounced the bill sufficiently. The Augusta *Chronicle*, aware of the possible outcome of the election of 1816, stated: "The storm of popular indignation . . . which rolls so furiously against our national representation does not astonish us." Believing that the members of the Georgia delegation had been outstanding and had "raised the character of [the] state to an eminence hitherto unknown,—and augmented its weight in the national scale," it wanted them to be re-elected.[12]

But the people of Georgia paid no attention to such advice, and in the election of 1816 for members of the Fifteenth Congress (March 4, 1817–March 3, 1819) they returned only one man of the previous House of Representatives, John Forsyth, to Congress; and he polled the smallest number of votes of the six elected. But in spite of political defeat, Wilde retained some popularity, for, although he was not a candidate for the Sixteenth Congress (March 4, 1819–March 3, 1821), he received a large number of write-in votes.

Wilde was neither a candidate for the Seventeenth Congress (March 4, 1821–March 3, 1823) nor for the Eighteenth Congress (March 4, 1823–March 3, 1825). A vacancy occurred, however, in the latter when, on the death of Senator Nicholas Ware, Representative Thomas W. Cobb went into the Senate. An announcement appeared that Wilde and William C. Lyman were to be candidates for the vacancy. Wilde, who won the election, served from February 7, 1825, until March 3, 1825.[13]

Wilde was not a candidate for the Nineteenth Congress (March 4, 1825—March 3, 1827) nor for the Twentieth Congress (March 4, 1827—March 3, 1829). But when a vacancy occurred in the House of Representatives for the latter Congress, he was suggested for it. Wilde withdrew his name and urged those people who wished to vote for him to support George R. Gilmer instead.[14]

When John Forsyth resigned as a representative to become Governor of Georgia, an election took place on November 17, 1827, for his seat. Since Wilde was the only candidate, there was little interest in the contest. Though elected on November 17, 1827, he was able to get to Washington only by January 14, 1828. During the Twentieth Congress Wilde was made a member of the Committee to Revise the Rules of the House on January 14, 1828, and a member of the Committee on Foreign Affairs on December 3, 1828.

During this time Wilde took an interest in agriculture. He introduced a type of wheat known as Malaga Wheat into the United States, and plants of it were distributed around Augusta to be tested by experimentation. And during the second session of the Twentieth Congress, he spoke briefly on the production of sugar in this country, mentioning various foreign markets and the tariff. He saw to it that several boxes of sugar cane were brought from "the vicinity of Velez Malaga," Spain, and distributed among planters around Augusta; the plant was supposed to be a hardy one. Wilde quite naturally would be interested in this crop because the main crop that he and White raised on their plantation in Florida was sugar cane.[15]

During the next three political elections Wilde was very popular, leading in the number of votes in two contests and coming in second in the other. In the returns for the Twenty-first Congress (March 4, 1829—March 3, 1831), he received the largest number of votes of all the candidates. In this Congress he remained on the Committee on Foreign Affairs, which had as two of the other members Edward Everett of Massachusetts and James K. Polk.

The latter was too much the slave of Andrew Jackson for Wilde's liking. After serving together on the Committee on Foreign Affairs, the two men later on were on the Ways and

Means Committee. Another member of this committee wrote to Wilde's son about the poet's dislike of the man destined to become the eleventh President of the United States:

In regard to my knowledge of your father[']s political life and opinions, from which you hoped to obtain information, I ought perhaps to have said in my former letter, that during the Session we were together in the House, circumstances of prior occurrence or the situation of his constituency, unknown by me except in a very general way, kept him in a state of inaction in the House. We were members of the Committee of Ways & Means, of which Mr. Polk was Chairman, but I could never prevail upon him to attend the Committee. I was indeed the only member of the minority who ever attended; & to all my urgency his only reply was his pleasant laugh, and "defend me from such company until you are Chairman."[16]

And in a letter of 1833 Wilde mentioned Polk in a list of representatives who were being considered for Speaker of the House:

With regard to the Qualifications of the pretenders we should not disagree. You have the measure of their intellect & honesty. Johnson[,] Wayne & Polk have not the talent, Stevenson has not the principle, & Sutherland has neither the talent or principle that a Speaker ought to have. Yet we must choose among these.[17]

In the election returns for the Twenty-second Congress (March 4, 1831–March 3, 1833), Wilde again received the largest number of votes. He was appointed to the Committee on Ways and Means, which for the second session had Gulian Verplanck as chairman and Polk as another member. Also he was on a committee to prepare a code of laws for the District of Columbia.[18]

Loyalty to either Troup or Clark had existed before the 1830's; but it generally was not openly expressed. In the election held in 1832, however, for the Twenty-third Congress (March 4, 1833–March 3, 1835), the newspapers definitely distinguished between the two: one list was called the Troup Ticket and the other the Clark Ticket. In the returns for this election, Wilde again showed tremendous popularity, coming in second after James M. Wayne. Of the nine representatives chosen, seven were of the Troup Ticket and two of the Clark Ticket. During the Twenty-third Congress Wilde again served on the Committee on Ways and Means, which during this time had Polk as chairman.[19]

Of the qualities that equipped Wilde to be a statesman, one of the outstanding ones was his ability as an orator. Paul Hamilton Hayne in 1885 stated that, in general, Wilde was remembered for just one poem, adding that "all his speeches are forgotten, his forensic ability is but a tradition." And the Augusta *Chronicle*, in praising the merchant class, felt that it was unusual that two of the most famous orators of the day—George McDuffie and Richard Henry Wilde—had come from it.[20]

Wilde had had long preparation not only in various law cases but also in dramatic productions. It is possible to find examples of his speeches which have a certain sense of drama in them, speeches that in the hands of a person unskilled in delivery would have been ineffective. As an example, Wilde, on May 19, 1830, made a speech in the House of Representatives in which he recommended the removal of the Cherokee Indians. This speech indicates his general method of presentation. First, he began with a generalized statement in which he showed the seriousness of his subject and suggested his humility in approaching it, for he "was not unmindful where, to whom, and of what he was about to speak. He was conscious how wide was the circulation of words uttered there; how eagerly they were caught up." Therefore, he was "deeply solicitous never to say anything which would dishonor himself or discredit the republic—for the rest, he was anxious only to express just thoughts in plain language."[21]

Then in a very long speech he made liberal use of sources dealing with the Cherokees, for "he had spared no pains in collecting information." He included such material as what the official policy of the United States had been toward the Indians for practically every year beginning in 1775, various compacts made with Indians, the number of Indians in the different states, the Cherokee Laws as published in the *Cherokee Phoenix*, and what the official attitude toward the Indians in various states had been.

Throughout his speech he emphasized the one theme that land does not necessarily belong to the first people who touch it but rather to those who cultivate it and care for it by hard work. Ending his speech in his best oratorical fashion, he declared that the Indians must perish and that there should be no lamentation if they do:

But alas! the Indians melt away before the white man like snow before the sun! Well[,] sir! Would you keep the snow and lose the sun!

It is the order of nature we exclaim against. Jacob will forever obtain the inheritance of Esau. We cannot alter the laws of Providence, as we read them in the experience of ages.

The earth was given for labor, and to labor it belongs. The gift was not to the red, or to the white, but to the human race—and the inscription was, to the WISEST—the BRAVEST—to VIRTUE—and to INDUSTRY!

Yet in spite of the emotional appearance of some of his statements, Wilde was noted for his coolness in handling difficult questions. An observer who heard him speak on the tariff and nullification, after saying that he kept his temper in discussing these bitter controversies, added: "To a lover of the Union, which binds these states, he has uttered words of fearful import, coming with a *sang froid* that was chilliness itself."[22]

The speech on the tariff, which Wilde thought to be "the best, or at all events the least bad" of his speeches, was heard by Henry Tudor, who wrote the following description of Wilde's delivery:

One of the most insinuating of the speakers whom I heard in this house was Mr. Wylde, the member from Georgia. There was a polished and gentlemanly style in his manner that was highly prepossessing, reminding me strongly of the grace and elegance so conspicuous in the address of Lord Lyndhurst. In addition to an expressive animation of feature, there was a smiling good nature of countenance, which, at the same time that it engaged the favour and attention of his auditors generally, must have in some measure disarmed the resentment of his tariff opponents. His arguments were forcible, well illustrated and elegantly delivered; and I could easily perceive some of his political adversaries, in defiance of his conciliatory demeanour, wincing under the lash of his well-pointed sarcasm with a gravity and ill-concealed asperity of visage which contrasted powerfully with the playful expression of his own. He denounced the tariff with an uncompromising opposition; and the only circumstance that appeared, according to our English notations, somewhat to diminish the effect of his oratory was, that he seemed occasionally, as I had also remarked in others, to read considerable portions of his speech from written papers. In many instances, I believe, the observations intended to be made are entirely committed to paper, and it then depends on the strength of the honourable member's memory how far he may seem to utter his sentiments from the extemporaneous effusion of the moment.[23]

One political adversary in the matter of the tariff was Tristram Burges of Rhode Island, who was notorious for hating any reference to his age. This gentleman, whom Wilde labelled a "Old Thersites," denounced not only Wilde's speeches but also his personality and called the representative from Georgia a "gallant gay Lothario of the South." Wilde bristled as he answered:

The gentleman ever *liberal* in epithets has indirectly favored me with another. Again I claim the judgment of our peers. We are both gray—both somewhat bald—neither very young & neither (tho' the gentleman may have been an Adonis in his day) either beautiful or seductive any longer. As to the rest it will be easy to determine whether the true Lothario is not him whose ardent fancy still revels in luxurious descriptions of female beauty, and whose sanguine choleric temperament kindles into fury at the slightest allusion to his age.[24]

Yet in spite of this sarcasm, Wilde was really a rather genial man—perhaps a little too genial to be an effective politician. A reporter who attended a festival at Appling, Columbia County, in 1833, agreed that a talk made by Wilde had "passages of almost unrivalled pungency of satire, purity of principle, and eloquent nobleness of patriotism," but yet it "bore too much of a please everybody aspect." Furthermore, Wilde's speech "so often praised and abused" each side that a "plain and unlettered citizen" admitted that "he was sometimes puzzled to know what it was really in favor of."[25]

During his terms as a member of the House of Representatives, Wilde received acclaim as well as violent attacks both from individuals and the press. For Speaker of the House of Representatives in 1834 he led on the first ballot, the other contenders being James K. Polk, Joel B. Sutherland, and John Bell. The position, however, finally went to John Bell of Tennessee. In addition, Wilde was at least thought of as a possible nominee for President.[26]

[36]

Wilde also received his fair share of condemnation. When an announcement appeared in the newspapers that there had been some "jockeying" between Wilde and Bell, which resulted in Bell's being elected to the chair of the House of Representatives in 1834, Wilde protested against the slander, saying that he and Bell "had no understanding of any kind, and never, directly or indirectly, concerted anything touching the election." Furthermore, the *United States Telegraph* in Washington attacked Wilde. In retaliation, on February 3, 1829, Wilde offered a resolution in Congress which stated, in part, that whenever future printers were chosen for the House, no person was to be eligible who had within the preceding two years been the proprietor, editor, or publisher of a newspaper. The printer for Congress was General Green, who was editor of the *United States Telegraph*, a leading Washington paper; and this paper supported the policies of Andrew Jackson. When an article appeared in the Milledgeville *Georgia Journal* attacking the *United States Telegraph*, the newspaper, believing that it was either written by Wilde or, at least, dictated by him, stated: "To be denounced in such terms by Mr. Wilde, a vain, silly coxcomb, inflated with the pride of place, and himself surprised at his elevation, gives us no uneasiness."[27]

But in spite of a few occasional criticisms of his actions, Wilde, in general, was a popular political figure during these years. In the election held in 1834, however, the citizens of Georgia, who had for three Congresses sent him to Washington with large popular votes, refused to re-elect him because of his opinion of Andrew Jackson.

Although President Jackson had been very popular in Georgia, during his second term he received much criticism from the members of Congress who were to support state rights. His opposition to the rechartering of the Bank of the United States, his dislike of nullification, his support of the tariff and the Force Bill, and his plan for the removal of the deposits—all made him unpopular with certain representatives from Georgia, including Wilde.

In 1832 Wilde was elected because he was believed to be "an upright and independent statesman, and . . . a firm and conscientious supporter of the administration." But a Washington newspaper in 1833 said that "Mr. Wilde [was] well

[37]

known in Washington City, whatever he [might] be in Georgia, as anything else but a friend of the administration."[28]

The State Rights Party was forming, as was the Union Party, in preparation for the election to be held in 1834. Since Wilde had not actively supported nullification, the Unionists attempted to get him on their ticket because he was popular politically. John Forsyth, a leading supporter of Andrew Jackson and the Union Party, wrote an official letter saying that that group wanted to nominate him, but it would like "some assurance he would act" with the other members of the party. Wilde answered almost immediately, stating that if he should be a candidate again, he preferred relying "on the kind and generous confidence of his fellow-citizens without distinction, to procuring the support of particular combinations, by assurances that he [would] act with them." When John Forsyth attempted again to secure him for the Union Party, Wilde did not answer.[29]

On December 12, 1833, at Milledgeville, a State Rights Convention was held, which nominated nine men, including Wilde, for the nine seats in the House. And a few days later a Union Convention was held in the same town, which nominated a Union ticket.[30]

A committee wrote Wilde a letter on December 14, 1833, asking whether he would be a candidate for the States Rights Party. Wilde, writing about a month later, said that his answer could be only "provisional." If he were nominated by a party, he wished it to be done "without impairing whatever little honor" he had already earned. He did not want to be discredited "in advance, by requisition of pledges or protestation," for "pledges are asked of men in trade, only when their credit or their honesty is doubtful—and when required of a politician, are generally regarded as evidence, that he would not otherwise be trusted." He felt that his past life was the only pledge that he could offer for his future conduct. If these opinions were agreeable to members of the committee, then he would be pleased "to receive the evidence of confidence and approbation" which would be indicated by their support.[31]

The State Rights Party was apparently content with Wilde's conditions and included him in its list of candidates for the Twenty-fourth Congress (March 4, 1835—March 3, 1837).[32]

Although Wilde preferred to be judged by his personal qualities rather than by the party he belonged to, the people of Georgia disagreed; and they, supporting Andrew Jackson, voted strictly according to party lines: the entire Union Party was elected and the entire State Rights Party defeated. Wilde wrote just after the election:

I arrived just in time to learn my defeat. We are routed horse[,] foot & artillery. The Union ticket i.e. Jackson—Van Burenism has succeeded by a majority of 2 or 3000. The causes of this were the same ardent not to say intemperate zeal of the State-Right Nullifiers: and the obtuseness and terror of our Yankee anti-Jacksonites who in their panic at the Bug-a-boo Nullification rushed without knowing it into the "Experiment." These men and many others are astonished & ashamed of their own success.[33]

There was some despair in Georgia as a result of this election, for the struggle had seemed to many to be between the power of the state and the power of the Federal government. A Boston paper said that the loss of Wilde would be deeply regretted, for he had been "universally esteemed in public life, indefatigable, spirited and faithful in his public relations." The paper felt that he had been "sacrificed to a blind and impetuous spirit of party."[34]

After being defeated, Wilde was invited to a public dinner to be given by fifty-six prominent citizens of Augusta. But, feeling that the offer was made just to soften the blow, he refused and instead sent the group a long and cheerful letter. He said that the Union Party had made him an offer, and that if he had accepted it, "the fall might have been avoided"; but he felt that he was "too old and stiff to shift [his] principles with any one's interests or resentments." Then he gave a long list of criticisms made by various people, which might account for his defeat. He agreed with one criticism, that he had not travelled about requesting votes, for he had "no passion for greetings in the market-place," was not "gifted with the eloquence of street corners," and had "an impatience of the arts of popularity." But after remarking that he did have a certain consolation, he humorously added: "It would be somewhat mortifying to have taken great pains, and yet failed to make myself acceptable. As it is, the election did not cost me above twenty visits and forty bows, at the rate of two each

[39]

visit, which is a very moderate expenditure of civility, even for a defeated candidate."[35]

Through 1835, Wilde had been elected, sometimes by large votes, four times (Fourteenth Congress, Twenty-first Congress, Twenty-second Congress, Twenty-third Congress); in addition he had been chosen twice to fill vacancies (Eighteenth Congress, Twentieth Congress). Only twice had he not been elected (Fifteenth Congress, Twenty-fourth Congress). After his return from Italy, he took part in one final political contest (Twenty-eighth Congress), but again he was defeated.

During his first term in Congress, the House of Representatives was "a vast, grand, magnificent, political amphitheatre." But the optimism that he had had during his first term gradually disappeared. By 1825 he felt that the United States "had fallen on evil times." Many of the men in public offices during this period when John Quincy Adams was president were concerned only with "the promotion of their own selfish views," and, as a result, the people had lost "all belief in political honesty." By 1830 Congress had become just a "tumultuous[,] hollow and glittering pageant."[36]

Yet from the standpoint of his physical and mental health, much of the life in Washington was satisfactory, for he wrote in 1831:

I assure you upon my veritable letter writing honor . . . that I am now in my usual health. Somewhat thinner perhaps and less ruddy—but with an excellent appetite—good spirits—sound sleep and as much activity of mind & body as I have had for two or three years back at the same session. I walk at least two or three sometimes four or five miles a day and read or write half a dozen hours. My passion for study has returned upon me with all its force & the fine collection of science & literature in all languages which our library opens to me is an inexhaustible fund of improvement & pleasure. Heretofore being here only during the session, I could merely glance at the outside of the books, now I have dipped into a few of them.[37]

Also he enjoyed being in the company of distinguished men in the city and the vicinity nearby—Verplanck, Everett, Kennedy, White, Pleasants. Generally there were pleasant conversation and good company at Miss Polk's boarding house and earlier at Mrs. Clark's. At the latter, located at the upper end of F Street where Wilde lived during his first session in Congress, he had met one night in 1815 a special visitor— General Andrew Jackson, whom Wilde found to be "a weather beaten old veteran rough as a nutmeg grater."[38]

Their paths were to cross many times. By 1833 Jackson found Wilde not to his political liking, as stated in a letter:

On yesterday the tariff bill would have passed the House of representatives had it not been for a very insulting and irritating speech by Wilde of Georgia which has threw [sic] the whole of Pennsylvania, New York and Ohio into a flame. I am told there is great excitement, and no hopes now of its passing this session.[39]

Wilde felt himself wrongly treated because of his opposition to Jackson. He was "*rightfully* entitled to be Chairman of the Committee of Ways & Means," but Jackson partisans overlooked him "in favor of Polk" because Wilde was "*for* a National Bank." He bitterly wrote to his brother: "I had been voted for as *Speaker* and failed only from the greedy and bargaining spirit of the West, and the *ardent* hatred of the Jackson party."[40]

The vast popularity of Andrew Jackson in Georgia had helped to defeat Wilde; and the poet, in *Hesperia*, when mentioning the home of Jackson at Nashville, Tennessee, paid tribute to his political foe:

> The Hermitage may claim an hour's delay
> For the old lion's sake. Behold him there
> No longer keeping all the chase at bay;
> Pain mingles with Defiance in his air:
> A forest king retiring from the fray,
> Thorwaldsen's noble Lion in his lair,—
> The wounds both bear attest the hunter's craft,
> But to the last our lion gnaws the shaft![41]

The statue of the wounded lion at Lucerne, Switzerland, by Bertel Thorwaldsen (1768-1844) seemed to Wilde an appropriate object to compare with Jackson.

The Augusta *Chronicle*, which for many years had its office next to that of Wilde, said in an editorial that although it had not supported Wilde's political beliefs, still it held his "many virtues" and "great talents" in high estimation. Furthermore, no one cherished towards Wilde "a warmer or more respectful personal regard and esteem" than did the *Chronicle*.

[41]

Nevertheless, "the field of politics was too rough, and its controversies too harsh and dissonant, for the highly intellectual refinement of his character." The paper, which believed that Wilde "valued political distinction only for the standing and influence it gave him in the best society," regretted that he, who had few equals "as a polite scholar," should have chosen the "field of politics, rather than that of literature" for his life's work.[42]

Wilde, for his part, was relieved that he was defeated in 1834. "After the scenes past in the H.R. *Honor* from a seat there [was] out of the question." Now able to travel to Rome, Naples, Germany, and England, he was happy to be away from "politics, a life in which [he took] no pleasure" and for which he felt, temporarily at least, that he was "not at all fitted."[43]

Italy: 1835-1841

Having "had enough of the World as it is called" and being "equally indifferent" to "the votes or the voices of the multitude whether exalting [him] to the skies or vilifying [him] below the earth," Wilde found refreshment in Italy. There he lived "among a people to whom [he did not] belong, to whom [he owed] nothing & [was] in no way accountable." The resources that "make life uselessly delightful" were his "destiny": "travel—study—science—literary occupation—the arts—the untroubled enjoyment of Nature."[1]

Wilde had "anticipations of twenty years" before he actually left for Europe. The lack of money had stood in his way. Shortly after the death of his wife in 1827, he ardently desired "to escape for a time from all that [was] associated with bitter recollections"; he longed to be among "strange scenes" in Europe, but "the state of [his] finances forbade" such a trip. In 1832 his "Florida cotton crop" failure prevented his leaving the country. But he saved what money he could, and in the spring of 1834 announced a definite plan: "My present intention is to go to England[,] France and Italy if the recess will afford me time." He wanted his friends to get him letters of introduction to various prominent people in Europe.[2]

Wilde had three reasons for going to Europe. His health was poor, and a "long sea voyage" might "churn or shake [his] bile into a wholesome state again." In addition, he was bored with politics. When a delegation of men from the State Rights Party had asked him in 1834 to be a candidate, he had not eagerly accepted. Rather he wrote that he was inclined to give up politics and "to seek occupation more agreeable to [his] taste, in a climate less unfavorable to [his] health." The political defeat in 1834 had decided him; having "been too rudely wakened," he had a temporary "hatred of [his] kind and [his] country and . . . determination to avoid both as much and as long as possible."[3]

His chief reason for the trip, though, was his love of languages. Although he had little or no formal training in any modern foreign language, he had studied independently. In 1821 he published a translation, beginning "They Say the Swan," of a poem by the Portuguese poet Luis de Camoens. By 1835 he had made translations from the Italian of Giovanni Zappi and Francesco da Lemene. An original poem "Lines for the Music of Weber's Last Waltz," written May 5, 1835, contained a note that the "first stanza was suggested by the beautiful passage of Dante commencing 'Era già l'ore &c' Purgatorio CVIII." A prized possession was his "two trunks of very discordant materials,—Italian literature & Congressional Documents." At one time Wilde wrote that his brother should send them to Washington because the books on the Italian language at the Congressional Library were "rather meagre," and Wilde needed "a resource from the graver, and duller reading of Public law Politics and Statistics."[4]

Even though he had considered the voyage to Europe for several years, he decided rather suddenly about May 15, 1835, "to embark from New York for Liverpool in the packet of the 1st June, & before [his] return to run over part of England, France, Italy & perhaps Germany." The ship *Westminster*, on which he wrote a poem entitled "A Farewell to America," dated June 1, 1835, was "a splendid new packet" bound for London on its first trip. Wilde knew a number of the passengers; and, since they were "all *great* folks and good *Catholics*," he attached himself to them, acting as "male attendant or cavaliere" to three ladies from Baltimore. They read their French and Italian faithfully every day and amused themselves by speaking these languages "by way of exercise." They finally arrived in London on June 25, 1835.[5]

In this city, "objects of interest & curiosity" passed before the eyes of the "back woodsman" with such swiftness that nothing left a distinct impression. He "*lived* years in the variety & rapidity of ideas." By July 4, he was in Paris, which did "not agree or wear" with him as well as England. He hired a "horribly expensive" carriage from Paris so that he could take short trips to nearby cities, such as Brussels. First-hand observation changed some of Wilde's ideas. "All the

[44]

talk about cheapness" in Europe was "nonsense." He wrote his brother: "At every stop you see and feel that you are cheated and imposed upon, without the possibility of helping yourself. You cannot eat any thing, drink any thing, buy any thing, sell any thing or pay for any thing without being duped." Though actual theft was "very rare," all begged, all lied, and all cheated. Some of the travellers he met, especially the English, were such a "disagreeable silly set of people" that he was not surprised "Byron shut his doors on all his countrymen abroad."[6]

After passing through Switzerland, "a country full of beauty[,] wonder & tradition," where "the Lakes and Glaciers and Tell & Byron . . . all conspired to make it fairy ground," he arrived at the gates of Italy on September 12; but reports of cholera hindered his progress. Finally several officials gave him bills of health to different Italian cities—and charged him "a small fortune" for them. Eventually he reached Florence, the city that was to be his home for the rest of his Italian trip.[7]

The moment that Wilde saw Florence, he fell in love with the city: "My eyes filled with tears, as I thought this would be the appropriate end of my wanderings—a place where it would be sweet to die!"[8]

During his first days he stayed at a hotel, the Chez Schneiderff; later he had a suite of rooms in the Palace Butourlin with two American friends, Mr. and Mrs. Sidney Brooks. Finally he had a handsome residence at Casa Vernaccia.[9]

Almost as soon as he arrived, he received a number of invitations to social events. One was to a "grand Ball at the grand duke[']s palace"; but he was rather disappointed at the lack of female beauty there, for, to tell the truth, the Florentine ladies were not "handsome." An American lady, a Miss Talmadge of New York, was able to shine at such a gathering. Wilde "had the honor of making a turn or two round the rooms [with her], enjoying the stare and whisperings of men and women, of which [he] took as much care as possible she should be unconscious by talking [his] prettiest all the time." In general, however, his routine during his early days in Florence was unexciting but restful:

Three hours, sometimes four of my days are given to reading or writing, translating, inspecting or copying manuscripts, or studying Italian history and legends. The rest I amuse myself in walking, visiting, seeing the churches, galleries, looking over curiosities, old books, hearing the news, & talking with some of my acquaintance. Visiting there is little of, except among the fashionables, or with the very few who maintain a strict intimacy. For the rest, you continue your acquaintance by meeting out of doors and chatting or walking together. With the opera in the Evening and a house or two where I sometimes go on the nights when there is no theatre, my hours and days and months wear away insensibly, with little care, & much freedom. I wonder three times a week that the day of the month is later than I thought, and am astonished to find myself the author of a volume, and half through another without ever having felt that I had a task and seeming to my own judgment as well as others, the idlest laziest dog in Christendom.[10]

The longer he remained in Florence, the more retiring his life became. One cause was his health. His "old enemies" were rheumatism, especially of the left arm; his liver, which "in spite of a diet almost entirely vegetable" was leading him "a dog's life of it"; indigestion; sore eyes; and "the attacks of age for which there [was] no cure." Wilde wrote to a friend about his "simple" habits of life: ". . . nearly all delicacies disagree with me. I rarely eat of more than one dish of meat—never touch pastry—am better when I drink only water without wine & sleep upon a hard bed from choice. This has been my habitual life for years." Any changes brought "injury" to his health and spirits.[11]

The arrival in Italy of his sister Kate and his two sons in the summer of 1838, as a result of his invitation, also helped limit his social life. Shortly after their appearance he wrote:

I have renounced what are called amusements and society, and live as retired as possible. . . . A walk in the country or to some of the Gardens with Kate & the boys, a visit to some of the galleries or curiosities, a rubber or two of whist in the Evening in which we have taught the boys to join us, and to play very keenly for a *Quattrino* i.e. the ¼ of a cent a game—these are our diversions.

Wilde had his hands full in trying to supervise the education of his sons. Their uncle had warned that the boys had never "studied in their lives." They had "no power of abstraction and their brains [were] yet to be taxed to a tithe of their

[46]

capacity." William, "somewhat smitten with antiquarianism," was "too indolent ever to make much progress in that or any thing else." John was interested in statues and novels, but nothing else; "to all manner of learning and application, he [had] a natural abhorrence, and in spite of his aptitude and quickness, he [fell] behind the tortoise." Yet Wilde made some progress; he kept after them constantly, and finally, among other subjects, they had "a smattering of French and Italian."[12]

Wilde know both Italians and Americans of importance while in Italy. Perhaps the most unusual person that he dined with was the sister of Napoleon, Caroline, the ex-Queen of Naples and the widow of Achille Murat. The only other American ever "admitted to her intimacy" had given Wilde a letter of introduction. This "most kind and affable" lady "gave [him] her arm and seated [him] at her right hand at table." Another acquaintance of nobility was the Marchese Malispina, who had been with Wilde in Naples. The two had a tender parting:

I was really grieved to part with him. I thought to get off by leaving a farewell card but he would come to see me and we separated like friends that had known and liked each other for half a century. It would seem ridiculous to our manners were I to describe the scene. Only think of two old gray headed fellows kissing on both cheeks like young lovers. . . . When the dear[,] warm-hearted [sexagenary] nobleman offered me the customary friendly embrace of his country. . . , I threw myself into his arms and the tears came into my eyes.[13]

The long poem *Hesperia* is dedicated to an American lady, Mrs. Ellen Adair White; but in the introduction Wilde gave her a fictitious name and called her a marchesa. During his stay in Italy he knew several ladies holding this title. For instance, at the dinner with Queen Caroline there were two ladies of this particular rank. And later, when he had published his work on Tasso, he wanted to make certain that the Marchesa Mary Bartolommei, who lived in the Via Larga, Florence, received a copy.[14]

The blot on the Italian trip was that Wilde probably had an illegitimate son by an Italian woman. The boy, named Niziero Nouvel or Novelli, was born November 13, 1840, with a midwife named Caterina Marzocchi in attendance. Nouvel was placed in the Ospedale degli Innocenti, a foundling home in Florence. It appears that the mother had been married at one time and had one or two legitimate children. From the foundling home Nouvel was given over to the custody of Giuseppe Mariana, a sharecropper, and his wife; and on August 20, 1854, he was confirmed in the Parish of Monsummano. For a while he worked as a farm laborer on the estate of the Cavaliere Martini of Monsummano and Florence. Wilde never acknowledged his son and never mentioned the boy in any of his letters. When the poet died in 1847, the boy was almost seven years old. In the six extant letters written between the years 1860-1868 from Nouvel to Hiram Powers, the latter, interested in the welfare of the boy, wanted to help him get a better position than that of laborer. Among other things, Powers told him about his dead father, though Wilde was never mentioned by name. Whether Powers was able to do much good is uncertain.[15]

If Nouvel were his son, perhaps a statement that Wilde made concerning the way that Byron spoke about women is not inappropriate. At least, it gives a reason for Wilde's not mentioning the child:

No degree of intimacy, no confidence whatever in the discretion of a correspondent justifies such communications and the greater the indiscretion of his fair favorites the less was he justifiable in betraying them. The highest eulogy a man of Honor can entitle himself to is that of never violating Faith to friend or enemy.[16]

Wilde, against his will, became a representative of American life to the Italians. He condemned most American tourists as "wandering Yankees," "the Goths and Vandals" that came "in schools like shad or herring." Yet to satisfy his Italian friends, he had his brother send "*Indian* curiosities, such as moccasins, pipes, belts, caps"; he added in a letter that "a few pairs of moccasins would put [John] on the best *footing* with the fair ladies of Florence." He supplied copies of the *Cherokee Journal* to a friend at Rome who spoke forty-two languages. Often he was struck by the Italian interest in American crops: he furnished details about cultivating Indian corn; he had live oak acorns, persimmon seeds, a gallon or two of chinquapins, and half a barrel of sweet potatoes sent to friends. As another touch of American life he attended a little Italian theatre, which was producing a comedy based on a tale by James Fenimore Cooper. Somewhat shocked, he remarked: "A curious coincidence! An American novelist furnishing a theme to the Tuscan stage."[17]

Yet some Americans in Italy, far from being "Goths and Vandals," became Wilde's good friends. George Greene, grandson of General Nathanael Greene of the Revolution, had married an Italian lady. Because of his enormous knowledge of Greek, Latin, German, modern Greek, French, and Italian, Wilde persuaded the young man to aid in the education of his sons. Another American, Horatio Greenough of Boston, took a fancy to Wilde; the latter spent hours in his studios, talking and playing billiards. The two saw each other almost daily for a while. Wilde acknowledged that if he had made any progress in understanding and appreciating the arts, much of the credit had to go to the influence of Greenough's conversation. Watching the progress that the American sculptor was making on his famous statue of George Washington, Wilde dedicated a poem to this artistic work.[18]

Another American artist, Hiram Powers, "a man of genius, of strange observation, and infinite simplicity . . . with a vein of humor & a fund of anecdote about his Western compatriots," after going to Florence in 1837, spent the rest of his life there. In 1839 Wilde wrote that "Powers' busts have made, are making & will continue to make, a strong impression here, & wherever else they are to be seen." He felt that one statue, "Eve at the moment of the Temptation," would be "exceedingly beautiful." And he believed that Powers, "by dint of exquisite delicacy of eye, minute and laborious finishing in the model, the invention of new instruments, and new methods of working the marble," would be able to convert the marble "into flesh." Unfortunately Powers had no patron to buy his works, and, as a result, "the spectre of Poverty [was] always before him." In *Hesperia*, Wilde celebrated this artist in four lines, the note to the stanza saying simply "Hiram Powers":

> Not Angelo's nor Donatello's skill
> In folds more graceful human form could twine;
> Nor his—my countryman—who, if he will,
> May rival yet the artist called "Divine."[19]

[49]

An American visitor, Charles Sumner of Boston, "a Prince of good-fellows socially, morally, & intellectually," was very unlike the man generally known in American history and hated by the South. The two men became good friends, although there was a difference in their ages, for in 1838 when they knew each other in Italy, Sumner was twenty-seven and Wilde forty-nine. On several points the two agreed. Early in life Sumner had said that he could not look upon politics "with any feeling other than loathing"; Wilde also did not care for politics. Both, however, were impressed by several politicians, notably Henry Clay; Sumner spoke of his "splendid and thrilling" eloquence. The chief interest they had in common, however, was in literature. As Sumner went from city to city in Italy, such as Venice, Ferrara, and Padua, Wilde asked him to look for books and manuscripts on Dante; Sumner seemed very happy to aid his friend. In a letter written after Wilde's death, William Cumming Wilde, in speaking of his father, called Charles Sumner "one of his most intimate friends."[20]

Still another traveller from New England was Edward Everett, who had served in the House of Representatives from 1825 until 1835; Wilde in 1828 had been appointed to the Committee on Foreign Affairs of which Everett was chairman. Beginning in 1839, Everett was in Europe, and there Wilde saw him again. After the death of Richard Henry Wilde, William Cumming Wilde, in preparation for a biography, wrote to various people asking for the return of Wilde's letters. Everett, in sending some, stated of his friend:

Allow me to add that I cherish a great regard for your father, & looked upon him as one of the most intelligent and accomplished of our countrymen. He not only possessed very extensive reading, but excelled in conversation. This with his amiable disposition & gentlemanly manners gave a great charm to his personal intercourse.— I found a very kind & respectful recollection of him among the men of letters & liberal opinions at Florence.[21]

The most vivid account of Wilde available is by Frances Appleton, the lady who was to become Longfellow's second wife. While a young girl of nineteen, traveling with her family, she kept a detailed journal of her trip to Europe, including the days in the spring of 1836 when she knew

Wilde. Wilde went with the family on various tours in Italy: to Rome, to Naples, to Palermo. One comment for May 2, 1836, stated: "For lack of other resources killed off some churches today. Mr. Wilde our cavaliere servante."

Wilde frequently went on drives with members of the Appleton family "to see the fashion"; at one party of Americans in Italy, Frances Appleton had a "long talk with Mr. Wilde" but had to confess it was "most learned & literary but sufficiently wearisome withal."

It is customary to think of Wilde as a melancholy, brooding man saddened by life. But Frances Appleton saw him otherwise; she could scarcely believe that he had written "My Life is Like the Summer Rose" because he was "so . . . antisentamental-looking [sic]." She found the poet to be affectionate toward an Italian youth named Marchio, who never talked "a sentence through in one language," who was "tickled by all the gentlemen & laughed at by all the ladies." Wilde hugged him "like a bear." At another time Wilde tried to be as pleasant as he could when he and Tom, the brother of Frances Appleton, took a trip to the baths of Nero in Rome:

Stopped at the baths of Nero, where Mr. Wilde & Tom resigned themselves into the hands of a demi-nudo guide & disappeared to enjoy a vapour bath by walking to the spring of hot water which makes this the best natural one in the world. . . . After a long time they emerged from the dark[,] steamy vaults in a fascinating state of dripfullness—hair[,] dress & whiskers all drooping "like flowers o[']er charged with rain" quite as well boiled as their eggs. Poor Mr. Wilde looked truly crest-fallen, his halo of grey hair hanging down his steaming cheeks, trying to raise his merry laugh but evidently having had quite enough of the vapour baths of Nero.

In her entries for June 2 and 3, 1836, as she was leaving "Firenze la bella," she believed that she would always remember parts of her trip: "How shall I miss the silver Arno & the sweet reflections of its 'fair white walls' . . . & Mr. Wilde's laugh. . . ."22

The Italian trip, however, was basically an intellectual rather than a social experience. During practically the entire stay, he was either studying Italian authors and manuscripts or writing about Italian poets and translating their works.

April 2, 1836, was a high spot in his life. Fewer days for

him had been "marked by interest higher, deeper, more intense, more painful and more delightful than this." Count Mariano Alberti, "an author & antiquarian," formerly a captain, came into possession of some manuscripts supposedly by the Italian poet Torquato Tasso. Although the Roman government would not allow the publication of these Alberti manuscripts, friends could see them. Wilde, invited with some others to a reading of the "treasures," described his reaction to the evening as follows: "We were sometimes all talking at once, even I forgetting my bad French & worse Italian & laboring to find words for wonder and for pity— At others we were nearly all in tears. . . . Such a scene occurs but once in one's life. There has been a fever in my blood & spirits ever since. . . . They will probably be yet published in England or France, and occasion a new life of the Poet to be written."[23]

A few days later Frances Appleton and some other Americans also visited Count Alberti:

Mr. Wilde hurried us . . . to pick up Miss Harper to go . . . to the house of a Count Alberti[,] who has been civil enough to permit us to come & see some immensely valuable manuscripts of Tasso illustrating particulars of his sad destiny. I never passed 2 hours more full of excitement & interest in my life. . . . Count Alberti delivered [one sonnet] in the most excited manner. Mr. Wilde looked equally so & drew suddenly out of his pocket a paper saying that, with his liberty, he would read to his compatriots a translation he had made from twice hearing the sublime original. It was very good but came in rather mal à propos here. The Count looked puzzled either at his audacity or thro' non comprehension of the English. We were "taken aback" & applauded frigidly. "Very pretty[,] Mr. Wilde," says Miss Seton, the old maid!—more unfortunate than our silence! . . . . Mr. Wilde says too: "If you publish these in America my translation shall illustrate this sonnet in the edition!"[24]

When the Grand Duke of Tuscany doubted their authenticity, handwriting experts examined them and Alberti sought verification. Wilde became convinced that internal evidence and some collateral proofs showed the manuscripts to be genuine. Later on, when the Roman government consented to publication, Wilde decided to translate the poems, an undertaking he called a "labor of love." He wanted to write a short work to accomplish the translations; what he "intended for a small pamphlet of 50 or 60 pages. . . swelled into a volume of two or three hundred." By June 17, 1837, the work was completed, though Wilde was able later to make a few changes.[25]

Getting the work in print was another matter. One copy went to America, where various literary men such as Henry Wadsworth Longfellow and Cornelius C. Felton tried to find a publisher. Another manuscript went to England with the hope that it might be published there at the same time as in America. But there was little success; Wilde believed only "Novels or Politics" were being printed. Joseph C. Cogswell, an American friend, started the idea of a prospectus to be sent around to various literary people. They would buy copies in advance from a printing of 1250 in all; but this method displeased Wilde. After asking Cogswell to recall the prospectus, he himself undertook the cost of the work, his only payment being 200 copies.[26]

After his return to America, Wilde stayed in New York for several months supervising the publication himself. Alexander V. Blake, a New York publishing firm, had the work ready by the first of 1842 under the title *Conjectures and Researches Concerning the Love, Madness, and Imprisonment of Torquato Tasso*. The work, appearing five years after the completion of the manuscript, had the following dedication:

To John W. Wilde, Esq.
My Dear Brother,
An affection like ours rarely shows itself in words, and, if I now allow it utterance, it is rather in homage to truth than in compliment to you. If I knew any one more worthy of my esteem and regard than yourself, I might spare you the pain of a dedication; but, in all that tries the heart, you only have always withstood the proof, and to you my first work must be inscribed, that flattery or falsehood may not stain the inscription.
Richard Henry Wilde.
Florence, 5th November, 1840.[27]

The work is not a full-length biography; rather it is a scholarly effort intended for the person who already knows something about Tasso's life. At one time Wilde called the work "an exercise in translation and composition"; nevertheless, he was really concerned with one key problem in Tasso's life: the reason for his madness and imprisonment.[28]

The book received praise for its "air of elegant scholarship and refined literary taste." The chief criticism was that Wilde "did not more clearly express his own opinion, and that he did not start by stating briefly what he wished to prove, and go on step by step to prove it." Robert Browning, who approved of the way in which Wilde wrote on only the one point in question, stated: "He relies upon the subject; is sure of the service he can render by an efficacious treatment of thus much of it; nor entertains any fear lest the bringing in of a Before and After, with which he has no immediate concern, should be thought necessary to give interest to the At Present on which he feels he can labour to advantage."[29]

One literary interest led to another. The first project was the work on Tasso. When that was completed, Wilde made an abridged life of the poet, added his translations, and included the combination as a part of his second literary project, entitled *The Italian Lyric Poets*. The plan was to write a number of biographical sketches of Italian poets, both major and minor, and to include translations of some of their poems. Although the work was never completed, it led into his third literary project, a biography of Dante. In addition to these three literary pursuits, to which he gave most of his time while in Italy, he also considered a book to be called "Legends of Florence" and a series of novels on Tuscan history; but he did not even begin these works.[30]

While working on Tasso, Wilde wished to see some rare letters by this Italian poet in the Medicean archives; therefore, he sought permission from the Grand Duke of Tuscany, which eventually came but too late. By that time he was "engaged in translating specimens of the Italian lyric poets, and composing short biographical notices of each author." Baffled by the "obscurities and contradictions abounding in the ordinary lives of Dante," he thought he would take advantage of the archives to clear up some points.[31]

Upon entering, he saw "suites of rooms whose large size and immense height would befit a royal palace, crammed with books and folio files of papers from top to bottom." Filled with "wonder and despair," he read widely for a while, but then decided that if he did not want to waste his time, "a very limited period" must be selected for his literary efforts. Therefore, "the life of Dante was chosen, and as materials increased, his times were added."

After deciding to write on Dante, Wilde began to realize how unqualified he was for his enormous task; he saw that he would have to read everything by or about the Italian poet. He was convinced that if he "really wished to explore the ground faithfully, there was nothing for it but [to] examine page by page and document by document every book and file that related to [his] epoch." Consequently, he planned his time: "Two or three hours of the morning, usually from nine to twelve, were given to the Riformagioni. As soon as [his] eyes became weary with the crabbed and sometimes faded characters of ancient parchments, [he] betook [himself] to the Magliabecchiana and remained until two, reading manuscripts in a more modern hand." In the afternoons and evenings he read printed works by Dante and biographies of the poet. Eventually he started writing, and the result of all his labors was a manuscript entitled *The Life and Times of Dante, with Sketches of the State of Florence, and of his Friends and Enemies*, of which the part dealing especially with Dante had the following dedication: "To the People of Italy This Life of their National Poet is humbly inscribed by their friend The Author."

During his search in "the ancient archives of Florence," Wilde found "some curious inedited matter respecting the poet himself and the means of reconciling some hitherto irreconcilable contradictions" in his life. His idea was to have at the end of the work a supplement "containing all the inedited proofs and [i]llustrations."[32]

Although only one volume of the proposed two-volume edition was completed, it is more nearly a biography than his work on Tasso. The manuscript pages are numbered to page 678, but one number sometimes serves for two or even three pages; furthermore, there is a fairly long introduction. Book 1 of Volume I, which goes to page 293 of the manuscript, has the following chapters:

Chapter 1 — Italy in the Age of Dante (beginning on page 1)
Chapter 2 — The Church (page 50)
Chapter 3 — The Nobles (page 62)
Chapter 4 — The Comuni or Towns (page 124)
Chapter 5 — Virtues and Vices (page 151)
Chapter 6 — Admn of Justice Etc (page 189)

Chapter 7 — Florence (page 197)
Chapter 8 — The Biographers of Dante (page 231)
Between Books 1 and 2 of Volume I is a sketch of Dante made by Seymour Kirkup.

Book 2 of Volume I, which treats Dante's life until his exile, has the following chapters:

Wilde, at first enthusiastic about this life of Dante, seemed to take great delight in the laborious study of manuscripts. Constantly he revised what he had written; every line was changed fifteen or twenty times, for by this biography he hoped to be remembered as an author. Charles Sumner, who saw Wilde in New York upon the latter's arrival in 1841, wrote Horatio Greenough: "He was full of Dante. I like to see a man instinct, as it were, with his subject." And Wilde read portions of the work aloud, for William Gilmore Simms heard him.[33]

Because of financial difficulties after he returned to the United States in 1841, he began to believe that he would not finish the work. As early as the fall of that year, he wrote: "I find it *impossible* to proceed with what I began in Florence." The next year he had almost completed the first volume, but he believed that he would have to return to Italy to finish the work. Simms, on seeing Wilde, wrote to a literary friend: "He speaks despondingly of the work—probably lacks impulse, and might be driven to the task by an application." After he decided to go to New Orleans, Wilde stated: "It may very possibly be years ere I take pen in hand . . . even to finish either the 'Italian Lyrics' or the 'Life & Times of Dante.'" He probably gave up working on the biography after October 10, 1842, the date he finished the first volume, according to a note on page 678 of the manuscript. Apparently realizing that he would never complete the book, he wrote on this last page: "And whether the leave we take of him be temporary or final. . . ." The sentence was never completed.

In very small letters on the last page but undoubtedly in Wilde's handwriting are the two words: "Deo Gratia!"[34]

In addition to reading and writing Wilde had other literary interests. By February of 1836 he had "written home a letter recommending . . . the attention of the Library Committee of Congress to a most rare and valuable collection of ancient works, comprising the library of Count Boutourlin in Florence," which was offered for sale and "could be purchased at comparatively a small price." But the United States did not buy the works.[35]

Wilde also took part in the discovery of a portrait of Dante. Giorgio Vasari in his life of Giotto stated that this early Italian painter had made a portrait of his contemporary and intimate friend, Dante Alighieri, in the chapel of the palace of the Podèsta in Florence. The palace later was used as a prison, and the chapel became an office in the prison, the name of the building being changed to the Bargello.

Carlo Liverati mentioned the fresco to Wilde. The latter read a note by Domenico Moreni in Filelfo's *Vita Dantis* in which Moreni said various attempts had been made to recover the portrait; Moreni himself had spent two years on the project but with no success. Wilde spoke to an Anglo-Italian, Giovanni Aubrey Bezzi, about the matter and said that since the latter was an Italian by birth, perhaps he would have some influence in getting permission to search for it.

Bezzi thought of an Englishman, Seymour Kirkup, an artist who had lived about fifteen years in Rome, as a person who could evaluate Moreni's statement. Kirkup thought the idea of attempting to recover the painting was good and offered money to aid in the experiment. After various English, American, and Italian friends and acquaintances agreed to help, Bezzi drew up a memorial in the name of Florentines, addressed to the Grand Duke Leopold II and asking for permission to look for the painting; the signers of the memorial said that they would pay for all expenses involved in the search.

After an expert, Antonio Marini, had removed the coat of whitewash from three walls, he found figures of saints and angels, and the portrait of Dante. Washington Irving wrote about the discovery as follows:

At length, on the uncovering of the fourth wall, the undertaking was crowned with complete success. A number of historical figures were brought to light, and among them the undoubted likeness of Dante. He was represented in full length, in the garb of the time, with a book under his arm, designed most probably to represent the "*Vita Nuova*," for the "Comedia" was not yet composed, and to all appearance from thirty to thirty-five years of age. The face was in profile, and in excellent preservation, excepting that at some former period a nail had unfortunately been driven into the eye. The outline of the eyelid was perfect, so that the injury could easily be remedied. The countenance was extremely handsome, yet bore a strong resemblance to the portraits of the poet taken later in life.

There was great excitement produced in Italy "by this discovery of a veritable portrait of Dante, in the prime of his days. It was some such sensation as would be produced in England by the sudden discovery of a perfectly well authenticated likeness of Shakespeare."

Shortly after the discovery of the portrait on July 21, 1840, Kirkup surreptitiously made a sketch of it. In 1841, when an attempt was made to restore the portrait of Dante, the result was far from satisfactory. As a result, Kirkup's sketch became more valuable than ever. After Wilde returned to America, he received an engraving of Dante's head made by Kirkup; Wilde's friend, Hiram Powers, sent it to him.

Discussions took place in Italy as to the person mainly responsible for the discovery. Wilde, told that Bezzi had been taking too much credit for himself, commented: "Mr. Bezzi's behavior in relation to this matter is to say the least *unhandsome*. I hope Kirkup will execute his promise of laying the truth in some way before the public." After Wilde's death, however, Seymour Kirkup took credit for practically everything. On some of the engravings he made, he said he promoted the discovery and on others he called himself the discoverer of the portrait. In a letter in which he mentioned Bezzi first, Kirkup spoke of Wilde only once: "The day after he came to propose the junction of another person of my acquaintance for this object. This was Mr. Wilde, an American, whom I accepted with pleasure as our associate in the affair." But Bezzi, strongly defending the part that Wilde had played in the discovery, remarked: "It was Mr. Wilde and not Mr. Kirkup who first spoke to me of this buried treasure."

Although Wide was happy about the discovery of the

portrait, he was not very much interested in who should receive credit: "As for me I have too much of other unpleasant work to do; and besides when I claim to be remembered in my day and generation it shall be for something that no one shall dispute with me."[36]

For his work on Dante—his translations, his unfinished biography, his part in the discovery of the portrait—Wilde received some recognition. He wrote to his brother: "Even the few and small additions I have been able to make to this branch of Florentine history, has procured me, so strong is the national devotion to Dante, a certain degree of literary distinction and the offer of some unmerited honors." A decree of November 30, 1838, reinstated the ancient city of Fiesole, on the outskirts of Florence; and on January 6, 1840, Wilde was offered an honorary title of nobility. A family tradition has been handed down that the title was that of Count.[37]

During the years in Italy Wilde had no source of income other than what he had saved from his law practice and the income that he received from the plantation interests in Florida. Always there was the threat that he would have to return home.

Yet, in spite of financial fears, the trip was memorable. He praised the entire country of Italy, of which he said: "Thy child in heart am I." Florence was "Italy's unfading fair" and "lovely to [his] eyes, [a]bove all other cities e'en more fair." He and his family left Europe and arrived in New York on January 18, 1841. He fully expected to "return to Florence in May or June" of the same year. Business affairs, however, prevented his going back, and by September of 1841 he realized it would be impossible for him to return at an early date to work further on the literary projects that he had "already devoted so many years['] labor to." He, his sons, and his sister Catherine dreamed of returning one day to Italy, where "of all countries on earth it seems . . . the one where life glides off the easiest & pleasantest, if you are only exempt from the sordid care of 'Quatrini' "; but by 1847 Wilde knew he would never go back and would have to be content with "having seen as much of Paradise" as he could.[38]

V

Georgia: 1841-1843

THE trip to Italy had satisfied Wilde's last basic desire. Realizing that he could not always remain in that country and looking toward the future, he stoically decided in 1836:

My design, if I remain there [in Georgia], as is probable, is to take up my abode in my hermitage on the Sand Hills, beyond the boundary of whose fence I am firmly resolved never to set my foot again. All the duties of my life have been fulfilled as nearly as I can fulfill them; all the objects that I greatly cared about will have been accomplished except such as are impossible. Nothing is left me worth pursuing as an object—no motive for any further exertion, and as I do not find any part of the world renders existence much more endurable than another, I may as well wait for Death at home. Sooner or later he will find me there.[1]

Understandably the break with Italy was a difficult one; a poem entitled "On Leaving Florence" expressed the bitter "pang" that he felt at departing. After "a long voyage" and "some heavy gales," Wilde, William, John, and Catherine arrived in New York on January 18, 1841, where Cornelius C. Felton, Charles Sumner, and Henry Wadsworth Longfellow were on hand at the dock, eager to greet them. Even the New York *Herald* proclaimed the news of their arrival.[2]

Though Wilde had managed to gather some local fame in Florence because of the portrait of Dante and his researches in the archives of Florence, it was Washington Irving, excited about his accomplishments, who gained prestige for him in America:

I have been—and *am being Lionized* to the utmost point that the most greedy Lion in the world could desire, & have been compelled to *roar* so long, so loud, and so often that I am hoarse and tired of the noise I make, and quite astonished at my own notoriety. Washington Irving has taken me and my literary fame and my works into friendly watch and ward and since he praises them so warmly I begin to think there must be more in them than I supposed.

Two poems in Georgia newspapers greeted Wilde on his return home: one began "Son of the South, we gladly welcome ye"; an introductory note to the other, entitled "Welcome Home," stated that Georgia had "always felt proud of the genius of her accomplished son."[3]

Financial problems had forced Wilde to leave Florence and continued to plague him. The "winding up of [his] unlucky planting interests in Florida" ate up the little money he had. The crops for 1840 had failed, and some land had to be bought back at a loss. Mrs. Ellen White, feeling that she could not carry out an agreement that her late husband had made with Wilde about the income from the Florida plantation, regretfully wrote that if she paid his annuity, she would be "left almost penniless." To add to his troubles, Wilde, who owed money in Italy to the banking-house of Emanuele Fenzi, was bitterly "vexed at their conduct" for thinking him a poor risk and requiring security from Hiram Powers.[4]

Wilde in 1841 and 1842 knew that both Augusta and the State of Georgia were "in a most wretched condition. The crop ½ short, all business suspended, some banks stopped and *all* soon [would]. It [was] utterly impossible to sell any thing, to collect debts, or to borrow, for there [were] none to lend & the banks [would not] discount any paper whatever." Many of his old friends, once "immensely rich," had been ruined. When Wilde tried to send money to Fenzi, a certain percentage was lost in the process: "Our notes must be exchanged for Northern money at a loss of 15 per cent. Northern money for a Bill on Europe 8 or 10 per cent more, commissions &c &c. One fourth is thus *lopped* off at once." The only solution, he felt, for both the state and the country lay in the establishment of another National Bank.[5]

For the sake of "economy," Wilde, his sons, and Kate moved in with John Walker Wilde and his family. The house, located on a street called today Pickens Road, belonged to Wilde; but he let his brother, who had been living in a residence over a bank, have it while he was in Italy. Supervising the raising of some crops, he designated himself "a corn planter"; there were not many profits, but at least everyone had "bread." The life was a retiring one for Wilde; sometimes he would endure a month "without going to town." Though he had little time for his Italian books and manuscripts, they remained his "friends & companions." Always there was the thrill of foreign literature; "next to *cash*," he said, "languages are worth having." And for the first time he began to study "a little German, hard as it [was]."[6]

With such limited resources, educating his sons posed a problem. Deciding to go even more deeply in debt, Wilde made preparations for them to enter Georgetown College on August 31, 1841. Friends helped him raise the necessary $300 for the advance fee, and he begged the administration of the school to allow each boy only 12½ cents per week for spending money. Wilde went to Washington also just to make certain that they reached the school safely. In February of 1842 he visited them, requesting permission that they not be required to go to their classes on a certain day. He was especially anxious for them to hear John Quincy Adams speak in the House of Representatives; they would "not probably have another such opportunity during the Session."[7]

When the boys planned a trip to New York to visit the Weyman household, Wilde, the protective parent, sent elaborate directions:

Don't go into crowds nor stand gaping or gazing in the streets or you'll have your pockets picked. Don't form any acquaintance or enter into familiarity with strangers. Keep your money & check in your *fob* or in an *inside waistcoat pocket*, all except what you want for *immediate use*. . . . See to your baggage and be wide awake or you'll be skinned. . . . At New York get into a *cab* and go straight to your uncle Abner's house at 35 Howard Street if it be day light when you arrive—or even as late as 10 at Night. If later[,] you had better go to a Hotel[;] the Astor-House . . . you will be most sure to get into. Get a room *by yourselves*. Don't let any one in with you unless it is a towns man or somebody you *well know*. . . . Trust no one . . . nor a room mate who may attempt to claim acquaintance with you, on my account or as a Georgian or in short in any way or else you'll be plundered. . . .

The boys, aged nineteen and eighteen, with such cautious advice constantly before them, managed to save their honor on the trip—and their money.[8]

Wilde wanted his sons guided constantly, not just during school hours. In particular, they should not waste their time on journalism. He wrote his brother: "Of all reading in the world newspaper reading in the general is the least profitable. It is about 19/20th waste of time. For a school boy especially, as it not only does no good, but actually distracts him from the great business of his life. Every moment of his time not given to study should be employed in good, wholesome, active exercise, to promote the growth and health of his body and allow his mind repose to prepare it for fresh exertion."[9]

Wilde raised enough money for their education during the 1841-1842 school year, but he could not make it through the next year. His finances required that he withdraw them on March 8, 1843. The question now was: What would the boys do? Wilde thought he had an answer for one of them. Will had always liked the sea, and entering the Navy might aid his health. Writing a strong letter of recommendation for his son, Wilde said that the boy had "an invincible love for the sea, [was] of very good character, disposition & habits," and had "a reasonable stock of French, Italian, Spanish, & Latin, and a little algebra." But since Will, unfortunately, did not receive the appointment, the two boys had to keep looking to their father for support.[10]

To have a source of income, therefore, Wilde returned to the practice of law, even though Charles Sumner was afraid that "the technical phrases of our common law [would] not be as acceptable as the verse of Dante; & that addresses to juries [would] be an indifferent substitute" for Wilde's literary labors. Wilde, not especially interested in returning to his old profession, wrote: "It is true I have been *forced* into two partial and temporary engagements of a professional nature by the temptation of good fees, my poverty and not my will consenting, but I went in like a Militia-man for a single tower [*sic*] of duty, and obstinately refused to enlist 'for and during the War' at any bounty whatever." His work took him to the Supreme Court twice, once as a consultant to Daniel Webster. In 1843, a lawyer friend said that there was some talk of getting Wilde for a proposed Court of Errors in Milledgeville; but the friend hardly believed Wilde "would be willing to make [himself] such a victim, to prove that Georgia [could] have a first rate Judge for $2000."[11]

As soon as Wilde resorted to law, the force of politics again faced him. He did not want to return to the same old pattern, for if he could return to Italy "long enough to complete the 2d Vol of Dante, and the Italian Lyrics," he would not exchange that period "for all the accumulated honors of the whole Georgia delegation in Congress from the adoption of the Constitution to the present moment, [his] own share of their laurels . . . included."[12]

Circumstances changed his mind. Thinking that he was going incognito to a political meeting of the Whigs in Charleston, he became uneasy when prominent citizens rose to praise him in hour-long speeches. Of the result, Wilde wrote: "As the last Orator sat down, a different peal arose, the most stunning I have ever heard. It consisted[,] as I have a vague idea[,] of my own name repeated uproariously from all quarters of the house." When the house would not cease, he stumbled to his feet and said something. This meeting marked his return to the political scene.[13]

Most assuredly in a "very savage mood of mind at the government" which had brought about such financial chaos to him and to the country, he decided he might be of some aid in trying to bring a Whig to the Presidency. Henry Clay was the hope of the party. When Wilde went to a convention at Milledgeville on June 13, 1842, for the purpose of nominating Clay for Whig president on the 1844 ticket, delegates picked him as the chairman of the committee of twenty-one. One of the group reasoned that it was foolish to nominate Clay two years before the national election, but the suggestion was quickly discarded.[14]

Wilde authored a report for his committee in which he spoke of "the long services, . . . great abilities, . . . frank and fearless character, . . . ardent, generous and uncalculating patriotism" of Clay. Ending with a rousing call for action, he concluded:

On, then, gallant countrymen! to win the heart of honest prejudice, by the friendly arms of truth and reason! On, to convict falsehood by evidence, and overwhelm self-conceit with ridicule. On, to inspirit languor and luke-warmness, by the thrilling eloquence of patriotic enthusiasm.[15]

Wilde admitted that just "as one thing leads to another," his report "involved [him] chin deep in politics." On June 14, 1842, the delegates made nominations for the eight seats in the House of Representatives for the Twenty-eighth Congress (March 4, 1843–March 3, 1845); one name was that of Wilde. Fearing "the loss of one or two years precious time, which would afflict [him] greatly," he addressed the convention and made the following resolution:

Resolved, that R. H. Wilde be excused from accepting the nomination tendered him for the reasons assigned to this Convention.

Since the resolution did not meet with a second, "the President of the convention refused to put it to the consideration of the body." Wilde reluctantly stayed on the ticket.[16]

Shortly after the nominating convention, the Augusta Chronicle, as an aid to its readers, printed sketches of the various political candidates. The description of Wilde mentioned his early life as a clerk in a merchandising store. The George McDuffie referred to, who had been born near Augusta and who eventually became a distinguished senator from South Carolina, was a close friend of Wilde's, although earlier the two had been alienated temporarily because of the Cumming-McDuffie duel:

[Wilde] gained a respectable support for himself, a widowed mother and her orphan children. For several years he was the co-laborer of Mr. McDuffie, as Clerk, in a merchantile house in Augusta, their days spent in the faithful performance of their duties, and their nights in reading and other strenuous efforts to improve their minds. Each afterwards studied Law and became distinguished in his profession. What a noble spectacle was afterwards presented in Congress, when these same merchants' clerks, then the Representatives of our admiring constituency in different States, were the acknowledged Champions of the House!—when on the re-charter of the U. S. Bank and the vetoes of Gen. Jackson, their united voices were raised in strains of eloquence that thrilled the nation and called forth the admiration of thousands! What commentary, too, this upon the folly and injustice of those who affect to despise the young and enterprising portion of our Merchants—and what encouragement to those youthful aspirants to cultivate their moral and mental qualities, rather than to spend their leisure hours in wild and reckless dissipation.[17]

In the months before the election held in October of 1842, there was perhaps a greater awareness of political parties than in any other election Wilde had been in, with the possible exception of the campaign of 1834. A political organ for the Democratic Party, such as the *Federal Union* of Milledgeville, seldom printed any news, especially any flattering news, about the Whigs. Nor did the Whig organ, the *Southern Recorder* of Milledgeville, give much attention to the Democrats. Each newspaper made personal attacks against the political candidates, and there were "sneering assaults on the intellectual attainments of Mr. Wilde."[18]

This election, in which the entire Democratic Party won by a small majority, was Wilde's last political try. He was, however, still anxious to get the Whig Party in power: in December of 1842, as chairman of a committee appointed to invite Clay to visit Augusta, he spoke at length about the man's excellent qualifications; he attended a Whig convention in Milledgeville in June of 1843; and on October 20, 1843, he was the chairman of a meeting of the Whigs of Richmond County. Shortly after these time-consuming political tasks, he headed for New Orleans.[19]

New Orleans: 1844-1847

At times Wilde thought highly of New Orleans, a "hurly burly city," where a person could "hardly walk the streets without being run over." If his sister "could see the quantities of children . . . and the ruddiness of their complexions," she "would imagine N.O. must be one of the healthiest cities in the Union." The city "would be over populated were it not for duels and yellow fever." To a friend he wrote:

Henceforth I am a creole of Louisiana . . . my permanent home is here . . . there were always until recently, times when I cherished the thought of returning one day or other to die among the scenes of my youth—among the friends of it—I would say— were there any left. But that thought is past. Fate has willed it otherwise, and I have now enough to do with her dunces not to struggle or repine any longer.[1]

By the first part of 1843 Wilde reluctantly concluded that he had to leave Augusta if he expected to practice law on a more active scale; his financial condition "in the present depressed State of the country," when all property was "unproductive," required the change. Bitterly despondent over money matters, he confessed:

Every struggle I make to do something only seems to sink me deeper and deeper in the slough of despond, and in spite of my dogged obstinacy, this eternal pulling against wind and tide depresses my spirits. Under the most favorable auspices, I must calculate the loss of two years, either in Balto or New Orleans, before I can support myself. How can I meet these expenses? And yet it is evidently worse to remain in Georgia doing nothing and with the certainty of never doing more.[2]

But where should he go? Both Baltimore and New York held out to him "some spice of temptation." With a special "hankering" for "the intrinsic charms" of the first of these, he visited the Maryland city in early 1843 where he delighted in "the indescribable titillating, tickling, teazing, laughing, writhing, wincing, thrilling, torturing pleasure of being Lionized." After being "admitted and *gazetted* as a member of the Bar of Maryland," he changed his mind and decided to try his luck in New Orleans. In early November Wilde expected to be on his way to the Crescent City.[3]

Long before going to Europe, Wilde had hopefully thought of the Louisiana city. A lady friend, however, had cautioned him against the "debility and hot weather" which required "a double allowance of the vital principle to subsist" and "a due degree of intellect to avoid utter stupidity." Summer there was terrible with "insects of various kinds, unpleasant odours and unpleasant sights of all kinds" in addition to "stewing in a damp warm-air." Also the "animosity between the French & Americans" in New Orleans was "bitter," extending "even to ladies and children." But Wilde would not be warned. Others praised the city where room existed for everyone who practiced "industry & honesty." In particular, he was lured by the success of his good friend William C. Micou, a lawyer and a former citizen of Augusta, who was thriving in the city.[4]

To get a little money for the trip, Wilde parted with some property including twenty-two of his negroes, seventeen of whom were men, "mostly good field hands." Soon after the Christmas of 1843, he started on "the most horrible journey" he ever made "for so long a space & time." The rain beat down the night he left Augusta and continued "in torrents" until January 18, when he arrived in Mobile, Alabama. His group was "run away with once, often stalled" in "what is technically called North Carolina travelling—i.e. walking half the time & carrying a rail on your shoulder to prize out." His general comment on the trip was that "never certainly had those who travel by land or water more need of the prayers of the Church."[5]

At Mobile Wilde saw "more Georgians" than he left in Augusta, and they treated him with joy and civility. Then journeying by steamer to New Orleans when "the weather smiled for a moment," he arrived on January 20, 1844, and received a kind and warm welcome from Micou and his family. Earlier Micou had written Wilde: ". . . make yourself

at home with us until you make your permanent arrangements."
Wilde, ever the gentleman, accepted the offer, and remained
with his friend, enjoying room and board, from January until
the latter part of October, 1844.[6]

Micou and his family treated Wilde "like a brother rather
than a stranger"; their kindness had "the rare quality of being
extreme but not oppressive." Micou's law partner, "a fine[,]
generous[,] whole-hearted man," had a very good law library.
This, together with their office, was put entirely at Wilde's
disposal. Also Micou in a certain law case was kind enough
to give up his own place in it to Wilde, "with all his notes, &
only half the responsibility."[7]

Summer in New Orleans was dreaded. During eight months
of the year, day and night were "too short for man[']s industry, & his power of enduring fatigue inadequate to gratify
his cupidity of gain." But from July to November, there was
no activity; the people who could went "somewhere, East,
North, or West, or into the country over the lake." It was
so dull in the summer that it became "common-Law in N.O.
that a judgt. [judgment] taken during the *sickly season*" was
"*prima facie* fraudulent and ought to be set aside."[8]

Wilde spent the summer of 1844 at Micou's home on the
Bay of St. Louis in Mississippi on the shores of Lake Borgne,
"about 60 miles from N.O." where it was "perfectly healthy,
with 100 Vols of French, Spanish, Roman, & Louisia[na]
law books for . . . companions, & fishing, shooting & bathing
for amusements." Others might "*die* of Dyspepsia & Ennui"
because of "the sterility & monotony of the Bay"; but Wilde,
in the "monotonous tenor" of his life, thrived on being a "complete Book-Worm eating [his] way diligently thro huge
tomes." If he expected to gain a reputation in New Orleans,
he had to know local law well; during the whole summer,
therefore, he was "preparing for the fight" ahead.[9]

The only unpleasant thing about the life was that now and
then the wind swept down "a swarm of starved musquitoes"
which sent the people near the bay "capering in all directions
like Cattle from Gad flies." These "*black* very savage" creatures, which blew "no trumpet of defiance" but made "war
without manifesto," fell upon people like "S. Sea Islanders
on the Missionaries and Cannibal like" devoured them. Wilde
himself suffered with "bleedings" from the pests. When

Wilde visited New Orleans on August 9 just for the day, he noticed that the "rascals" were even worse in the city.[10]

Yet the summer of 1844 was a mild one, and the members of the Committee of Public Hygiene in New Orleans were "in absolute despair for want of a well authenticated case of yellow fever, whereupon to report" so that they might "seem to *do* something for their money." Most of the people along the Bay, therefore, had left by the middle of October.[11]

With a jolt Wilde soon realized that "making fortunes" in New Orleans was just a dream of *"El Dorado."* Each year the city was "overrun with starving lawyers" who worked for little or nothing, ran into debt, and left town if they managed to "get a little clients['] money."[12]

All kinds of problems faced determined lawyers. The judges were strict, and it was "not easy for a silly or superficial blockhead to stand the test." Wilde had to study "tooth and nail at the Civil Law, in all its codes & versions, French, Spanish & Louisianian." Competition was "so great & the old established barristers of reputation so numerous" that a new lawyer needed "much time to make his way." Yet he knew that in time he could master the "technicalities of a very intricate, absurd, & often self-contradictory code of practice."[13]

Not much could be said for the clients, for "the whole population" was as "shifty and shifting as the lawyers." Character was of no value; never had Wilde "seen such universal sharpers." "Even most of the men of property & standing" were no exception. For instance, there was a crafty physician, one of the very richest men in the city but as mean as he was rich, who tried to cheat Wilde out of some land; but the poet refused to "allow this Shylock to cut his pound of flesh" contrary to an agreement that the two had made. And the City Bank, for whom Wilde "must have done $1,000 worth of work," "behaved like the shabbiest set of Yankees," even though Wilde was "mainly instrumental in saving them some 20 or 25,000$."[14]

Micou had been a life-saver for the first months in New Orleans. But Wilde, with "about $30 left," felt that he should start out on his own. Resolved to keep out of debt at all sacrifices, his schemes had to be "of the most rigid economy practicable." He rented a single, small second-floor room at 14 Exchange Place, "the Inns of Court in New Orleans," had his name put on the door, and tacked a sign downstairs which announced "R. H. Wilde atty at Law upstairs." The room, conveniently located just opposite the post office, did not have "an article of furniture except a grate"; for these bare walls and dingy floors he had to pay a high rent. A law partner was a necessity because the courts were "8 mo. in perpetual session," and a man could not be "there & in his office both." Yet for Wilde it was "as hard to suit one's self with a partner, as with a wife, a house, servants, a horse or any other necessary Evil." But Sam R. Plummer filled the bill and eventually became a good friend.[15]

Wilde lived at the St. Louis Hotel, the most economical one he could find, but "not sufficiently so" for his limited resources. Later his children joined him to add to his financial distress. At the end of 1845 Wilde made out the following itemized list of expenses: "office rent $25 lodging 40$ board for 3 $85 Postage five, candles &c $25," for a total of more than $175 a month.[16]

Of his general financial situation, Wilde wrote: "The Devil, or some equally good natured friend who is kind enough to take charge of regulating my pecuniary destinies, seems to have sworn I shall never have a dollar, without instantly finding a use for it." Further commenting, "I never remember in my life to have been so perfectly destitute," he thought about "the hangers on of the Bar who ought to be thrown over it"; they intimated that he charged and got "such enormous fees, that even Banks" which employed him would not "be able to pay dividends." Though for the year 1845-1846 he "received in Cash . . . just $200," the rumor persisted that he had a "lucrative business." Supposedly he "confined himself to important cases," and always had "a *minimum* charge of five hundred dollars."[17]

All was not gloom in New Orleans, however. For one thing, Wilde's health was basically good. To be sure, he still had his customary troubles. During a "sudden cold spell" he had a little rheumatism and once had "a returning sense of weakness" in his ankle. At rare times he also had his old trouble with his eyes, but his cure—consisting of taking sulphur internally and using an eyewater prescription he got in Florence —helped somewhat. He had to get Kate to have this prescription filled in Augusta because there were "not many, if any" druggists in the Crescent City that he "should be willing to trust."[18]

Yet on the whole his complaints were few. Even occasionally feeling that his health had "never been so good these 20 years," he no longer had to depend on "carbonate of soda" and did not have many headaches. Though for exercise he walked at least two miles every day, he was "growing *fat* on French & Roman" food. The chief beverages drunk—"claret & Mississippi water"—agreed with him; the latter cured "everything except yellow fever." Believing "in this system of *hydropathy*," he sent two hogsheads of the water all the way to Augusta to his brother. John Walker Wilde was to follow directions: he was to let the water stand for a while so that the muddiness would work itself clear; or he could put a "small salt spoonful of powdered alum in each cask"; also he might add a little ice to cool it. Wilde added in the directions: "Call me 'horse'—aye *old horse* if you please in case you don't say after a week you never drank water like it." Wilde also enclosed "some 9 or 10 boxes of veritable table claret." The regular daily dose was half a bottle of Mississippi water a day and half a bottle of claret—"the largest half claret." Wilde, for his own use, apparently emphasized one half of the mixture a little too much, for he finally decided he would have to abandon wine "for fear of the gout."[19]

Wilde had much social life in New Orleans, especially during his first two years. On one particular night, he dined out, then went to a large private party, and after that to a masquerade. Every week he had two or three dinner invitations, where he always met "some agreeables." During one week in the winter of 1845, his social schedule listed four balls, "besides Theatre, Operas, Lectures[,] foot-races & bull-fights." The situation changed as warm weather approached: the Italian opera closed, the "belles & beauties" left, and his friends fled to Europe. Unhappily, Wilde lamented: "I am without a place to spend my evenings. . . . From 7 to 10 hang heavy on my hands, and you have no idea of the trouble those three hours cost me. Men have hanged themselves on much less provocation."[20]

One entertainment he attended was in the ball room of the St. Louis Hotel, "the French centre of fashion," which excelled "the American tenfold." Amid a display of "really fine"

Creole beauty, he was dazzled by the room, the most beautiful he had seen in New Orleans with its "four immense Chandeliers," which "shed a flood of Gas Light from porcelain imitations of Wax Candles." A beautiful young Creole condescended to speak to him, and from a bouquet she was carrying "a small fragrant rose dropt off most opportunely." Wilde gathered it up and with her permission "preserved" it "as a memorial."[21]

Always women—in New Orleans, in Augusta, and elsewhere—made life pleasant. Wilde admitted that he had lost his heart several times, but it had always been returned to him "as a damaged commodity wholly unmerchantible." He admitted his one weakness: "to see—or hear—a friend—a female friend especially—a pretty woman above all in the dishabille of her person—heart—or understanding—*in confidenza*—as my Italians say—that I must confess is a foible of mine, to which I have sacrificed many graver & it may be better things. . . . O! the ingratitude of the Sex, to deny me in my old age *almost* the only gratification I have derived from my idolatry."[22]

All the world was ready to marry him "by Report," whether or not he wished it. "Even a little Fairy at the last child[']s *fancy* ball" told his fortune to that effect. He commented on the marital situation in general, a "great folly for a veteran" like him: "It must be a most delightful companion who never becomes tiresome. Even Adam & Eve must have yawned in Paradise, or the Serpent would never have found a chance to break in upon their tête à tête."[23]

Though Wilde spoke almost as a flirt to women, he nevertheless firmly believed "a male coquet is a detestable character." He had a number of lady friends—married, widowed, single— to whom he expressed undying love and devotion, but always in a playful mood, far from serious.[24]

In Augusta Julia Cumming, "the fair Julia," "more blooming and beautiful than ever," was the wife of a friend, Henry Cumming. In his correspondence with Mary Parmelee (the wife of another friend of Augusta, Thomas Parmelee), Wilde, "the humblest of her slaves," confessed his literary interests to one who had so often shared his "griefs and losses." And after Maria Hopkins Walker, the daughter-in-law of a Mobile friend, left the St. Charles Hotel in New Orleans, where she had been staying, "the Heavens wept, the men raved and the women laught. . . ." When she wrote Wilde later on, her "charming" epistle greeted him "most opportunely on the Sabbath morning (after church)—and . . . Heaven was no more remembered."[25]

The widows he knew were cautious—and so was Wilde. Mrs. Ashley, the widow of General William Ashley, whom Wilde had known in Congress, was a "most agreeable person." But she had had two husbands, "a fair share for any one woman"; to "become a third," supposing it possible, would be like "making one's will—a memento of mortality." This lady delighted in Wilde's "wit and spirit of fun & mischief," but she prudently kept him "carefully at full arm[']s length, looked frightened when he approached her, and seemed as if she was thinking of the Scotch proverb 'they ha' need o' a lang spune that sip soup wi' the deil.' "[26]

Mrs. Emily Tubman, the widow of a rich merchant in Augusta, was unusually attractive. Wilde frequently recalled he "as the lovely and accomplished girl who came so near stealing" his heart "at first sight." He, when a "young briefless barrister, never . . . dared to trust himself in her company." When she decided to go to Europe on a trip, Wilde wrote his brother: "Tell Madame T. I am quite out of patience with her for having so little taste as not to go and take me with her, when I should finish Dante, immortalize her in prose and poetry, and be buried in Sante Croce."[27]

The single women that Wilde preferred were younger than he. And sometimes his attitude was puzzling, at least to John Patterson Wilde. The son once could not grasp the attitude that his father took toward a young woman that both men were interested in. Wilde replied: "You are a very *literal* young gentleman. I really have *not* the least idea of becoming your rival." He had enough sense to know she would prefer a younger man, for he was not near enough his "dotage to think otherwise."[28]

Miss Charlotte Cleveland of Augusta, with whom Wilde corresponded, was "always a great friend & favorite." Other letters went to Caroline Stanford, "Cara Carissima," living with the Parmelees in Augusta. This attractive girl had "been playing the deuce with Augusta, setting the town on fire." If only Wilde "were within finger-reach instead of pen-reach" of her, how she "should be—pinched!" Women who attacked

[74]

his modesty he summarized as follows: "O! the ingratitude of this world of petticoats!" How wonderful it would be if he were only twenty years younger with his "present reputation"; then he would revenge himself on the whole sex, and on Cara first. When he adoringly read her letters with their "infinite craft—witchcraft . . . spells and charms" in them, he begged the Lord to "preserve" him, sinner that he was. He tried to entice her to come to New Orleans "so as to double" his pleasure in going to the operas. Possibly she could persuade Thomas Parmelee to establish himself in the Crescent City and make a fortune; then the two—Wilde and Cara—would amuse themselves "by helping . . . to spend it." In one letter he signed himself "Old Harry," but between the two words he wickedly drew a figure of the Devil.[29]

Wilde had male visitors as well as female to cheer him up. Among his political friends the most distinguished was Henry Clay, to whom the poet introduced Sir Charles Lyell. The latter, an English professor on a geological tour through the Valley of the Mississippi, visited New Orleans at the end of February, 1846, saw the poet at the Hotel St. Louis, and left the following description:

We were very fortunate in finding our old friend, Mr. Richard Henry Wilde, residing in the same hotel. . . . Mr. Wilde took me to the Houses of the Legislature, where a discussion was going on as to the propriety of changing the seat of government from New Orleans to some other place in Louisiana. . . .

Before we left New Orleans, Mr. Wilde received a message from his negroes, whom he had left behind at Augusta, in Georgia, entreating him to send for them. They had felt, it seems, somewhat hurt and slighted at not having been sooner permitted to join him. He told us that he was only waiting for a favorable season to transplant them, for he feared that men of color, when they had been acclimatized for several generations in so cool a country as the upper parts of Alabama and Georgia, might run great risk of the yellow fever, although the medical men here assured him that a slight admixture of negro blood sufficed to make them proof against this scourge. "No one," he said, "feels safe here, who has not survived an attack of the fever, or escaped unharmed while it has been raging." He mentioned the belief of some theorists, that the complaint was caused by invisible animalcula, a notion agreeing singularly with that of many Romans in regard to the malaria of Italy. . . .

During our stay in New Orleans, Mr. Wilde introduced us to his friend Mr. Clay, the Whig candidate in the late presidential election and I was glad of the opportunity of conversing with this distinguished statesman. . . .[30]

Wilde at several times had his say about culture in New Orleans. Believing that the city was beginning to revive in its interest in the arts, he felt that it was a glorious place with a "generous feeling" which needed to be carefully directed. On the other hand, he regretted that the city lacked some necessities: for instance, a public library and at least one good bookstore. At one time he wrote: "You can't conceive any thing so dull as New Orleans except a Quaker meeting."[31]

Hoping to encourage cultural progress, Wilde took part in obtaining a statue of Benjamin Franklin by Hiram Powers for the city. Almost as soon as he arrived, Wilde, aided by others, brought up the suggestion, "not from any enthusiasm for Franklin," but from "a strong and kind feeling" for Powers. The first meeting to stimulate enthusiasm was a failure, for there were "not over an hundred present." The citizens, who "adjourned for a week, & squibbed and agitated for the arts & Franklin in the mean time, invited all [their] female friends, and reserved seats for the ladies." For the second meeting, held in a church, "the Sacred Musical Society agreed to attend in the choir, and had a new piece composed for the occasion." This attraction, in addition to "the distinguished Orators expected to be heard, filled the Church to overflowing." Wilde spoke "in a speech of an hour, made without any notes, but with all [his] heart." Delivery without notes had at least one advantage: Wilde was "spared the vexation of putting on and pulling off spectacles." Since there was great enthusiasm, manifested by "loud and long continued cheers," a committee of which Wilde was a member sent an official letter for the statue of Franklin, " a commission from the Crescent City— the spontaneous fruit of her love for the arts and her admiration of the Artist." The intensity of the second meeting, however, did not continue, and it became more and more difficult to make the payments to Powers. Eventually the statue was unveiled in 1873; and a description of it, with a mention of Wilde's name, is available in a recent guide to the city of New Orleans.[32]

To break the monotony of life in his new home, Wilde traveled frequently. One important trip was to the Supreme Court from early December, 1844, until the first part of February, 1845. He not only visited in Washington, but also slipped in quick trips to Richmond, Charleston, and Augusta. The summer and fall of 1845, from late June to late November, found him on an extensive trip to Baton Rouge, St. Louis, Chicago, Niagara, Saratoga Springs, various places in Canada, Boston, New York, Philadelphia, and finally Augusta. John Walker Wilde, seeking relief for his ailments, and John Patterson Wilde were with him part of the time. In 1846 he spent the entire time from early July to late November in Augusta with his loving relatives.

The presence of his sons in New Orleans gave Wilde his greatest happiness. Scarcely managing "to swim himself" and "entirely unable to sustain the expense" of the boys in the new home, he nevertheless was delighted to have them there, though they "might all sink together." John, who had been reading law, decided to come first. Wilde had him outfitted in Augusta because in New Orleans a person could get "nothing done or only at enormous prices." Early in December, 1844, the boy left for the city. Though he lived there with his father after arrival, Wilde "put him to board in a French family" so that he would have practice in another language; soon he began to " 'Parlez-vous' passably ill." Wilde examined him every day on law problems, and after a private and public examination John was admitted to the bar in May of 1845. But since he had no experience, he just joined a group of starving lawyers, his only income being a few weeks of copying work.[33]

John Patterson Wilde was a special problem to his father. He was a great sufferer from morbid melancholy, partly because of bad health and partly because of "natural temperament." Wilde, thinking the son's blood might be "thick," recommended the use of sulphur, which had been "very serviceable" to Wilde himself— "a *tea spoon* full every night for a month." He also suggested "cheerful society, healthful exercise, never pushed to *fatigue*, and rational amusement." Whenever John felt "a nervous irritability coming on," he should "find some amusement or employment in the open air, or visit or talk, and above all never lose an opportunity of laughing," for there was "nothing so good for the spleen." The young boy had a temper that he could not control; Wilde wished that his restless son could "curb the outward demonstrations of ill-humor at inevitable evils." The poet wrote that Pat, as he was affectionately called, was "never contented anywhere, or in any condition. Dissatisfied on going to Europe. Repining while there, and enjoying nothing. Vainly longing for it after [his] return. Discontented in New Orleans. Finding N.O. a paradise when [he was] at the Sand-Hills. . . . Ever languishing after the future, or repining over the past—the present . . . perpetually" escaped him. Furthermore, John, "very susceptible" and "always in love with a new face," was "full of torments and despondency" when anything went wrong.[34]

Wilde's elder son, William Cumming Wilde, had been in Augusta "getting a knowledge of business," because the concerned father was anxious to place him "in a situation to become happy[,] useful & independent." On a certain trip during the summer of 1845, Wilde's companion was James Robb, the owner of the Mechanics Traders Bank of New Orleans. The two men became friends; and Robb, "a liberal, frank[,] unostentatious lover of the arts, and a gentleman at all points," agreed to help Will at a future date. The boy came to New Orleans in December of 1845 and soon managed to get a position in the early part of 1846 with Peter Conrey, a dealer in exchange, "without salary or compensation of any kind." "Very hard worked as [an] out of door clerk—out in all weather," he "never murmured" and apparently "committeed no mistake." But he made a blunder: he went to a perfectly respectable "stylish party" attended also by Mr. Conrey. The latter, thinking it "impertinent in a clerk" to associate with the "master," sent the father a "polite note" next day, saying there was "no further occasion for Will's services." This son, who had worked for a month, was thus *dismissed* without a cent." As a result, he was "very melancholy"; he "filled up." In December of the same year Robb, according to his agreement, hired Will. The young man was "indisposed" for a while, but the banker "kept the place open for him for nearly a fortnight." Getting up from a sick bed, Will returned to work and eventually became a favorite with the banking house. He had a good salary, was "as busy as a bee," and growled most when he had "least to do."[35]

The two sons were such exact opposites that Wilde said of them: John Patterson Wilde "gets tired and growls at not a tenth of the work that poor Will does or strives to do." To both he was devoted: "My wish has been always to live with my sons as friends, enjoying their love & confidence without losing their respect."[36]

Though money was scarce, the poet had "*fame* enough." Even before Wilde left Augusta, two newspapers in New Orleans, knowing of his plans, elaborately praised his talent both in law and literature and expressed their pleasure at the thought of adding him to the notables in the Crescent City. As soon as he arrived in New Orleans, he was "much courted fêted & caressed." In several cases he felt that he had performed extremely well. If his comments seem vain, Wilde had an answer: "How can one write of one's-self without *Vanity?* . . . Vanity is the greatest rogue of all the passions except Love."[37]

In one case in the United States District Court he had to answer "a bull-headed, well-meaning but most captious barrister who was at once party and client." The man attacked Micou and Wilde "with accusations of professional discourtesy and illiberal practice." Wilde's "blood being up" but his "head perfectly cool," he "gave the learned counsel a homily which he was very much at a loss how to take, whether as complimentary or ironical, tho' he was the only person in the Court room . . . that had any doubt on the subject, the question remaining balanced in his mind only from the influence of extreme self-love." Wilde "placed some of his complaints in so comic a point of view" that this "renowned fire-eater . . . was obliged to laugh heartily at them himself." But Wilde's victory was not complete. A lady who had "an old spite" against him and who took care to let him know "all the *disagreeable* things," though she was "polite enough to hide the medicine in honey," said a friend of hers gave "a great deal of exaggerated praise" to the speech, but also added that "there was . . . a sort of affectation about it, an excess of Elegance."[38]

In the United States mint case, Wilde said that he had "the credit of being the first man in [Louisiana] who succeeded in shewing that the *United States can* be sued in some cases." In general, he felt that a rank was quietly being accorded him "among the heads of the profession." On May 13, 1847, when the Association of the Bar of New Orleans was organized, Wilde became a member and soon was appointed to the committee on membership. This group of important lawyers was succeeded in 1855 by the New Orleans Law Association, which eventually became the Louisiana Bar Association.[39]

A. Oakey Hall, traveling in the city, wrote a description of the lawyer Wilde in 1846 or 1847:

I crossed the vestibule and listened to him for half an hour. He was addressing a bench of four judges. . . . I recognized in the speaker a tall gentleman of commanding appearance whom I had often met walking dignifiedly, and with smiling face, among the busy groups with cane in hand, which he held rather in compliment to his slightly-furrowed brow and flowing gray hair, than to assist footsteps which had lost none of their juvenile elasticity. . . . [He had settled] in New Orleans, and [was] shedding on the severer features of its rough-and-tumble life the chastening influence of his refined taste and classically stored mind. He had for a moment forgotten his classics and his poetry, . . . and was deep in the mysteries of the question whether twenty-five bales of cotton belonged to a hook-nosed stuffy gentleman seated at his side, (and dignified as "my client" by lips which in their day had smiled upon admiring throngs in drawing-rooms and saloons,) or whether they belonged to a broad-backed Kentuckian who was seated by the grate-fire mumbling some chestnuts.[40]

In the last few months before his death Wilde was an important figure in the establishment of a law school. The Constitutional Convention of 1845, which began its sessions in August, 1844, in a country town, adjourned to meet in New Orleans in January, 1845. The Constitution was adopted on May 14, 1845, a portion of it being: "Art. 137. A University shall be established in the City of New Orleans. It shall be composed of four faculties, to-wit, one of law, one of medicine, one of the natural sciences, and one of the letters." This convention was followed by the legislative incorporation of the University of Louisiana on February 16, 1847.[41]

A newspaper notice about the law faculty of the University

listed "Hon. R. H. Wilde, Second Professor." His position was that of "Professor of Public[,] International and Constitutional Law in the University of Louisiana." Several of Wilde's friends took "a warm interest in this projected institution," but he felt that he had been *"forced"* into this new position. He wrote to his brother: "As vexations never come single they have elected me a *Professor* here. . . . I have begged & entreated & implored to be excused. The Chief Justice, who is . . . very much my friend, and has the University greatly at heart will listen to nothing, but that I *must* serve. I told him I am under bond to be in Washington next winter; and could not deliver my course: he said the others would take my place as substitutes 'till my return—*He* would lecture in my stead, if there was no other remedy. What was to be done? Alienate one of my best friends & the Chief Justice too?"[42]

Although he had "an utter want of faith in the scheme," he intended to prepare himself for his work by being familiar with as many books as possible in his field. Wilde's prediction of failure was far from accurate, for the school became successful and developed into Tulane University. But the yellow fever saw to it that Wilde, whose lectures were to begin "next winter," was only briefly associated with the school.[43]

Although Wilde had gained recognition as a lawyer, he often thought of the adage: "Wine is often drunk in honor of poor fellows who would be glad to have the empty bottles." Since he planned to live in New Orleans and there was little money to be had from law, he had to find income elsewhere. He still had some slaves in Augusta, living with his brother; positive that they were of "infinite trouble" to John Walker Wilde, he sent directions for shipping them to New Orleans. The bibulous Isaiah was warned that the yellow fever killed "all drunkards the first season." Another slave, Betty, was instructed that she must learn to dress hair—a profitable business. These two, as well as the others, arrived in 1846. But Isaiah, though he had not "egregiously misbehaved" in New Orleans, kept up his reputation of being rarely sober; Wilde doubted if he ever would be. He got some work as a carpenter. Betty had a little employment as a hair dresser, but Wilde's hopes for having the others work at an iron foundry were unsuccessful, for white hands were abundant. The slaves were "quartered" on him and had to "bivouac in a small room adjoining" Wilde's office and "at night in the office itself."[44]

Some money came from houses being rented in Augusta. Wilde even considered land speculation in New Orleans as a sugar planter, though he was cautious because he had "no talent for managing slaves & no experience in any business but Law." Will also aided financially by turning over his entire salary to his father.[45]

Wilde and his two sons had earlier moved to the St. Charles Hotel to "spare Will a walk." Finally deciding that to pay $100 a month there at the same time that he had servants was "monstrous," Wilde planned to get a place of his own. Early in 1847 Kate was informed: "The House is bought and $1,000 paid on it. . . . There was no living at the St. Charles rates, and it costs as little to starve in a house of our own as to rent one." Wanting Kate to come to New Orleans to be with them, he tempted her by saying there was "a little Catholic chapel not far off, a thing not without its influence" on the purchase he made.[46]

Since William Wilde had to remain in the city during the summer of 1847, Wilde decided "to summer it" also. Of his son he stated: "I can never leave *him;* and as half the young men in the Bank are unacclimated *all* cannot go." Surrounded by his two sons and his sister Catherine, who had accepted his invitation, Wilde prepared to endure a New Orleans summer with its expected yellow fever plague. Aware that something might happen, he wrote to his brother in August, 1847, a little more than a month before his death:

Tho' the best part of my life is over and I set no great value on the remainder for myself, as I have a *chance* of Independence by a few years more, I would not lose that chance on my children's account & your[s]. Few partnerships of weal & woe have lasted longer or been less interrupted than our[s], and I still hope to wind it up by our both retiring with a Competence.[47]

Encouraging John Walker Wilde not to worry, he complained that the newspapers magnified the threat of the yellow fever for various reasons, one being that "the Creoles desire to *scare* off the Americans." Furthermore, the "South Carolinians & Georgians [were] rarely subject to it at all." It seldom attacked women, or men over fifty; Wilde and Kate were surely safe. The family lived "in one of the cleanest &

healthiest streets in the city." When the servant Bill was taken with "the acclimating fever," Wilde wrote: "I attended to him constantly, felt his pulse and his head, and am satisfied from all his symptoms & complaints, that I have had a dozen worse fevers. You see the thing has not half the terror you suppose."[48]

The clue was prudence. Will, the one most exposed, avoided night air, carried his umbrella always, changed his clothes frequently when heated, and was otherwise very cautious. Wilde refused "to be frightened at shadows."[49]

But the yellow fever did attack a woman—Catherine Wilde. She survived; and Wilde, in the last letter that he ever wrote, reported on September 4, 1847: "As yet we have no new case, and it is not impossible, the rest of us may escape altogether or have it only lightly, as we are all prudent." Shortly after receiving this letter, John Walker Wilde sadly added the following postscript to it: "My beloved Brother's last letter to me. He was taken sick the next day, at midday Sunday 5' & died at sunrise on Friday the 10' Sep: I received the dreadful intelligence by the side of my children's graves at half past seven o[']clock in the morning of Wednesday the 15' September 1847." The news of Wilde's death came to John Walker Wilde in a letter from William Micou, who personally had felt "no such sorrow, since the loss of [his] own father."[50]

Wilde died at 4 A.M. on that dreaded morning of September 10, 1847, a victim of the yellow fever. This particular year was a terrible one in the number of lives taken, for there were at least twenty thousand cases of yellow fever during the season, a vast number out of a population of from seventy to eighty thousand; often seventy or eighty people died daily. An appeal was made for strangers to stay away from the city and for "all persons who [had] not had the fever to remove out of the city until the epidemic [had] disappeared." During the week in which Wilde died, "the mortality in [the] city [was] visibly on the decrease." In Lafayette and New Orleans, ninety-four died on September 7; seventy-three on the 8th; seventy-four on the 9th; forty-six, including Wilde, on the 10th; and thirty-eight on the 11th.[51]

While Wilde was sick, his son John Patterson Wilde was "nearly dying . . . of the fever," and "it was weeks before they dared to communicate" the news of the death of his father to him. Catherine, who watched over her brother during his sickness "like an Angel of Mercy," stated that "his last moments were peaceful and happy, he was perfectly tranquil and sensible, that [as] he was dying he spoke of each member of his family and desired to be remembered to each, he desired a Catholic priest might be sent for and died a convert to the Catholic faith."[52]

At a time when many people were dying from yellow fever, it seems unusual that the New Orleans papers gave so much space to his death; yet "the press [seemed] to have vied with each other in the touching and eloquent eulogiums pronounced upon his character." He was praised for his "eminent scholarship, and charming eloquence, . . . his private virtues, high sense and honor, and singular amiableness of disposition." One New Orleans newspaper, in its obituary, said: "The ripe scholar, the elegant gentleman, the polished statesman and lawyer, we do not expect soon to meet again in any one person, as they were happily united in him. In the death of Mr. Wilde the community has lost one of its most distinguished ornaments, the country one of its richest and most cultivated minds."[53]

After Wilde's death on September 10, 1847, the body was placed in a vault in New Orleans in St. Louis Cemetery No. 2. In 1854 it was removed and taken to the place on the Sand Hills near Augusta where Wilde's wife and their first-born child were buried. There was a tombstone for the child but none for Caroline Wilde.

For over thirty years the body of Wilde remained in this spot. Then in 1885 a prominent citizen of Augusta, Charles Colcock Jones, Jr., interested in preserving the traditions of the city, wrote a pamphlet entitled *The Life, Literary Labors and Neglected Grave of Richard Henry Wilde*, which had as its purpose the honoring of the poet by Augusta. Jones asked whether "the bones of this lawyer, statesman, scholar, poet, [should] be permitted to lie longer in an unmarked and obliterated grave in the obscure corner of a vegetable garden?" He distributed his work to a number of people such as John Greenleaf Whittier and Paul Hamilton Hayne, and they in answer commented on Wilde and his poetry.[54]

In 1886, to some extent as a result of Jones's pamphlet, the Haynes Circle of Augusta made arrangements to remove Wilde's body to a more appropriate spot. One member of

[84]

the committee stated: "The body was in a leaden coffin or case, and the case was not opened. A shovel struck the foot and broke a small place which showed the end of a slipper. James R. Randall, who was one of [the] party, seemed much depressed."[55]

They deposited the body in a certain section of Magnolia Cemetery, which later was to hold also the graves of Paul Hamilton Hayne and James R. Randall. This section today is known as the "Poets' Corner." The grave, the only one on a lot, contains a small flat stone, made of white marble, about two feet high, with the following words: "Richard Henry Wilde. His remains are buried here. His public monument is on the 1200 block of Greene Street."

The Haynes Circle supervised the erection in 1896 of the monument on Greene Street in honor of Wilde. The memorial bears the following inscription:

Erected by the Haynes Literary Circle of Augusta, Georgia, 1896
Richard Henry Wilde,
Born
Sept. 24, 1789,
Died
Sept. 10, 1847.
Poet,
Orator,
Jurist,
Historian,
Statesman.
"MY LIFE IS LIKE THE SUMMER ROSE,
THAT OPENS TO THE MORNING SKY,
BUT ERE THE SHADES OF EVENING CLOSE
IS SCATTERED ON THE GROUND TO DIE."
WILDE

Survivors and Descendants

RICHARD Henry Wilde was survived by two sisters, Catherine and Ann; one brother, John; and two sons, William Cumming and John Patterson.

Catherine Wilde, who never married, helped to rear Wilde's sons; when their mother died in 1827, they were only three and two years old. She had lived in Richard Henry Wilde's household and had gone to Italy with him and the two boys. Upon their return all the family stayed mainly at Wilde's old home near Augusta, where John Walker Wilde was also living. After Richard Henry Wilde moved to New Orleans in 1846 he persuaded her to come there. She watched over her brother during his last illness when it was almost impossible to get much nursing and medical aid because of the numerous deaths. Catherine Wilde died on October 25, 1853, in New Orleans and was buried in the Wilde family vault in Magnolia Cemetery in Augusta.[2]

John Walker Wilde, after serving from 1836 until 1851 as cashier of the Georgia Railroad and Banking Company and from 1832 until the first part of 1851 as judge of the Mayor's Court in Augusta, considered a change of residence because of his bad health. He went to San Francisco, California, in 1851. Eventually his family joined him in that city, where he became a partner in the banking firm of Tallant and Wilde. He died on August 3, 1862, and was buried in Laurel Hill Cemetery, San Francisco. He had numerous survivors.[3]

Ann Cecile Wilde, the youngest of the children of Richard and Mary Newitt Wilde, and her husband, Dr. John M. Anthony, who was a cousin of Dr. Milton Anthony (or Antony), the founder of the Medical College of Georgia, had one child surviving infancy—Mary Ann Anthony, born on February 22, 1842. The three moved to Arkansas, but on the death of her husband in 1854, Ann Anthony moved with her daughter back to Augusta, Georgia. Mary Ann Anthony married John Benjamin Pournelle in 1858; this union produced seven children. Ann Cecile Wilde Anthony died on October 13, 1886, and her daughter, Mary Ann Anthony Pournelle, died on February 3, 1936.[4]

Richard Henry Wilde's younger son, John Patterson Wilde, was working as a lawyer in New Orleans during the last years of his father's life. He aided the Duyckincks in their entry on Richard Henry Wilde in *Cyclopaedia of American Literature*. Catherine Wilde in a letter to Mrs. Hiram Powers said that John Patterson Wilde would probably remain single "because he admired the ladies too much"; indeed he never married. He continued as an attorney to the end of his life, and in the 1857 city directory of New Orleans was listed as a partner in the law firm of Wilde and Marks. He died on March 11, 1861, "at the residence of his brother, William C. Wilde, in Jefferson City."[5]

Richard Henry Wilde's older son, William Cumming Wilde, and his wife, Virginia Wilkinson of Augusta, Georgia, whom he married in late 1850 or early 1851, had five children: Richard Henry or Harry Wilde; Virginia Wilkinson or Jenny Wilde; James Wilkinson Wilde, who died at the age of eight months; Emily Wilde; and Caroline Wilde.[6]

Before the death of his father, William Cumming Wilde was working as a bank clerk in New Orleans for the Mechanics Traders Bank run by James Robb. Later he held various other positions, such as correspondent for the New York *Herald* and teacher.[7]

In addition to writing some poems of "fire, poetic luster and exquisite finish," William Cumming Wilde prepared a biography of his father, which was to be published with the poetical works of Wilde. John Patterson Wilde said that his brother was "a man of rare literary taste and cultivation of fastidious taste, who [had] inherited his father's poetical genius." In 1858 William Wilde wrote that the biography was awaiting publication; for this undertaking he had written to various men who owned letters written by Wilde, asking for their return.[8]

The obituary for the wife of William Cumming Wilde appeared in the *Daily Picayune* for June 4, 1888. He married again, this time to Miss Mary Goodale. Soon after the marriage, the two moved to the country, "in order, as he expressed it, 'to listen to the songs of the birds, and to let the eye rest upon an expanse of beauty as broad as its sight of heaven.'" There William Cumming Wilde contracted pneumonia and died as a result of it in 1890.[9] Thus, the biography of his father, together with the letters collected, was never published.

In 1917 Emily Wilde, a daughter of William Cumming Wilde, gave to the Library of Congress certain writings by Richard Henry Wilde, consisting of a manuscript of *Hesperia*, Volume 1 of his work on Dante (all that was completed), his translations of some Italian lyric poets together with introductions, and a collection of original verse. She was planning to send the biography and the letters to Augusta, Georgia, but they were destroyed in a fire. William Cumming Wilde did accomplish one thing of literary importance: he arranged the publication of Wilde's long poem entitled *Hesperia*.

The first child of William Cumming and Virginia Wilde was born late in 1851 and was named Richard Henry. In the city directories of New Orleans he was listed as having at least two occupations during his brief life: he was a member of a detective bureau called Wilde, Pearson & Co. (1878) and he was also a clerk (1880). This young boy, known as Harry Wilde, was described as being an author who "had a purely local reputation as a newspaper writer, for his verses. He died young, a great loss it was felt to the city which did not boast many young poets."[10]

The next child was named for her mother, Virginia Wilkinson Wilde, but she was generally called Jenny Wilde. She became a famous designer for some of the beautiful carnival parades and tableaux in New Orleans. Some of her work is in the Louisiana State Museum. In addition, she wrote a book of verse entitled *Why and Other Poems*. She died while on a cruise to England. Her body was returned to New Orleans, and she was buried next to her brother in Metairie Cemetery in a tomb that she had designed.[11]

Emily, the child who survived longest and who worked for a while as a bookkeeper, according to the New Orleans directory for 1893, lived with her sister Jenny until the latter's death. After that she moved to California to be with the family of John Walker Wilde, and there she died.[12]

The youngest child of William Cumming and Virginia Wilde, Caroline, was the only one of the five children who married. She became the wife of Eugene Giraud, a civil engineer. Caroline died at Austin, Texas, in March of 1902, and a funeral service was held for her on March 12 at Immaculate Conception Church, Baronne Street, New Orleans.

The marriage of Caroline Wilde and Eugene Giraud produced two daughters. One of them, Frances, became a Roman Catholic nun and died in a convent at Roswell, New Mexico. The other child, Virginia Giraud, who married John Crockett of New Orleans and then moved to Los Angeles, California, is, together with her children and grandchildren, the only direct descendant of Richard Henry Wilde.[13]

Part Two
SELECTED POEMS

Lament of the Captive

My Life is like the summer rose
That opens to the morning sky,
And ere the shades of evening close
Is scattered on the ground to die:
Yet on that rose's humble bed
The softest dews of Night are shed
As if she wept such waste to see
But none shall drop a tear for me

My life is like the Autumn leaf
That trembles in the moon's pale ray;
Its hold is frail — its date is brief
Restless — and soon to pass away;
Yet ere that leaf shall fall and fade
The parent tree will mourn its shade,
The wind bewail the leafless tree
But none shall breathe a sigh for me!

My Life is like the print that feet
Have left on Tampa's desert strand
Soon as the rising tide shall beat
Their track will vanish from the sand
Yet, as if grieving to efface
All vestige of the human race
On that lone shore loud moans the sea
But none shall thus lament for me.

FROM *POEMS*: *FUGITIVE AND OCCASIONAL*
Manuscript owned by Mrs. Virginia Crockett, Los Angeles, California

I

Introduction

In at least two places—in his biographies of Tasso and Petrarch—Wilde speaks about the intensity of feeling necessary
for the poet:

> Poets are . . . like the rest of our species. What is most
> deeply and strongly felt by them is apt to be most clearly and
> forcibly expressed.

> No one is continually on the rack of violent emotions:
> they cannot be and live. Yet if we glance over a poet's biography
> to find he did many things like the rest of the world, and some-
> times, it may be, even diverted himself at the expense of his
> own craft, we begin to distrust the transports and lamentations
> that admitted of so much commonplace interruption. The ques-
> tion however is one of intensity not time. Men who describe
> strongly, must in general have felt deeply, but agony and
> rapture are occasional incidents, not habitual modes of existence,
> and must inevitably give place to long intervals of apathy or
> languor. They are often recalled no doubt, and keenly remem-
> bered, but not every joy or every pang, is embalmed in rhyme,
> and blazoned to the world.

Even objects of nature by themselves are insufficient; they
must in some way be related to human feelings if poetry is to
result:

> But the heart seeks, and has forever sought,
> Something that man has suffered or enjoyed,
> And without human action, passion, thought,
> Nature, however beautiful, is void:
> 'Tis from deep feeling Poetry is wrought;
> Such is the spell her master minds employed.
> What wins for Arden's wood one Briton's tear,
> But pensive Jaques with his poor stricken deer?[1]

[93]

In his original poems Wilde's favorite verse form is the quatrain of iambic tetrameter, iambic pentameter, or anapestic tetrameter, with a rhyme scheme of *abab*. His frequent use of the anapestic foot is unusual. Occasionally he employs feminine endings in lines 2 and 4. He, however, also uses several other forms, especially the sonnet and the eight-line stanza with various rhyme schemes.

Within these metrical forms, Wilde chooses several Romantic subjects that he uses frequently. He praises the present moment, as did the Cavalier Poets. He exalts women at times and at other times condemns them. In an exalted mood, he sometimes celebrates those who fought for freedom. He even has an occasional humorous poem. But in most of his original verse, Wilde, weary of life and having known grief and disappointment, looks back to happier days of youth and friends. And memory is powerful:

> For me, tho' my life has long since lost the hue
> That hope to the scenes of futurity gave
> When such rainbow [-] like tints on their darkness she threw
> As the sun on the mists of Niagara's wave:
>
> Tho' joy [']s golden beams seldom brighten or cheer
> The dreary and tiresome path that I tread
> And no ray of glory to mark my career
> Shall shine on me, living, or light on me, dead,
>
> Still so sweet and so soothing is memory's power
> (Tho sacred and solemn and pensive it be
> As the mild summer evening's first star-illumed hour)
> Tis dearer than hope [,] joy or glory to me.

All he can look forward to is the grave. The mood is one of farewell—whether to past joys, to friends, to a woman, to America, to Florence, or to earth. Even the album he writes in is a "record of departed years." Many of his translations—and, in general, his translations are superior to his original poetry—have this same subjective, melancholy brooding.[2]

One question must be asked about this type of poetry: To what extent are the poems autobiographical? Was Wilde really "melancholy's slave" and weary of life?[3]

In a letter on the subject of "The Lament of the Captive," Wilde said: "Whatever *my* life may be like, whether roses or thorns, the public is in no danger of being troubled with my confidence." Furthermore, Edgeworth Baxter in his speech at the unveiling of the Wilde monument stated that everybody who knew Wilde agreed that his outward appearance was "one of cheerfulness and sunshine." This contrast between his external appearance and what he spoke and wrote about is clearly described by a reporter who attended a festival at Appling, Georgia, and, after hearing a speech by Wilde, reported it in his paper:

The allusion to his "flagging spirit," loss of interest in the scenes of the world, and rapid progress to "that rest which he coveted, the grave," was in bad taste for the practiced statesman and politician; and though it might have passed tolerably well in the anonymous poetical effusion of a romantic youth or lovesick girl, yet in contrast with the athletic frame, and gay, animated, and smiling countenance of the speaker, his age, business habits, and the matter-of-fact gravity of the subject and the occasion, was altogether *outre* and ludicrous.

And the *Augusta Chronicle* showed that it was aware of the amusing side of Wilde when it stated: "An Irishman by birth, Mr. Wilde seems to have inherited all the playful humor and the rare endowments of genius, as well as the good taste and discriminating judgment of the gifted nation from which he is descended."[4]

If Wilde is posing in many of his poems, an influence that must not be overlooked is that of the English poet Thomas Moore, who wrote many poems similar in both spirit and meter to those by Wilde. A survey of the issues of the *Augusta Chronicle* for a typical year when Wilde was writing his poems gives an estimate of the great popularity of Moore. In the available 93 issues of the paper for 1817, which was then semi-weekly, 29 poems appeared, 11 of them by Moore. No other poet had more than two poems published in that year.

Yet Wilde apparently was despondent at times. John Forsyth spoke of his "morbid sensibility," and Wilde wrote to his friend John Patterson, shortly after the death of Caroline Wilde, that he wanted to travel: "I know & care not where, provided only it is among strange scenes. I have suffered much in body & mind since I saw you & desire to escape for a time from all that is associated with bitter recollections." In the next few years, 1828-1830, he wrote much original poetry.[5]

Furthermore, Wilde looked for autobiography in the poetry of Tasso. After listing all the works probably written to Laura and all those to Leonora, he planned to discover in the following way whom Tasso loved: " 'The loves and transports' which he 'wept and sung,' being *true*, then, *what* they were may be deduced, with some degree of certainty, from a careful examination of his writings." He used this same method of analysis in his essay on Petrarch in *The Italian Lyric Poets*: "Giving credit to Petrarch then, for only as much sincerity as is necessary to explain his poetic success, it may be possible from his own verses, to trace, at least in outline, the story of his love."[6]

The best answer to the question is that there is a limited amount of autobiography in Wilde's original poetry. However, he was an early Romantic poet in America and often was just choosing subjects used earlier by Romantic poets in Europe.

Edgeworth Baxter said that Wilde's poetry is "always without affectation" and that it is "original and sincere." The statement is not accurate, for most of his verse seems to be highly affected and of little merit. The poems, as well as his speeches and letters, are verbose. Francis Lieber wrote to Charles Sumner: "Wilde was here, and has given me 4 very acceptable letters indeed, except that they are written in too high a strain, about my reputation in America and Europe."[7]

A good criticism of Wilde's original poetry is that of Lewis Parke Chamberlayne in the *Library of Southern Literature*:

The fault of all these poems as lyrics is Wilde's fatal fault—he never could develop his theme, hardly ever even show the theme in progression. Separate ideas are thrown off one after another, but of movement or growth there is none. This same trait is shown in his excessive use of exclamatory sentences, and lines consisting of disconnected words, all nouns, or all verbs, or all adjectives—word-lists, in short.

Wilde . . . treats his subjects more like an orator than like a poet. The "Ode to Ease" is a mass of negatives, and "Solomon and the Genie" a series of questions. . . . Even in the descriptive passages, in which his accumulation of detail has a certain effect, he does not so much produce a picture as recount the objects he would like to combine into one.[8]

Although Wilde enjoyed writing, he apparently did not consider himself a good author. Surprised that Rufus Griswold wanted to include him in *Prose Writers of America*, he said that he rarely kept copies of his prose works and in fact he hoped that the greater part of them had been destroyed. Furthermore, no one thought more humbly of his pretensions as a "rhymer" than he did.[9]

He seldom sought publication of his original verse, and when he did it was for a specific reason. During the controversy about "The Lament of the Captive," he sent Verplanck the poem "Solomon and the Genie" for publication but added: "It is not now my purpose to acknowledge any thing, & I don't wish ever to be known as sending you the inclosed."[10]

Trying to be a literary man was not compatible with being a lawyer. Wilde felt that literature did "no good to an advocate's reputation"; in fact, it often impaired a person's usefulness. When he decided that he would go to New Orleans to practice law, he said that he would have to give up his "literary amusements" immediately. And three years later, writing from New Orleans, he stated that a passion for Dante "can't live in the atmosphere of Law and Commerce. It is like putting some innocent warm-blooded animal into carbonic gas."[11]

"The Lament of the Captive"

THE most famous poem by Wilde, that beginning "My life is like the summer rose," has had various titles such as "The Lament of the Captive," "My Life is Like the Summer Rose," "Summer Rose," "The Complaint of the Captive," "Fragment," "Lines," and "Stanzas." The lines, a portion of a proposed epic, were written with the travels of Wilde's brother, James, in mind. In a letter to an "intimate friend," probably James K. Paulding, Wilde spoke of the background for the poem:

The lines in question, you will perceive, were originally intended as part of a longer poem. My brother, the late James Wilde, was an officer of the United States Army, and held a subaltern rank in the expedition of Colonel John Williams against the Seminole Indians, of Florida, which first broke up their towns and stopped their atrocities. When James returned, he amused my mother, then alive, my sisters, and myself, with descriptions of the orange-groves and transparent lakes, the beauty of the St. John's River and of the woods and swamps of Florida, a kind of fairy-land—of which we then knew little except from Bartram's ecstacies—interspersed with anecdotes of his campaign and companions. As he had some taste himself, I used to laugh and tell him I'd immortalize his exploits in an epic. Some stanzas were accordingly written for the amusement of the family at our meetings. That, alas! was destined never to take place. He was killed in a duel. His violent and melancholy death put an end to my poem; the third stanza of the first fragment, which alludes to his fate, being all that was written afterwards. The verses, particularly "The Lament of the Captive," were read by the family, and some intimate acquaintances; among the rest, the present Secretary of State, and a gentleman then a student of medicine, now a distinguished physician in Philadelphia. The latter, after much importunity, procured from me, for a lady in that city, a copy of "My Life is

Like a Summer Rose," with an injunction against publicity, which the lady herself did not violate; but a musical composer, to whom she gave the words for the purpose of setting them, did; and they appeared, I think, first in 1815 or 1816, with my name and addition at full length, to my no small annoyance. Still, I never avowed them; and though continually republished in the newspapers with my name, and a poetical reply, I maintained that newspapers were no authority, and refused to answer further. I resisted even the inclination to say that there was no *personal* allusion in the lines—no small effort of self-control considering how vexatiously certain the contrary assumption appeared.[2]

Available are four fragments of the epic and two lyric poems. In the first part of the fourth fragment is "the supposed indignant address of a savage chief to one of the American officers." The man who is captured by the Indians and sings the famous lines is Juan Ortiz, the last survivor of an expedition to Florida in 1528 led by Panfilo de Narvaez.[3]

Since James Wilde was killed in a duel in January of 1815, the lines were written before that time. The young student mentioned in the above letter was probably Dr. Charles Delucena Meigs (1792-1869), who, after graduating from the University of Georgia in 1809, studied in Philadelphia and then went to Augusta to practice. In a letter to William Cumming Wilde in 1856, he said that he saw "The Lament of the Captive" between 1812 and 1814. The date of composition, therefore, was probably about 1813 or 1814.[4]

It is difficult to identify the lady of Philadelphia to whom a copy of the poem was given. But the Library of Congress has sheet music with the following inscription on the cover:

My life is like the summer Rose
Written by
R. H. WILDE, ESQ.
(of Georgia)
Composed & Dedicated
To
Miss Adelaide Richards
By
CHARLES THIBAULT
Copy right secured.
New York Published by Dubois & Stodard 126 Broad Way

Perhaps the lady Wilde referred to was "Miss Adelaide Richards" and the composer was Charles Thibault. Although the music is not dated, the New York Library, which also has a copy, lists it as 1822; perhaps another edition had appeared a few years earlier.

The verses had the title "Song" in the *Analectic Magazine*, XIII (April, 1819), 352. The Augusta *Chronicle*, in reprinting the poem, added the following note: "We have copied from the 'Analectic Magazine' a poetical effusion from the pen of R. Wilde, Esq., of this city. It breathes the true spirit of poetry. The verse is easy and harmonious and the sentiment finely expressed." This comment suggests that the editor of the *Chronicle*, who had his office next door to Wilde's law office, had never seen the poem in print before. The first publication, therefore, that can be dated precisely is that in the *Analectic* of 1819.[5]

These three stanzas of eight lines each involved Wilde in one of the most interesting controversies of the day. About 1822 a gentleman of Savannah sent a copy of "The Lament of the Captive" to Scotland in the hope that it would be included in a periodical called the *Coronal*, published in Greenock. The editor, Mennons, probably published it in another of his publications, the Greenock *Advertiser*.[6]

Dr. Meigs informed William Cumming Wilde that the poem (entitled "Song") appeared in the Cork, Ireland, *Mercantile Chronicle* in 1823, the author being "an American lawyer." An Irishman named Patrick O'Kelly saw the verses and plagiarized them in a poem entitled "The Simile," in which he made only a few minor changes. R. Shelton Mackenzie said that O'Kelly was "in the habit of 'conveying' odds and ends of other men's productions and passing them off as his own."[7]

One editor, who believed that O'Kelly was the original author of the lines, said that he wished "to pluck the stolen laurels from the honorable plagiarist of Georgia. . . . The white feathers of the singing Swan of Killarney . . . have not been long suffered to remain as felonious ornaments in the black wings of the Georgian Gander." But the article entitled "The Authorship of 'My Life is Like the Summer Rose'" by James Wood Davidson has proved conclusively that O'Kelly's poem was a forgery.[8]

The controversy about the Wilde-O'Kelly authorship had an unusual result. Anthony Barclay, born a British subject, who was for a while consul at New York and for more than fifty years a resident of Savannah, discussed, on a Wednesday evening in August of 1834, with some friends the charge of plagiarism brought against Wilde. Since somebody suggested that Wilde had copied a Greek original, Barclay thought of doing a Greek translation of the poem.[9]

Then, after completing the Greek translation, he also made a Latin version. He prepared the various versions—Greek, Latin, O'Kelly, Wilde—side by side and sent the Greek, as a joke, in a letter signed "Terence Doyle" to a pastor friend. The pastor, who attributed the Greek to Alcaeus and wrote to James L. Petigru to see whether the latter could find a volume of the works of Alcaeus in Charleston, called on Barclay the following Monday and told him about the similarity between the Greek version and Wilde's poem.

Since the works of Alcaeus could not be found in Charleston, a copy of the poem was sent to the president of the University of Georgia, who called the Greek "pure and ancient."[10]

Various manuscript copies of the Greek forgery were circulated in Georgia and elsewhere. In November, 1834, Barclay moved to New York and, without his permission, a copy of the Greek poem was given to the editor of the New York *Albion*, who in turn sent it to Sumner Lincoln Fairchild, editor of the *North American Magazine*. The latter magazine in its December, 1834, issue, in an article entitled "Plagiarism," probably by Fairchild, printed all four texts.

Wilde protested to the magazine in a five-and-one-half-page letter. A similar letter, but shorter, was sent to the editor of an Augusta paper, in which Wilde stated: "The lines in question. . . , good or bad, are mine alone; neither Alcaeus nor O'Kelly has the smallest right to them." Furthermore, he wrote to Barclay within the next few days, asking for a published acknowledgment that Barclay had translated Wilde's poem. Barclay, in reply, wrote Wilde a letter stating that the latter was indeed the author of the poem.[11]

An article appeared in the *New York Mirror* of February 28, 1835, probably by Wilde's friend James K. Paulding, who was then editor of the magazine, which contained the letter from Wilde to Barclay, the letter from Barclay to Wilde, Wilde's account of the reason for writing the poem, and various other documents.

At times other authors were also claimed for the poem. Finally in 1871 an account of the whole controversy was published with the following title:

Wilde's Summer Rose; or the Lament of the Captive.
An authentic account of the origin, mystery and explanation of Hon. R. H. Wilde's alleged plagiarism; by Anthony Barclay, Esq., and with his permission published by The Georgia Historical Society. Savannah: 1871.[12]

This poem, which has had great popularity, has been translated into several languages. It has been set to music often. And it has been imitated or parodied several times.[13]

Criticism of the work has been varied. Edgar Allan Poe did not care for it. In his "Chapter on Autography," he included Wilde's handwriting with the following comment:

Richard Henry Wilde of Georgia has acquired much reputation as a poet, and especially as the author of a little piece entitled *My Life is Like the Summer Rose*, whose claim to originality has been made the subject of repeated and reiterated attack and defence. Upon the whole it is hardly worth quarrelling about. Far better verses are to be found in every second newspaper we take up. Mr. Wilde has only lately published, or is about to publish, a life of Tasso, for which he has been long collecting material.

His MS. has all the peculiar sprawling and elaborate tastelessness of Mr. Palfrey's, to which altogether it bears a marked resemblance. The love of effect, however, is more perceptible in Mr. Wilde's than even in Mr. Palfrey's.[14]

John Greenleaf Whittier praised the poem, stating: "His touching lyric was one of the first poems which attracted my attention when a boy. It is a perfect poem."[15]

Perhaps the best known criticism of the poem is that of George P. Marsh, who, in the course of a lecture delivered at Columbia College in 1858, remarked:

I know . . . in the whole range of imitative verse, no line superior, perhaps I should say none equal, to that in Wilde's celebrated nameless poem:

Yet as if grieving to efface
All vestige of the human race,
On that lone shore loud moans the sea.

Here the employment of monosyllables, of long vowels and of liquids, without harsh consonantal sounds, together with the significance of the words themselves, gives to the verse a force of expression seldom if ever surpassed.

And Paul Hamilton Hayne commented on the poem and also on the statement made by Marsh:

Technically the song has serious faults, and Marsh's dictum to the effect that in the blending of *sound* & sense, that line before the last is unrivalled in English verse, strikes me as *absurd.* I would undertake during a single morning & in Tennyson's works *alone*, to match it over & over again, but what matter? [T]he *sentiment* of the little lyric is so embodied that the very *commonplaceness* of it is endowed with *perpetuity.*

There isn't a particle of creative imagination in it; (such as one sees for example, in Swinburne's masterly lyrics, like "The Garden of Proserpine") nor a scintilla of originality; yet for one person that Swinburne's *chef d'oeuvre* has gratified & thrilled, Wilde's has gratified & thrilled hundreds! Everybody can comprehend the homely lines, and they appeal to a universal instinct.[16]

A statement widely circulated is that Lord Byron admired the poem greatly. It is difficult, however, to trace this comment further than Miller's *Bench and Bar of Georgia*, where it is made upon the authority of W. H. Torrance.[17]

FRAGMENT I[18]

Who knows not that of late, though patient long,
    And loving peace, till peace herself grew vile,
Our country raised at length her battle song,
    And hurled defiance to the haughty isle,
    That still with open force, or secret guile,
Urges reluctant nations to prolong
    The flame that lights their own funereal pile,
Claiming from power the right of doing wrong,
Owning no law save such as suits the strong?

Who knows not, too, how many a gallant band,
    Such as e'en Sparta's self were proud to own,
Rushed to the summons, seized the glittering brand,

Ere the first spirit-stirring trump had blown,
Eager their country's injuries to atone,
And all her glory, all her danger share:
For who that hears my rude harp's faltering tone,
Had not some brother, friend, or kinsman there,
To claim full oft a wish, a sigh, a prayer?

I too had once a brother! He was there
Among the foremost, bravest of the brave:
For him this lay was framed with fruitless care;
Sisters for him the sigh in secret gave;
For him a mother poured the fervent prayer—
But sigh or prayer availeth not to save!
A generous victim in a villain's snare,
He found a bloody, but inglorious grave,
And never nobler heart was reached by baser [glaive]!

. . . .

FRAGMENT II

The morn breaks gloriously!—the wind is fair—
The bugle sounds, the boatswain's whistle cheers,
The word is past—for parting all prepare,
And many a lovely cheek is wet with tears:
Brief space such scenes allow for woman's fears!
A few fond words—a kiss—a short embrace—
Thus sever they who meet no more for years!
Perhaps who never meet on earth again!
But mad Ambition only stops to trace
His score of millions spent and thousands slain!
The dreadful reckoning of the human race
With him, war, pestilence, and all his train,
He sees not, or, if seen, regards with cold disdain!

All are embarked!—the signal-gun they fire!—
The gallant pinnace bounds before the wind,
And dances on the waters! Mast and spire
And tower and tree and town are left behind!
And those who watch the bark receding, find
Distance and sorrow's mists obscure her sail:
The bar is past—the fresh'ning breeze is kind—
The pilot parts—round go the laugh and tale,
And joyous thus the song floats far upon the gale!

Sons of the deep! Ye spirits brave,
    Whose victories saved a nation's fame,
From whom the ruler of the wave
    First learned the pangs of fear and shame!
To you the cup is flowing free,
    To you we fill, where'er you roam,
Whether you brave the stormy sea,
    Or dare the thunderer on his home.

Skilful and bold—in hardship nurs'd—
    By horrour taught—by peril tried—
In danger and in glory first—
    Your country's hope, her joy, her pride!
To your loved names, ye gallant few,
    Our souls the song of triumph raise,
And after years shall swell for you
    "The fondly lingering notes of praise."

Long may your flag its lustre shed
    O'er the wild waters of the main;
Long may the laurel crown your head,
    And never, never wear a stain.
To you, with soul-enamouring beam,
    Dear woman's melting eye shall turn,
Your deeds shall be the sage's theme,
    And o'er the story youth shall burn!

FRAGMENT III

"By heaven!" said Jacques, as carelessly he flung
    His tired limbs to earth, "this life for me!
'Tis sweet, when every sinew is unstrung,
    Outstretched at length beneath the greenwood-tree,
To rest from every care and sorrow free—
Keenly to feast on coarse and homely cheer,
    To mark our soldiers' rude but honest glee,
Then lay us down without a hope or fear,
And soundly sleep till *reveillée* we hear!"[20]

      . . . .

FRAGMENT IV

'Tis many moons ago—a long, long time,
    Since first upon this shore a white man trod;
From the great waters to the mountain clime,
    This was our home—'twas giv'n us by the GOD
    That gave you yours. Love ye your native sod?
So did our fathers too! for they were MEN—
    They fought to guard it—for their hearts were brave—
And long they fought!—We were a people then!
    This was our country—it is now our GRAVE—
    Would I had never lived—or died this land to save!

. . . .

When first ye came, your numbers were but few,
    Our nation many as the leaves or sand;
Hungry and tired ye were—we pitied you—
    We called you brothers—took you by the hand;
    But soon we found ye came to spoil the land:
We quarrelled—and your countrymen we slew,
    Till one alone of all, remained behind—
Among the false he only had been true—
    And much we loved this man of single mind,
    And ever while he lived to him were kind.

He loved us too, and taught us many things,
    And much we strove the stranger's heart to glad;
But to its kindred still the spirit clings,
    And therefore was his soul for ever sad;
    Nor other wish nor joy the lone one had,
Save on the solitary shore to roam,
    Or sit and gaze for hours upon the deep
That rolled between him and his native home;
    And when he thought none marked him, he would weep,
    Or sing this song of wo[e] which still our maidens keep:

LAMENT OF THE CAPTIVE

    My life is like the summer rose
        That opens to the morning sky,
    And, ere the shades of evening close,
        Is scattered on the ground to die:[21]
    Yet on that rose's humble bed
    The softest dews of night are shed;
    As if she wept such waste to see—
    But none shall drop a tear for me!

My life is like the autumn leaf
    That trembles in the moon's pale ray;
Its hold is frail—its date is brief—
    Restless, and soon to pass away:
Yet, when that leaf shall fall and fade,
The parent tree will mourn its shade,
The wind bewail the leafless tree,
But none shall breathe a sigh for me!

My life is like the print, which feet
    Have left on TAMPA's[22] desert strand,
Soon as the rising tide shall beat,
    Their track will vanish from the sand:
Yet, as if grieving to efface
All vestige of the human race,
On that lone shore loud moans the sea,
But none shall thus lament for me!

Hesperia

For some time Wilde contemplated the writing of a nationalistic poem on a large scale. By 1827 he had firmly in mind a work which would be "an acquisition to the lighter literature" of the United States and especially of Georgia. The work was "to record the living manners of the age, as displayed in language[,] costume, customs & habits"; these characteristics were to be woven into narrative or set in anecdote. A possible title for a long work was to be *Georgia Lyrics*. A friend suggested such material as a description of emigrants from North Carolina to Georgia, squirrel hunts, barbecues, country weddings, and singing schools.[1]

America was a subject for poetry, according to Wilde. He wrote his brother about a poem written by the latter based on a work by Bulwer-Lytton: "The novelist (Bulwer) does not seem to me particularly happy in this same apostrophe, and I know not why you should borrow any one[']s wit or humour who have so much of your own. There are many subjects peculiar to our country yet untouched[,] rich in mirth, & almost fitted to your hand. Irving and Halleck are strong only on American ground."[2]

The book-length poem *Hesperia* appeared twenty years after Wilde died. Some portions were written before his trip to Italy, for the Library of Congress has a manuscript dated June 21, 1828, which contains working versions of the stanzas beginning "O would to Heaven we were alone once more," "Those days are gone—will they return agen?" and "Must I not coin false smiles—and obey the beck." Although the poem apparently was incomplete at the time of his death, his son William Cumming Wilde had it ready for the press when he wrote: "I go on to Boston in a few weeks where my father's great poem Hesperia will be issued from the press of Ticknor and Fields." The book finally was published in Boston by that firm in 1867. The title page stated: *"Hesperia, A Fragment by the Late Fitzhugh De Lancy, Esq.,"* Wilde's pseudonym.[3]

Similar to *Childe Harold's Pilgrimage* by Byron, the poem consists of four parts. Each refers to a section of the United States. Places of interest in these four sections—Florida, Virginia, Acadia, and Louisiana—are described, as are various people of historical interest. But the boundaries Wilde uses are not the present-day boundaries:

> Virginia, as laid down on some old British maps, extended from the Hudson to the St. John's, E.F. On the other hand, those of Florida as claimed by Spain reached to, and even beyond, St. Helena. The boundaries of their respective colonies were a fruitful source of war between European states. In the division of my subject, I have taken with names the license this uncertainty permitted. You cannot expect Poetry even now to be more exact than her sister Geography once was.[4]

Wilde at one time or another probably visited all the places he describes in the work. In a letter in which he described in detail a trip that he took along the Canadian border and into Canada, he made the following comments about Niagara Falls:

> The grand cataract swallowed up every thing. Highly raised as my curiosity and expectations were it more than equalled them. It is matchless. . . .
>
> The immense column of water rushing from inland. . . , the sea green colour, the foaming rapids above resembling closely the breakers on a lee shore, the roaring waters, the showers of foam, the deep abyss and the Rainbows all give a grandeur and awful sublimity to the scene which once felt can never be forgotten. We viewed them from above and below—on the American & the English side, and rambled all around Goat Island which is in the centre. But the most grand & captivating and terrific sight of all, is from the end of a slender foot bridge, above the fall, projected into water some distance and resting on rocks. There you lean over and look down . . . if your head is able to stand it. The sight has a strange fascination. It produces a delirious propensity to plunge in.[5]

In *Hesperia*, as in his shorter lyrics, Wilde looks to the past: the poet remembers when he first met the Marchesa, to whom the work is dedicated, and he remembers when they parted. In the present, he, "the wreck of love and time," writes the poem which will reach her from the grave and which will tell her of the love for her that he never openly expressed while alive.[6]

The name of the Marchesa is the feminine form of Manfredi di Cosenza, whom Dante mentions in *Purgatorio*, Canto III. Aubrey H. Starke identifies the Marchesa as Mrs. Ellen White-Beatty and gives the following pieces of evidence: her name was identified with that of Wilde in several descriptive titles of "The Lament of the Captive"; she was married to Colonel Joseph White and therefore Wilde could not marry her ("the one adored in vain"); Wilde describes her father, General John Adair, in several passages in *Hesperia;* Escambia, her home in Florida, is familiar to him; and of the names "Ashley, Argia and Adria" in *Hesperia, Argia* is from the Greek word for "white" and *Adria* must be an anagram for *Adair*. Furthermore, Mrs. Ellen White-Beatty can be identified with each of the geographical divisions of the poem.[7]

The completed work shows Wilde as an early Romantic poet in America. Although he disliked Wordsworth "in toto," he, like the English poet, wrote of the grandeur of nature. Byron, with his descriptions of wild scenery and his melancholy brooding, and Thomas Moore, with his sentimental recalling of the past and his Irish wit, were the two English Romantic poets that Wilde most admired.[8]

Included here are the important dedication and certain representative stanzas which illustrate Wilde's interest in the use of American settings, his importance as an early Romantic poet in America, and his searching for materials suitable for poetry.

ALLA NOBILLISSIMA DAMA, LA SIGNORA MARCHESA MANFREDINA DI COSENZA.

It were useless to ask your pardon for these lines, since before you read them the writer will be past the reach of love or anger.

You once advised me to attempt a poem of some length, in hopes that an occupation suitable to my inclinations might divert my inexplicable weariness of life and spirit.

You may remember my telling you some of the difficulties of such an undertaking. Few write well, except from personal experience,—from what they have seen and felt,—and modern life, in America especially, is utterly commonplace. It wants the objects and events which are essential to poetry,—excludes all romance, and admits but one enthusiasm.

In addition to these inherent obstacles came my own want of invention, and the impossibility of adopting a foreign story, because the scenes and manners to be painted were unknown to me.

You urged me no further. Years have intervened. Perhaps you have forgotten the subject, and supposed it forgotten. It was treasured up, however, like every wish of yours, and though it could not be literally fulfilled, has given birth to the rhymes I send you.

> "Utinam modo dicere possem
> Carmina digna Deae."

They were written in different lands at distant times; some of them so long since that they are obsolete. They do not constitute a poem, for they have no plan. The charm they had for me will be felt by no one else,—that of recalling the scenes we visited together, or those otherwise associated in my memory with you.

To some of the minor pieces in the notes, I pretend no claim. You will readily guess the places or persons that connect them with yourself. Others, like portions of the text, written before my task assumed the character that changed its destiny, were meant to relieve the monotony of mere description, and supply the want of incident and adventure.

Adopting a somewhat loose and general geographical division of the immense country over which we wandered, my recollections of our travels naturally assumed a fourfold distribution,— FLORIDA, VIRGINIA, ACADIA, and LOUISIANA,—each one being supposed to include a large part of its ancient boundaries.

I have called the whole HESPERIA, for want of a better title. You must not suppose, however, that I mean any invasion of the classical prerogatives of your native, and my adopted country. The word, as you well know, comes from *Hesperus*, a name given to Venus when the star of evening, and signifies a setting, or the West.

The Greeks, therefore, who lived to the eastward of Italy, naturally called it Hesperia. But inasmuch as, since that time, the West has moved westward, the appellation may now without violence be applied to America, especially as an Italian discovered it. Hesperia Maxima might be more precise, to distinguish it from Spain as well as Italy; but the term is equivocal, and might savor of national vanity. We will call it Hesperia Nova if you like.

Ausonia and Italia will still be left to your native land, names beautiful enough for any country on earth, even her who bears them, and whose love and fame (another excuse for my temerity) I have endeavored to blend with America's and yours. If you are still dissatisfied, call my verses what you please. To the "ten thousand rents in her imperial garment," I would not add one more to save all I have ever written from the flames.

Intended at first merely to sketch scenes and objects, my rhymes insensibly and involuntarily became the depositary of thoughts inseparable from them in my mind, though always buried in my own bosom:—

"Per suo amor m'er io messo
A faticosa impresa assai per tempo,
Tal che s'i'arrivo al desiato porto,
Spero per lei gran tempo
Viver, quand'altri mi terra per morto."

Considering the time and manner of their utterance, my words surely cannot wound the most scrupulous delicacy, since the sentiment they indicate reaches you only from the dust. If I err, however, you are mistress of my verses' destiny. There is no other copy in existence. They were written for you alone. When you have read them, their office is fulfilled, and my offence may be expiated by their sacrifice. I have often been on the point of destroying them myself; but the patient labor of so many solitary hours, the only confidant of so many cherished thoughts, had become dear to a distempered fancy, and could not be parted from, while life remained.

Farewell! Forgive my madness, and think of me sometimes as your friend.

F. DE L.

Palermo, 18—.

. . . .

Could we our country's scenery invest
With history, or legendary lore,
Give to each valley an immortal guest,
Repeople with the past the desert shore,
Pass out where Hampdens bled or Shakespeares rest,
Exult o'er Memory's exhaustless store,
As our descendants centuries hence may do,—
We should—and then shall have—our poets too![9]

[112]

But now!—'tis true in this our day and land
All that is written perishes, alas!
Like feeble traces from the sea-beat strand,
Or evening's dews from morning's sunny grass:
Smote by the stroke of dull oblivion's wand,
As all have passed before us, we shall pass,
Nor leave one trace of us or ours behind,—
One glorious deathless monument of mind!

We have not even found—and shall we find?—
One lay like his, that in the wizard's glass
Beheld his ladye-love,—the gentle, kind,
And knightly SURREY,—he whose genius as
The morning-star was herald-like assigned
To the far-flashing glory whose bright mass
With jealous splendor his mild beams outshone.
Such usher of our dawn alas! we've none!
                    (Canto I, Stanzas XI-XIII)
        .   .   .   .

Hail to thee, Florida! bright fairy-land!
Here shall my wandering verse its course begin:
Beauty hath left her footsteps on thy strand;
Lake, fountain, gulf, and forest well might win
Our praise and wonder. Nature's lavish hand
Hath half redeemed thee from the curse of sin,
And in thy lap with such profusion showers
Her gifts, that men have called thee "land of flowers."
                    (Canto I, Stanza XXIV)
        .   .   .   .

We met! . . . this is the night! . . . 'Tis now five years
Since first I gazed—and spoke—and loved in vain!
Alas! how often have I wept hot tears,
Musing upon that hour, its bliss, its pain,—
False hopes, deep griefs, and too prophetic fears,—
The breaking heart, and the unbroken chain,—
Constraint and absence,—sickness, misery, doubt,—
Fierce pangs within, a heartless world without!
                    (Canto I, Stanza CVIII)
        .   .   .   .

Hark! is it thunder bursts upon the ear,
Startling a scene as quiet as the grave?
Impossible! the sky is bright and clear,
The forest sleeps, the winds are in their cave,—

[113]

Yet it continues!—Are there breakers near?
Does Erie mimic thus the Ocean's wave,
Not in hue only, but in power and sound,
Or does an earthquake fright the trembling ground?

It is NIAGARA! draw near the shore,
What greater marvel has been, or can be?
The ocean-cataract whose ceaseless roar
Has far outlived Fame's immortality!
Say was it to the Deluge Nature bore
This mountain-torrent of an inland sea?
Time's wonder till the sun and stars expire,
And the earth perishes in quenchless fire!

Above the frightful fall's deceitful brink
The raging waters urge their frantic way
O'er rock and rapid;—on the verge they shrink,
And seem to linger with a fond delay:
Into the gulf at length they slowly sink,
To lose themselves in vapor, foam, and spray,
And when they rise, returning on their course,
They reel as if with horror and remorse!

Approach! look down the dizzy precipice,
And gaze upon the yawning deep below:
One step will plunge you into the abyss,
And end at once, forever, mortal woe.
Death the destroyer! how sublime is this,
Thy thundering avalanche of liquid snow!
What subtle fiends throng round its giddy verge,
Tempting Despair to perish in the surge!

What desperate delirium thrills the brain
Of the devoted, standing thus upon
The margin of eternity!—in vain
Instinct and Reason urge us to be gone:
We rave like maniacs who have burst their chain,
Mocking at death!—so stood I there with one
Who but for me all doubt had madly dared,
Before or with me!—Wherefore were we spared?
                    (Canto III, Stanzas XXVII-XXXI)

. . . .

No, no! as evening's dews to sun-parched bowers,
So to young burning breasts has verse been given
To soothe and cool the flush of feverish hours,

[114]

Even with the tears exhaled from earth by heaven:
Such drops renew the bloom of passion's flowers,
And calm the weary soul, "parched, wrung, and riven,"—
Bless those that shed, and those on whom they fall,
Ay, and the world that mark them, one and all!

But when the ebbing pulse wanes faint and slow,
And into twilight sinks each lingering ray;
When on our head falls fast untimely snow,
And coming winter clouds the cheerless day;
No dews the Night, no tears the eyes bestow,—
No words the soul, to mourn its own decay;
Within—around—a dreary silence reigns,
And Life is all exhausted but its pains!

Or if no frost the waste of years deform,
With flushing cheek and festering breast we breathe,
Proving—far worse—volcanic passions' storm,
Whose outward calmness mocks the fires beneath,
As coming earthquakes wear a tranquil form,
And the sword slumbers in its quiet sheath;
Or as typhoons and desert winds alike
Are silent as the serpent till they strike.

These have no voice; yet, might their ruins speak
The past and present eloquently well,
Homer and Hesiod's tongue to theirs were weak;
Angels alone might utter what they tell,
As, fiend-like, on themselves their rage they wreak,
Yet never dare to burst the seal-bound spell.
Thus fane, tower, palace, desert-buried deep,
Thebes, Tadmor, and Elora's secrets keep.

For souls like such, all poetry is past;
Not even in history their thoughts survive,
Like crowded cities into lava cast,
Oblivion-doomed, embalmed while yet alive;
Into the hardening rock that holds them fast
They petrify and live, but cease to strive,
As more than one enchanted realm o'erthrown
Saw all things turning at a word to stone.

Above the stifled heart or nation's grave
Years, centuries, millenniums ev'n may pass,
But o'er their barren dust no laurels wave,
Forth from their ashes springs no blade of grass:

Thus seas, in tempest frozen, cease to rave,
Joining the icy ocean's Alps of glass
To threat the sunless sky with horrid forms,
Whose calm or shock exceeds a thousand storms.

No, no! the prison may send forth its mirth,—
Fire-tortured metals in the flames refine,
Ores in the dark recesses of the earth,—
Pearls in the sea's unfathomed caverns shine,
Gems in the mountain's living rock have birth,—
But never Poetry in souls like mine!
When there are none to love, hear, blame, or praise,
What God or man or statue utters lays?
                     (Canto IV, Stanzas CVII-CXIII)[10]

IV

Poems: Fugitive and Occasional

WILDE wrote hundreds of original poems, many of which he destroyed. A number were designed to be set to music. While he was in Italy, he made a collection of his original verse; the manuscript is owned by Mrs. Virginia Giraud Crockett of Los Angeles, his great-granddaughter.[1]

This manuscript is reproduced in its entirety on the following pages. Any notes given are by Wilde himself; all of the editor's notes have been put at the end of the book.

The manuscript is incomplete, although it is in excellent condition. It runs from page No. 1 to page No. 217, with the following pages missing: 15, 16, 23, 214, 215, 216.

Multa quidem scripsi: sed quae vitiosa putavi
Emendaturis ignibus ipse dedi.
Tum quoque, cùm fugerem, quaedam placitura cremavi
Iratus studio, carminusque meis. —Ovid. *Tristia.* Lib. IV El. X

TO IOLE[2]
Sweet Iole! with pure and warm emotion,
I lay these worthless offerings at thy shrine,
And with them a true heart whose fond devotion
Is such as sister saints might feel for thine:
Grant me thy prayers!—and oh! disdain not mine—
But if henceforth none ever hear or see
Our cherished creed avouch'd by word or sign
It is because men call idolatry
The worship we have always deemed divine.
The World's misjudging incredulity
Allows no sacred light on earth to shine
Or understands it not if seen—and we
Must the true faith in our soul's cell confine
Or brave the persecutor's cruelty.

[117]

Nearly all the following trifles were written many years since.

This is said as an apology for the hours wasted in their composition, rather than by way of excusing their faults which if not incorrigible might have been long ago corrected. In choosing them from a mass of others, it is almost needless to add that they were not selected for any peculiar merit. The charitable may perhaps discover a better reason. Whatever personal application they have—or had—relates to feelings blameless in themselves, to occasions long since forgotten, or to persons beyond the reach of mortal praise or censure. Nothing therefore forbids their publication. A few indeed have been already published in magazines or journals; and some claimed, disclaimed and re-appropriated. One in wandering through the world, like other personages of doubtful parentage, has met with various adventures, and at length pretended to a noble origin: while more than one it is feared, have circulated in society on the assumption of belonging to those who never heard of them. It is time therefore such vagrants were given up to justice, and the critics will assist the public to pass sentence.
Florence.

SOLOMON AND THE GENIE[3]

"At the sight of so terrible a figure, the fisherman would have fled, but was too much terrified. 'Solomon, Solomon, the great Prophet!' exclaimed the Genie, 'pardon, pardon, pardon! I never more will oppose your will!' The fisherman hearing this took courage, and said 'Thou proud spirit what is it thou talkest of? It is 1800 years ago since the prophet Solomon died. Tell me your history and how you came to be shut up in that vessel.' The Genie, turning to his deliverer with a fierce look, said, 'thou art very bold to call me a proud spirit. Speak to me more civilly lest I kill thee.' 'What' replied the fisherman 'would you kill me for setting you at liberty? Is that the way you reward the service I have done you?' 'I can't treat you otherwise' replied the Genie, 'and that you may be convinced of it listen to my story: I am one of those rebellious spirits, who opposed themselves to the will of Heaven. The other Genies owned Solomon the great prophet, and submitted to him. Sacar and I only resisted. That potent monarch caused me to be seized and brought by force before his throne.' "

Arabian Nights

[118]

Spirit of Thought! Lo! art thou here?
Lord of the false fond ceaseless spell
That mocks the heart, the eye the ear:—
In human bosoms dost thou dwell
Self-exiled from thy native sphere,
Or is the human mind thy cell
Of torment?—to inflict and bear
Thy doom?— the doom of all who fell.

Since thou hast sought to prove my skill
Unquestioned thou shalt not depart,
Be thy behests or good, or ill,
No matter what, or whence thou art:
I will commune with thee apart,
Yea, and compel thee to my will
If thou hast power to yield my heart
What Earth and Heaven deny it still.

I know thee Spirit! thou hast been
Light of my soul by night and day,
All-seeing, though thyself unseen,
My dreams—my thoughts—and what are they
But visions of a calmer ray—
All, all were thine—and thine between
Each hope that melted fast away
The throb of anguish, deep and keen.

With thee I've searched the earth, the sea,
The air, sun, stars, man, nature, time,
Explored the universe with thee,
Plunged to the depths of woe and crime,
Or dared the fearful height to climb
Where amid glory none may see
And live, the *Eternal* reigns sublime
Who is, and was, and is to be!

And I have sought, with thee have sought
Wisdom's celestial path to tread,
Hung o'er each page with learning fraught,
Questioned the living and the dead;
The Patriarchs of ages fled—
The Prophets of the time to come—
All who one ray of light could shed
Beyond the cradle or the tomb.

And I have tasked my busy brain
To learn what haply none may know;
Thy birth, seat, power—thine ample reign
O'er the heart's tides, that ebb and flow,
Throb, languish, whirl, rage, freeze, or glow,
Like billows of the restless main
Above the wrecks of joy and woe
By ocean's caves preserved in vain.

And oft, to shadow forth I strove
To my mind's eye, a form like thine,
And still my soul like Noah's dove
Returned, but brought alas! no sign:
'Till wearying in the mad design
With fevered brow and throbbing vein
I left the cause to thread the mine
Of wonderful effects again.

But now I see thee face to face
Thou art indeed a thing divine
An eye pervading time and space
And an angelic look are thine,
Ready to seize, compare, combine,
Essence and form—and yet a trace
Of grief and care a shadowy line
Dims thy bright forehead's heavenly grace.

Yet thou must be of heavenly birth
Where naught is known of grief or pain;
Though I perceive alas! where Earth
And earthly things have left their stain:
From thine high calling didst thou deign
To prove—in folly or in mirth—
With daughters of the first born Cain
How little Human Love was worth?

Ha! dost thou change before my eyes?
Another form! and yet the same,
But lovelier, and of female guise
Such as our heart's despair can frame
Pine for, love, worship, idolize,
Like Her's [*sic*] who from the sea-foam came,
And lives but in the heart or skies.

Spirit of Change! I know thee too,
I know thee by thine Iris bow,
By thy cheeks ever-shifting hue
By all that marks thy steps below,
By sighs that burn and tears that glow—
False hopes—vain joys that mock the heart
From *Fancy's* urn, these evils flow
Spirit of Lies! for such thou art!

Saidst thou not once that all the charms
Of life lay hid in woman's love
And to be lock'd in Beauty's arms
Was all man knew of Heaven above?
And did I not thy counsels prove
With all their pleasure, all their pain
No more, no more my heart they move
For I alas! have proved them vain!

Didst thou not then, in evil hour
Light in my soul Ambition's flame
Didst thou not say the joys of Power
Unbounded sway—undying fame
A Monarch's love alone should claim?
And did I not pursue all these,
And are they not when won the same
All Vanity of Vanities?

Didst not to tempt me once again
Bid new deceitful visions rise
And hint though won with toil and pain
"Wisdom's the pleasure of the Wise"
And now when none beneath the skies
Are wiser held by men than me
What is the value of the prize
It too alas! is Vanity

Then tell me!—since I've found on earth
Not one pure stream to slake this thirst
Which still torments us from our birth
And in our heart and soul is nurst
This hopeless wish wherewith we're curst,
Whence came it, and why was it given?
Thou speak'st not!—Let me know the worst
Thou pointest!—and it is to Heaven!

[121]

Note.

I was not aware until long after this poem was written of certain points of resemblance between it and Mr. G. Lewis's tale called Amorassan or the Spirit of the Frozen Ocean. In some of the following passages the imitation may be supposed not wholly involuntary: it was however, if I may trust my memory, unconscious.

"The spell was complete; thrice had he pronounced it in the awful name of Solomon, the powerful and the wise; and now a thick gray cloud descending into the room, hovered a while over the chafing dish and then spread itself through the whole apartment. Gradually it dispersed, and now Amorassan beheld a female figure, the faultless perfection of whose form & features assured him she was no terrestial being. . . .

"With her hands folded on her bosom, the Spirit stood fixed before Amorassan silent and motionless."

Amorassan.—Tell me, thou frosty being, know'st thou the word Virtue.

The Spirit.—I have sometimes heard it mentioned but it is no concern of mine.

Amorassan.—No? And Vice then?

The Spirit.—Oh! that I have heard mentioned much oftener: but that is no concern of mine either. I used to hear of such things when I lived in the Court of Solomon.

Amorassan.—Of Solomon the wise?

The Spirit.—Aye; the wise . . . as he was called. I was his slave, and in his latter years his constant companion. It was in my society he learned, that every thing on Earth is Vanity."

[NO TITLE]

Farewell fair Florence! not I hope forever,[4]
    Once more I yet may see thee—Who can tell?
With thee and thine it is a pang to sever
    I had not thought to feel again. . . . Farewell!

Florence farewell! the memories earthly cherished
    That for long years in my hearts core did dwell
By Time and Death and Chance and Change have perished
    Thou and thine only now are left! . . . Farewell!

Farewell! farewell! . . . and if indeed forever—
    The thoughts untold that in my bosom swell

Can never be forgotten!—never! never!
   Blessings on thee and thine! . . . Farewell! Farewell!

Farewell! once more—If the enfranchised spirit
   May haunt the spots it loved in life so well
'Till Earth dissolve with all it doth inherit
   Mine shall be with thee Florence still! . . . Farewell!

FRAGMENT[5]

     . . . .
'Tis many moons ago—a long long time
Since first upon this shore a white man trod—
From the great water to the mountain clime
This was our home—'twas given us by the God
That gave ye yours—Love ye your native sod?
So did our fathers too, for they were men,
They fought to guard it for their hearts were brave,
And long they fought—We were a people then!
This *was* our country—it is now our grave—
Would I had never lived or died this land to save!

When first ye came your numbers were but few
Our nation many as the leaves or sand:
Hungry and tired ye were—we pitied you—
We called you brothers—took ye by the hand—
But soon we found ye came to rob the land:
We quarrelled—and your countrymen we slew,
'Till one alone of all remained behind
Among the false he only had been true
And much we loved this man of single mind
And ever while he lived, to him were kind.

He loved us too, and taught us many things,
And much we strove the stranger's heart to glad:
But to it's [*sic*] kindred still the spirit clings
And therefore was his soul forever sad;
No other wish or joy the lone one had
Save on the solitary shore to roam,
Or sit and gaze for hours upon the deep,
That rolled between him and his native home,
And when he thought none marked him he would weep
Or sing his song of woe which still our maidens keep.

[123]

My life is like the summer rose
That opens to the morning sky,
And ere the shades of evening close
Is scattered on the ground to die:
Yet on that rose's humble bed
The softest dews of night are shed
As if she wept such waste to see
But none shall drop a tear for me.

My life is like the Autumn leaf
That trembles in the moon's pale ray;
It's hold is frail—it's date is brief—
Restless—and soon to pass away—
Yet when that leaf shall fall and fade
The parent tree will mourn it's shade,
The wind bewail the leafless tree
But none shall breathe a sigh for me!

My life is like the print that feet
Have left on *Tampa's** desert strand
Soon as the rising tide shall beat
Their track will vanish from the sand
Yet, as if grieving to efface
All vestige of the human race
On that lone shore loud moans the sea
But none shall thus lament for me.

*The Indian name of a bay in East Florida called by the Spaniards Espiritu Santo. It was in the neighborhood of that bay that Juan Ortiz was long held in captivity by the Indians, and the verses are founded on his story.

TO ----------------------

Farewell! . . . I take no formal leave,
    Though lingering round each much loved spot,
For me, I wish no heart to grieve,
    Though mine has ne'er one friend forgot.

But who would deem that there could dwell
    Beneath the careless mirth they hear
Thoughts, for their depth unfit to tell
    Feelings, unbreathed to mortal ear?

A fountain sealed—sepulchral lamp—
    A sibyls leaf—a funeral urn—
A dim drear vault, where cold and damp
    Death and decay's pale vapours burn.

Such is, or such at least may be,
    For aught thou knowest, the soul I bear—
No more!—Why should I claim from thee
    In weal or woe of mine to share?

I go!—Farewell!—again farewell!
    The first slight pang of parting o'er,
With the forgotten past I dwell,
    And thou wilt think of me no more.

Like waters of the silvery lake
    That o'er the chance-thrown pebble close,
The slight heart-thrill my follies make
    Will soon subside to calm repose.

And I shall be as one unknown,
    Or if once known remembered not—
Like a fantastic shadow flown,
    Or fleeting vision soon forgot.

'Tis wise!—'tis well!—I do not ask
    One tear, one sigh from thee or thine:
They chose indifference for their task
    Deep sad remembrance, I, for mine!

FORGET ME NOT

Forget me not! where'er we rove
    Whate'er may be our varied lot
In stately hall or shady grove
    Forget me not! . . . forget me not!

Forget me not! O! I could see
    Unmoved my name Oblivion blot
So I were but the same to thee
    Forget me not! . . . forget me not!

Forget me not! on land or main
    O! let me never be forgot
In weal or woe—in Joy or Pain
    Forget me not! . . . forget me not!

[125]

Forget me not! by every scene
    We saw—by each familiar spot—
By all we loved—by all we've been,
    Forget me not! . . . forget me not!

Forget me not! by every hour
    Together passed in wood or grot
By the heart's spell of nameless power
    Forget me not! . . . forget me not!

Forget me not! though severed far,
    By thy dear home—thy nurse's cot
Thy native land—thy natal star
    Forget me not! . . . forget me not!

THE SIGNS OF LOVE

The sleepless eye,
    The frequent tear,
The deep drawn sigh,
    Of Hope and Fear
        Are they not Love's?

But sighs may feign
    And tears betray,
And Guilt and Pain
    And slow decay,
        Are they not Love's?

Then would'st thou know
    The false from true,
Through bliss and woe
    Still keep in view,
        What signs are Love's?

The silent tear,
    The secret sigh,
Unheard by ear,
    Unseen by eye,
        These, these are Love's!

The looks which hide,
    Not those that shew,
What one beside,
    Alone should know,
        These, these are Love's!

Pangs whose kind art
   Veils their excess,
That one fond heart
   May feel them less:
      These, these are Love's!

The powers that reign,
   With tranquil air,
O'er untold pain
   And mute despair;
      These, these are Love's!

The breast that aches
   But never swells,
The heart that breaks
   Yet never tells,
      These, these are Love's!

[NO TITLE]

The dream of life is over,
   The light of love is gone,
O! who would be a rover
   On earth like me alone.

My early joys are blighted,
   My friends are with the blest,
Deserted and benighted,
   I long to be at rest.

My leave of life I'm taking,
   I feel this cannot last
Yet though my heart is breaking,
   It's sighs are for the past.

I feel my moments flying
   But ere I cease to be
My latest prayer when dying
   Will be blessings upon thee!

LINES IN AN ALBUM[6]

Dear Record of departed years!
   Our thoughts recess—our Memory's fane—
Sacred to all our Hopes and Fears,
   To Love and Grief—to Joy and Pain.

Recalling many a faded face,
  And picturing many an altered mind,
On every page we find a trace
  Which those we loved have left behind.

The Heart's Eolian lyre that flings
  To every passing breath its tone
Thrilling from wild deep wond'rous strings
  A sweet sad music all it's own.

Shrine of past spells—and long lost powers
  Map of the soul—affection's chart—
Memorial of fast fading hours—
  I hail thee, scripture of the heart!

TO _____ [7]

Farewell! . . . a word we shrink to speak, or hear,
  Of cherished hours the melancholy knell,
Nor heard, nor spoke, without a boding fear
  That it *may* be forever. . . . Fare ye well!

Farewell! . . . and if forever, will ye not
  Think of your friend and the last look he gave?
One thought from you, though by the world forgot
  Were as a flower to deck his nameless grave.

Farewell! farewell! . . . His pilgrimage of woes
  End when, and where, and howsoe'er it will,
Can only bring an aching heart repose
  And bid a throbbing brain at length be still.

Farewell! once more . . . if e'er his soul finds rest
  He might but leave with those he loved a spell
To keep them happy—blessing all and blest
  It should be breathed in his last word—Farewell!

[NO TITLE]

Light be the turf on thy tomb!
  Bright be the place of thy rest!
Thy spirit has fled in it's beauty and bloom
  To its home, the abode of the blest.

The depth of our love and our woe,
  And all that this trial hast cost

No hearts save those only, can know
    Who have owned such a treasure and lost!

We cherish thy memory here,
    While in humble affliction we bow,
And Heaven will pardon our sorrow a tear,
    Since thou ne'er cost us one until now.

SONNET

Friend of my early days! the same kind soul
Whom as a fair, mild, studious boy I knew,
The tide of feeling bursts from all control
To hail once more those times, those scenes, and you!
Mine was a melancholy youth 'tis true
Born to the orphan's heritage of woe,
Slight leisure love or hope or joy it knew
And soon was quenched the buoyant spirit's flow:
Therefore perhaps, those hours so bright and few
Of happy boyhood on my memory glow
With all imaginations brilliant hue
Sun beams from showers reflected—Even so
Returns the vision of the past anew
Shining through tears the souls celestial bow!

TO 8

    Utinam modo dicere possem
Carmina digna Deae.

              Ovid.

Seek other bards to hymn thy praise,
    It is no theme for lips like mine;
Worthy of purer, holier lays,
    A harp and minstrel more divine.

This proud, worn heart may once have known
    Some chords that might have claimed thine ear,
Perhaps there lingers yet a tone,
    Thou would'st not all disdain to hear.

But I have stirr'd for good and ill,
    Too deeply all its secret strings,
Joys maddening note, Grief's freezing thrill
    And Disappointment's fiery stings.

Extreme and passionate in all,
Love—Hatred—Pleasure—Pain—Disgust—
In stormy flight and endless fall
Above the clouds—below the dust.

No, 'tis too late! . . . There was a time
I could perhaps have struck a sound,
Which like the Vespers hallowed chime
Might wake a sacred echo round.

Such strain would well become thy name
A heavenly anthem sweet and calm,
Like incense from the altar's flame
Breathing a more than earthly balm.

But now. . . . No more! . . . that time is past—
I must not wake one note for thee,
The seal is set—the die is cast
And I fullfill my destiny!

Aye! leave me to my wayward fate,
My praise thy virtues would but stain,
And worth, I may not consecrate,
I prize too highly to prophane.

Then seek somewhere to hear thy praise
It is no theme for lips like mine,
No! it belongs to holier lays,
A harp and minstrel more divine.

LINES FOR MUSIC

Fare thee well! the words are spoken
Can they be unuttered ever? . . .
Fare thee well! my heart is broken
But we meet no more wherever!
Never!—never—no, no, never!
No we meet no more forever!

Fare thee well! with bitter anguish
Now I feel that we must sever—
Years like ages, did I languish
Thus to part with thee forever?
Aye! forever . . . Ever! . . . ever!
Never more to meet, no! never!

Fare thee well! thou unforgiving,
Henceforth 'twere a vain endeavour
Faith to find among the living,
Thou hast broke that dream forever!
Ever! ... ever! ... yes!, yes, ever!
Never to return! ... no! never!

THE GUINEA FOWL

On the device of a seal with the legend "Come back!"

There is a sort of feathered scold
Whose note is (if the truth be told)
Much like a vixen's clack,
Morn, noon, and night the sound you hear,
Still ringing in your deafened ear,
"Come back! Come back! Come back!"

When forced to leave a pleasant home,
Upon the world's wide waste to roam,
Our sinking hearts alack!
Feel all their devils doubly blue,
If some of this discordant crew
Cry out, "Come back! Come back!"

But if with travel, toil and pain
Worn out, we're hastening home again,
Our fancy has a knack ...
Of making even discord sweet,
Which seems our own return to greet,
With Wel—"come back, come back!"

My song, much like the throat it mocks,
As shrill as winds and hard as rocks,
(Since rhyme is growing slack)
As it began perforce must end
By crying out with every friend
"Come back! come back! come back!"

LINES
ON THE FIRST LEAF OF AN ALBUM[9]

Here Memory, and here too Oblivion dwells:
One o'er the tablet weaves his drowsy spells
The other in the fount her pinion wets
Who writes remembers, she who reads forgets!

[NO TITLE]

I knew that this must end—at first
I said it would be so—
Nor do I grieve to prove the worst
Of long foreboded woe:
I do not shrink from what I bear,
I only feel what thou must share.

I even smile to hear thee chide
My silence—yet suppress
My once free thoughts, because I hide
My pangs, to make thine less:
Though my heart breaks, I do not dare
To add my own to thy despair.

I muse forever on the past
Although I only mourn . . .
O'er what I knew could never last
And know can ne'er return:
And thou who sigh'st because I seem
A dreamer—must not know my dream.

I once believed the great relief
Of my full heart would be . . .
In every joy and every grief
To share them all with thee;
But I have learned that there are woes
Which I must feel yet ne'er disclose.

Whate'er they are, it matters not
So they are never known—
By me they cannot be forgot,
But must be mine alone:
They will go with me to the tomb,
But shall not cloud thy brow with gloom.

[NO TITLE]

The future bard of Paradise in youth,[10]
   Wearied, some half hour on a moss bank slept,
And female beauty, innocence and truth,
   Watch o'er his slumbers for an instant kept.

He waked—and found—placed there while he reposed,
    This sweet Ausonian couplet in his hand—
"Eyes! mortal stars, if thus ye wound me closed,
    Open—who could your witchery withstand?"

The circles of their being touched no more—
    He never saw her!—Though in after years,
Fair Italy received him on her shore
    Aye! and baptised his genius with her tears!

Quenched were those eyes in darkness, want and strife,
    He never saw her!—Yet our fancy deems,
To the last moment of his stormy life
    A lovely vision haunted all his dreams.

SONNET TO LORD BYRON[11]

Byron! 'tis thine alone on Eagle's pinions
In solitary strength and grandeur soaring
To dazzle and delight all eyes out-pouring
The electric blaze on tyrants and their minions:
Earth, Sea and Air, and Powers, and Dominions,
Nature—Man—Time—the Universe exploring
And from the wreck of Worlds, Thrones, Creeds, Opinions,
Thought, beauty, eloquence, and wisdom storing.
O! how I love, and envy thee thy glory!
To every age and clime alike belonging,
Linked by all tongues, with every nation's story,
Thou Tacitus of song!—whose echoes thronging
O'er the Atlantic, fill the mountains hoary
And forests, with the name my verse is wronging!

[NO TITLE]

Heaven's sovereign spares all creatures but himself
That hideous sight a naked human heart.
                    Young.

There is a narrow cheerless cell
    Silent and sad, and cold and deep,
A living grave, which yet full well
    Can its dark dreadful secrets keep.

[133]

A whited sepulchre—it seems
    Goodly enough in outward shew,
And he who marks it, seldom deems,
    How much corruption lurks below.

But yet though fair and bright above,
    Beneath, the worm hath left her slime,
O'er withered Hope, and ruined love,
    Corroding grief and festering crime.

A prison-house—whose tortures shun
    The light, yet rend the soul like steel,
A horrid mystery, which none
    Can quite suppress, nor quite reveal;

It is the dungeon of despair,
    At half its feelings heaven might start,
It's very thoughts would taint the air,
    It is, it is—*The Human Heart!*

[NO TITLE]

The full levee, the crowded hall
    The gay salon I once could tread,
Mix in the mask, the fête, the ball,
    And share them too—those times have fled!

With listless eyes, the giddy throng
    So joyous once—so tedious now—
I mark to loathe and scorn—and long
    To wear my thoughts upon my brow.

And yet I know and feel full well
    The change is not in them but me—
Life has lost Hope's delusive spell
    And is—but one sad phantasy.

Fled is the dream that ne'er returns—
    Broken charm that ne'er unites—
And my soul faintly dimly burns
    Like a past revel's dying lights.

Why should I ghost-like haunt the scene
    Of former joys in silent gloom
The mournful shade of what I've been,
    The living tenant of a tomb?

[134]

No! no, to crowds a long farewell
　　Give me a desert or a cave
The Hermits grot—the friar's cell
　　Or better still than all—a grave!

REPLY TO SOME MELANCHOLY VERSES BEGINNING "WHY DO WE LIVE?"

Why do we live?
　　　　The answer lies
In every flower that springs:
　　In every star that decks the skies,
In every bird that sings:
　　　　In all that makes the Earth so fair,
　　　　What would we have which is not there?

Why do we live?
　　　　Is there no ear
Such cruel words would wound?
　　Is there no eye whose ready tear
Would answer to their sound?
　　　　We live because our death would throw
　　　　On others all our weight of woe!

[NO TITLE]

In youth's first flush when hearts are light
　　And hopes are high, and spirits gay,
When all the Earth around seems bright
　　And life one joyous holiday.

It is not then, when hall or bower
　　With careless festive steps we tread,
Affection's deepest, purest power,
　　Upon unsuffering souls is shed.

'Tis when unuttered miseries melt
　　When our long cherished hopes decay—
When bitter disappointment's felt—
　　And some desert—and some betray—

O! it is then, one fond true heart
　　Is tried and proved, and loved and prized,
Like sibyl's leaves the wasted part
　　But makes the rest more idolized!

THE POET TO HIS LYRE

And would they tame thee down my lyre
    Checking thy fall and swell
To make thee what—harmonious wire
    A modulated shell?
Ah! where were then thy native fire
    And thy heart-moving spell?

No! let them teach their tuneful art
    To nightingale or dove
Thou canst not be a thing of art
    Below it—or above—
Thou'rt but the echo of the heart
    The murmur of it's love.

No! as beneath the moonbeam pale
    To every breeze that springs,
The sweet wild minstrel of the gale
    Her fitful music flings,
So must thy master's strange sad tale
    Thrill from thy trembling strings!

AT NIGHT

When life is young
And Hope has flung
    O'er all to come her rainbow light
How deeply thrill
Our pulses still
    To the light step that comes at night!

When those we loved
Away have roved
    And home has lost it's chief delight,
How brisk—how free,
How cheerfully,
    Sounds their returning step by night!

When Fortune parts
Two kindred hearts,
    And threatens all their joy to blight,
What hopes, what fears,

What smiles, what tears,
    Wait the light step that comes at Night!

When Love is kind,
And hearts are twined,
    In fond affection pure and bright,
How quick the ear,
That waits to hear,
    The loved light step that comes at Night!

WRITTEN IN AN ALBUM

When the lone exile sees at last
    His loved his early home once more,
How rushes on his mind the past
    How his full heart at length runs o'er!

Yet every face and spot he knew,
    Are seen with mingled joy and pain,
To mark of all he left, how few,
    Hearts, hopes, or scenes unchanged remain.

And thus perhaps, in after years,
    To turn these leaves will but recall,
Moments of smiles, and days of tears,
    Friends, joys, hopes, loves, all lost! all! all!

SONNET

Calm mother of the night! on whose wild brow
Love—Solitude—High thought, and Peace have thrown
Immortal loveliness which shines even now
As in creation's infancy it shone;
When first serenely from thy starry throne
On Earth thou gazed . . . , as on thy sleeping child,
And watched its couch in silence, and alone,
And tranquilly upon its slumbers smiled.
Now bowed with years—and more—with crimes defiled,
Its infancy and innocence are o'er
While there eternal Beauty pure and mild,
Lonely and sweet and pensive as before
Falls on our hearts—and all their passions wild
Beneath thine eye maternal throb no more!

[137]

WRITTEN ON THE LEAF OF AN ALBUM
UNDER TWO DOVES BILLING

Ye dear little doves,
Whose innocent loves,
    So pleasantly rhyming, our poets delight;
And billing, and cooing,
Wedding or wooing,
    Your bills on our billets-doux sweetly unite.

I protest my heart thrills,
At the sight of your bills,
    Such accounts, and discounts, I should like to arrange
But say what ye will,
It were much better still,
    To exchange both your bills for a bill of Exchange.

SONNET FROM THE PORTUGUESE OF CAMOENS[12]

Flow on silver stream to the Ocean!
    Through thy margin of osiers and willows
Thou fleest with eager and tremulous motion
    To court the embrace of its billows:
'Till sinking at length on their bosom to bliss
    In the transport of constant devotion
They welcome their wanderer home with a kiss
    Of the deepest and purest emotion.
Thy stream like the loitering Scamander's
    Through mazes tow'rd pleasure is winding
But alas! for my poor heart that wanders
    Amid objects forever reminding
Sad thought, that Life vainly meanders
    Lost hopes, and past joys never finding!

EPIGRAM ON A DULL PREACHER
FROM THE ITALIAN OF RONCALLI[13]

On the miseries of life and mankind's wretched lot
A very long lesson you teach:
But sure the worst misery of all you've forgot
The misery of hearing you preach!

SONNET FROM THE PORTUGUESE OF CAMOENS

My years were short and troubled upon earth,
And all my moments wretched though so few;
The bitter boon Fate gave me at my birth
Ere my fifth lustre ended she withdrew.
Strange lands and unknown seas I wandered through
Seeking for life some palliative or cure,
But that which no kind chance before me threw
Nor travel, toil, nor peril might procure
Nor all that mortal man could dare or do
Devise—attempt—encounter—or endure.
On Lusitania's nursing breast I grew
My home Alemquer and the sea my grave:
A tyrants jealousy the cause that drew
Destruction on my head—it's cause a slave!

EPITAPH ON A POET FROM THE ITALIAN OF RONCALLI

Beneath this stone a poet's bones lie cold:
Innumerable odes he made—and sold—
Think, reader think, how many lies he told!

SONNET FROM THE PORTUGUESE OF CAMOENS

'Campo nas Syrtes deste mar da vida' &c

To thee sunny isle in this ocean of life,
    Last hope of the shipwrecked I fly!
Thou art dear as are moments of bliss after strife
    Or bright spots in a storm-clouded sky:
O'er the foes whom I shun there's no conquest but flight
    And if place changes fortune, at last I change mine
The victory's sure—and I hail with delight
    O'er love and ambition a triumph divine:
I'll while life away, in these calm shady bowers
    Where the murmur of waters falls sweet on the ear,
Where the Autumn brings fruits and the Summer gives flowers
    And the Nightingale's love song is heard all the year;
Where buried forever past cares, and lost powers,
    Content and Repose shall become doubly dear!

[139]

[NO TITLE]

Cast up a wreck by Fortune's tide,
    The ebbing wave in this lone bay
Has left me by the ocean's side
    Mouldering in sure and slow decay;
    Love, Hope, Fame, Power, have past away
And with them Joy and Grief and Pride
    I live but in my thoughts, and they
Are of the things that long have died!

TO ....

But yesterday, these flowers
    Hung blooming on their stem;
But yesterday, my hours,
    Were bright and gay like them:

Tomorrow, faded—perished—
    They will be flung away;
So the fond hopes I cherished,
    Must wither with today!

LINES WRITTEN IN MARY[']S 'RELIQUIARIUM'

Hail to these venerable wrecks of Time!
    Precious and rare memorials of the brave,
The wise—the good—the great of every clime
    Where Man is not—or should not be—a slave!

To these most sacred treasures of the heart
    In deep, devout humility I bow,
Linger before the shrine, and loath to part
    Repeat my '*ave*' and renew my vow.

An unknown lonely Pilgrim from afar,
    By shipwreck on the World's wide desert cast,
My only guide a solitary star,
    I reached this Temple's vestibule at last;

And bending thus, as at Loretto's fane,
    I pour most fervently my secret prayer,
That after years like centuries of pain,
    I too, the Virgin-Mother's Peace share.

Offering alas! it is not mine to make—
　　I have none worthy of Madonna's name,
To meditate and worship, for her sake—
　　Not to record my piety, I came.

But yet if more than silver, gems, or gold,
　　Avail the widow's mite, and sinner's tear,
A tribute never to be bought or sold,
　　The honest tribute of the heart, is here!

[NO TITLE]

Mary farewell! Like the ill-omened toll
　　Of tocsin, curfew hour, or passing bell
That word of fear and misery strikes the soul
　　With an unutterable pang—Farewell!

Farewell! to one so lov'd, so idolized,
　　So praised—so flatter'd—humble verse can tell
No novelty—thou know'st how thou art prized—
　　How much thou wilt be missed & mourned—Farewell!

Farewell! farewell! the parting hour is nigh,
　　When silently, the bursting heart must swell,
With all that Earth but utters in a sigh,
　　The exstacy of wretchedness!—Farewell!

Farewell! once more—how many an hour of years
　　Are in those words! O! that they were a spell
To save thy heart from woe—thine eyes from tears—
　　And I would die in breathing them!—Farewell!

Farewell! farewell!—if on the loveliest scene
　　At Twilight's hour, the Day's departing knell,
Should but recall the half of all I've been,
　　Wilt thou not long for me?—Farewell! farewell!

LOVE AND REASON[14]
ON THE DEVICE OF A SEAL
REASON GIVING WINGS TO LOVE
WITH THE LEGEND
"SE VEDE, VOLA"

Venus once bound on Cupid's eyes
　　A fillet stolen from Fancy's bow,

[141]

And sent him wandering from the skies
    To seek his fortune here below.

With face of sun-shine soul of mirth
    He roved through wood and mead and bower
Making a sweeter heaven on earth
    Such was of Fancy's spell the power.

Sometimes he thought he chased through air
    The loveliest butterflies—and laugh'd
While wounding many a bosom fair
    To see them fluttering on his shaft.

Reason who found an infant boy
    Blindfold, alone, and far astray
In hopes to give the urchin joy
    In pity tore the web away.

Love saw—but with returning sight
    Vanished the charm by Fancy given
Earth now for him held no delight
    And the boy longed and pined for heaven.

Her own rash kindness Reason blamed
    And the fond spell would fain restore,
It might not be—her power it shamed
    The fillet would unite no more!

"Go! then," she cries and o'er him flings
    Down pinions of most rosy hue,
"Go say 'twas Reason gave thee wings!"
    The urchin smiled, obeyed and flew!

Lovers, who listen to the tale,
    Mark well the moral it supplies,
Do not let Reason rend Love's veil
    Remember if he sees he flies!*

*Every one will at once trace the origin of these lines to Moore's
Love and Reason and Lord Byron's—"Love has no gift so grateful as
his wings."

[NO TITLE]

Bright as the diamond of the mine
    Soft as the azure of the sky,
Of earthly things the most divine,
    Is woman's eye.

Gay sweet and warm as laughing beams
    Sporting around a sunny isle,
Or glittering spray from falling streams,
        Is woman's smile.

Melodious as the soft south breeze
    The voice of waters, song of birds,
Or ripple slight of summer seas,
        Are woman's words.

Delicious as the breath of Spring
    At morn upon the mountain's tip,
While flowers their odours round her fling,
        Is Woman's lip.*

Pure soft and mild as silver light
    That smiles upon us from above
Shed by the orbs that rule the night
        Is Woman's Love!

*Notes
". . . [Manu,] the great lawgiver of Hindustan's long catalogue of things
pure and impure, says the 'mouth of a woman is constantly pure,' and
he ranks it with the running waters and the sun beams. He suggests
that their names should be agreeable, soft, clear captivating the fancy
auspicious, ending in long vowels, resembling words of benediction."
                                              Tod's Rajahst'han.
                                              Vol. 1. p. 611

[NO TITLE]

At home, with other friends, in after years,
    When scenes together trod, thou shalt recall
And Italy returns mid smiles and tears
    Florence—Rome—Naples—Baiae—Paestum—all!

With them may come the thought of one whose name
    Might never else have crossed thy lips or mind:
One, who with thee and them, found more than fame,
    And less than Memory would not leave behind.

FEMALE INFLUENCE[15]

I own I love the boundless sway
    To woman's gentle spirit given
It cheers life's dull and dreary way
    And smooths the path to hell or heaven.

And she too, in her joys and woes
    Such is great Nature's mingled plan
Seeks in her turn support—repose—
    Affection—Confidence—from man.

The son upon his mother's heart
    In all his boyish cares relies,
In every grief she bears a part
    And every little want supplies.

The daughter in her sire's embrace
    Feels of her wildest whim secure,
How could he frown on such a face
    Or chide a thing so sweet—so pure?

Of mutual hearts—maturer years
    Marriage, and love—I will not sing
Most know—or may—their smiles and tears
    Hopes, Joys, "and all that sort of thing."

But even in Piety, love shares,
    Men's orisons Madonnas claim,
While *Joseph* hears most female prayers
    Or would—but for his luckless name.

SONNET[16]

The friendless captive in his lonely tower
Which air and light and liberty denies,
Forgotten victim of despotic power
Consumes his bitter life in useless sighs:
For him in vain suns rise, and set, and rise,
And moons of tranquil beauty wax and wane,
On the calm azure of the star-lit skies,
For mountain, stream, and wood, and earth and main,
Are hid forever from his grief-worn eyes,
Which drop their fruitless tears like desert rain,
Only to rust the more his cankered chain.
So I heart-prisoned, from whose love hope flies
Reft of all life, save what is wrung from pain,
In darkness nurse the worm that never dies!

ON BREAKING THE CHAIN OF A LOCKET

I've worn it in my bosom night and day
    A talisman of bliss . . . and now the chain

Which bore it breaks—Is it an omen say!
    That we too sever ne'er to meet again?

Aye! 'tis the curse of gold to sunder so,
    All all the ties that love and nature twine
Take the freed pledge!—'tis yours—yes take it—go!
    The severed chain and broken heart are mine!

[NO TITLE]

What Alchemy's empiric art
    Found not with all its boasted powers
Life's true elixir—is a heart
    Blended by mutual love with our's.

Unbounded wealth—perpetual youth—
    Eternal life—what are they all
Compared with fond unwavering Truth
    Heaven's only relic since the fall.

Who that has loved and been beloved
    Would change for all the world can give
The one bright spell his heart has proved
    Without which 'tis not life to live.

Birth—Riches—Talent—Glory—Friends,
    All man can ask or fate supply
Are nothing 'till affection lends
    It's own delicious Alchemy.

Whence has all Joy and Beauty birth?
    Who lights the sun the stars the wave?
Whose magic gladdens Heaven and Earth?
    Whose eye first pierced beyond the grave?

Love! Love, Almighty love! reply
    All those who worship and rejoice—
But absence-tortured votaries sigh
    And bitter Memory finds no voice!

[NO TITLE]

It *was* as if he had been cast
    Alone upon a desert shore,
Silent but for the tempest's blast
    Deathlike but for the ocean's roar.

It *is* as if at once he found
    To minister unto him there
One who made all enchanted ground
    A gentle spirit of the air

It *was* as if his heart had died
    And turned his bosom to a tomb
Where young affection hope and pride
    Lay wrapped in everlasting gloom.

It *is* as if an angel came
    And rolled the marble weight away
Relighted the extinguished flame
    And called it back to life and day.

It *was* as if the fiery wind
    Over his life and thoughts had blown
With withering breath—and left behind
    But wrecks the soul's Simoom had strewn.

It *is* as if Armida's art*
    Restoring all that was destroyed
Watering with tears the wasted heart
    Had filled with flowers the aching void.†

Notes. *See Tasso's Gerusalemme Liberata Book XV
      †"Watering the heart whose early flowers have died" Byron

ON A SUN-DIAL NEAR VENICE[17]

with the inscription "Horas non numero nisi serenas."

Let others in some dreary clime
    Of fogs and storms, and snows and showers,
Scan the slow lapse of lingering Time,
    I only count unclouded hours.

Beneath calm, pure, and brilliant skies,
    Where all is sunshine, mirth, and flowers,
I seize each moment as it flies
    And truly tell the cloudless hours.

When Heaven withdraws its cheerful ray
    From pleasure's waste and leafless bowers,
I take no heed of night or day,
    I only note unclouded hours.

Learn then from me this rule of life,
    When Fortune smiles or danger lowers
In bliss or woe in peace or strife
    Learn but to mark unclouded hours.

ODE TO EASE[18]

"Otia, judicio semper amata meo."
                              Ovid.

I never bent at *Glory's* shrine
    To *Wealth* I never bowed the knee
Beauty has heard no vows of mine
    I love thee *Ease*, and only thee.
Beloved of the Gods and men
    Sister of Joy and Liberty
When wilt thou visit me agen
In shady wood or silent glen,
By fading stream or rocky den,
Like those where once I found thee when,
    I listened to thy Syren voice
    And made thee mistress of my choice?

I chose thee Ease and Glory fled
For me no more her laurels spread
Her golden crown shall never shed
Its beams of splendor on my head,
And when within the narrow bed
To fame and memory ever dead
    My wretched corpse is thrown:
Nor stately column sculptur'd bust
Nor urn that holds within its trust
The poor remains of mortal dust
    Nor monumental stone. . .
Nor willow waving in the gale
Nor feeble fence with whitened pale
Nor rustic cross, memorial frail!
    Shall mark the grave I own.
But to all future ages lost
Not even a wreck tradition-tost
Of what I was when valued most

By the few friends whose love I boast
 In after years shall float to shore
 And serve to tell the name I bore.

I chose thee Ease! and Wealth withdrew
 Indignant at the choice I made,
And to her first resentment true,
 My scorn with tenfold scorn repaid:
And vowed my folly I should rue
 In poverty's benumbing shade.
Now noble palace, lofty dome,
Or cheerful hospitable home,
 Are blessings I must never know:
My enemies shall ne'er repine
At pomp or pageantry of mine
Or prove by bowing at my shrine
 Their souls are abject base and low;
And worst of all I shall not live
To taste the pleasures wealth can give
 When used to soothe another's woe.

The peasants of my native land
Shall never bless my open hand
 No wandering bard shall celebrate
 His Patron's hospitable gate
No war-warn soldier, shattered tar,
Nor exile driven from afar
 Nor hapless friend of former years
 Nor widows prayers nor orphan's tears
Nor helpless age relieved from cares
Nor innocence preserved from snares
 Nor houseless wanderer clothed and fled,
 Nor slave from bitter bondage led,
 Nor youth to noble actions bred,
 Shall call down blessings on my head.

I chose thee Ease! and yet the while
So sweet was Beautys scornful smile
So fraught with every lovely wile
Yet seemingly, so void of guile,
 It did but heighten all her charms:
And Goddess, had I loved thee then,

[148]

But with the common love of men
My fickle heart had changed agen
Even at the very moment when
    I wooed thee to my longing arms:
For never may I hope to meet
A smile so sweet, so heavenly sweet!

I chose thee Ease! and now for me
    No heart shall ever fondly swell
No voice of rapturous harmony
    Awake the music-breathing shell
Nor tongue of witching melody
    It's love in faltering accents tell
Nor flushing cheek, nor languid eye
Nor sportive smile nor artless sigh
    Confess affection all as well.
No snowy bosom's fall and rise
Shall e'er again enchant my eyes
    No dewy lips profuse of bliss
    Shall ever greet me with a kiss
Nor sweet low tone pour in mine ear
The trifles Love delights to hear:
    But living loveless, hopeless, I,
    Unmourned and unloved must die.

I chose thee Ease! and yet to me
    Coy and ungrateful thou hast proved,
Though I have sacrificed for thee
    Much that was worthy to be loved.
But come again, and I will yet
Thy past ingratitude forget:
    O come again! thy witching powers
    Shall charm my solitary hours.
With thee to cheer me heavenly queen,
And conscience clear, and health serene,
And friends and books to banish spleen,
My life should be, as it has been,
    A sweet variety of joys:
And Glory's crown and Beauty's smile,
And treasured hoards, should seem the while
    The idlest of all human toys.

[149]

BELPHEGOR[19]

The Subject from Macchiavelli

In the great council hall of Hell
    There once was held a consultation,
The subject was—'tis strange to tell—
    How to encourage population.

'Twas long ago—I can't tell when—
    But ere they heard thy name, *Gastronomy*,
And *Malthus* had not taught them then
    The true political economy.

Causing less talk and discontent
    Than Panama's debated mission
An Envoy to the Earth was sent
    Belphegor got the new commission.

A devil of parts—and not without wit
    Handsome and graceful as Apollo
And then in salary and outfit
    He beat all other envoys hollow.

With grave enquiries charged, he came,
    To Earth—a Duke, or some such matter—
And when the women heard his fame
    Wives, widows, maids, began to flatter.

One vixen dame whose charms and art
    Might make the devil himself light-headed,
First caught his eye and then his heart
    'Till they in short were fairly wedded.

But now began Belphegor's woes
    His spouse's tongue forever wagging
Gave the poor devil no repose
    Still teasing—scolding—never flagging.

He ran at last—who would not run
    To scape such matrimonial cooing
Through every clime beneath the sun
    With his Eurydice pursuing.

At length one day almost o'ertaken
    He heard her voice—he knew it well—
And with a dreadful panic shaken
    He scampered off direct for Hell.

> Arrived at Court he told his story
>> "Learn Sire," he said, "from my miscarriage
> To fill your realm and raise your glory
>> You've but on Earth to favor marriage."

DIALOGUE[20]

> Written in Mrs. I_____'s Album
> beneath the figure of Cupid sharpening arrows

Fortune. Cupid! you rogue, what sharpening darts!
Pray are they tipped with Gold or Lead?

Cupid. How can you ask? You know men's hearts
I aim at them and not the head!

SONNET FROM THE PORTUGUESE OF CAMOENS[21]

> "Cycnis qui non sine causâ Apollini dicati sint
> . . . cum cantu et voluptate moriantur."
>> *Cic. Tuscul. Quaest. Lib I*

They say the swan, though mute his whole life long,
Pours forth sweet melody when life is flying,
Making the desert plaintive with his song
Wond'rous and sad and sweetest still while dying.
Is it for Life and Pleasure lost, he's sighing?
Grieving to lose, what none can e'er prolong:—
O! no, he hails it's close, on death relying
As an escape from violence and wrong.
And thus, dear Lady! I at length perceiving
The fatal end of my unhappy madness,
In thy oft-broken faith no more believing
Welcome despair's sole comforter with gladness,
And mourning one so fair is so deceiving,
Pour out my soul in notes of Love and Sadness!

EPIGRAM FROM THE ITALIAN OF DE ROSSI

> "How very soon your roses die!"
>> Said Love to Flora with a sneer:
> "True" was the blushing nymph's reply
>> "And yours, do they last all the year?"

[151]

[NO TITLE]

No wonder if thy pulses thrill
    To harmony almost divine
And yet it caught with all its skill
    An eloquence much less than thine.

Yes! when the witching syren sung
    Her unpremeditated song
'Twas but thy hearts dear native tongue
    Which thou hast pined to hear so long.

Thy soul was as a living lute
    Tuned to the music of the spheres
Untouched before it's chords were mute
    But now it echoes all it hears.

Thou hast not heard indeed on earth
    Sounds that so flashed through all thy frame
But thou hast known them ere thy birth
    Even in that Heaven from whence they came.

And when again the angel choirs
    (Late may it be and I at rest)
Receive thee home from kindred lyres
    Congenial sounds shall hail thee blest!

[NO TITLE]

It was a just reproof! ... and yet I thought[22]
    But no! ... Shall I deserve reproach again?
No by the Gods! ... My nature overwrought
    Has yet enough of Pride to hide its pain!

I have borne much in silence once—and now
    Shall I at last play woman with my tongue?
No! ... I will shew so smooth, so calm a brow
    That none shall dream how sore my heart is wrung.

Even thou thyself shalt deem my feigning true—
    A smile—a hollow laugh—a bitter jest
Would but betray me to the vulgar view,
    Thy garb *Indifference!* becomes me best!

Gay with the gay, and solemn with the wise
    Dull with the plodding—sportive with the fair—

Thou shalt distrust my love or doubt thine eyes
　　To mark how perfectly my mask I wear!

The hand that would not perish in the flame
　　If the heart bade it, is unworthy thine—
The mind that shrinks from any pang but shame
　　Would well deserve thy utmost scorn and mine.

There is no sterner task of soul to teach!—
　　No matter!—It *is* taught—The silent spell
Closes upon my murmurs—look—act—speech
　　Shall all obey thee!—Well—perhaps too well!

LINES WRITTEN IN AN ALBUM[23]

Of Human Life from youth to age
　　This Book an apt sad emblem seems;
Hope promises to fill each page
　　With Friendship, Love or Pleasure's dreams.

Time wears apace—but day by day,
　　Hope's promises are all forgot
Some flowers are scattered by the way
　　But here's a blank—and there's a blot.

At length they fill—revolving years
　　Add their memorials, sad, or kind,
But some are sullied by our tears,
　　And some have left a stain behind!

And when in after times we turn
　　Our Memory or our pages o'er
'Tis but too oft alas! to mourn
　　O'er all we knew—and know no more!

The hand that traced *those* lines is old—
　　The spirit that flashed *here* has fled—
And *these* recall warm hearts—now cold—
　　The changed—the absent—or the dead.

Then why should we embalm the past
　　Since the fond record only tells
That Love and Hope and Life at last
　　Are broken charms and baffled spells?

[153]

I do not know. . . . They say that Eve
    Some flowers of Eden chose to keep
O'er all she prized and left to grieve,
    O'er all she loved and lost to weep!

[NO TITLE]

    Beatus qui te videt est
      Beatior qui te audiet
    Qui te basiat semideus est
      Qui te potitur est deus.
           Buchanan

Happy is he who sees thee smile,[24]
    Still happier he who hears thee speak,
He half a God who dares awhile
    Breathing fond vows to flush thy cheek.

Thy hand to press—thy lip to touch—
    O thou hast ne'er such favors given—
'Twere bliss too much for man too much
    For all except a saint of Heaven!

To clasp thy form and hear thee sigh—
    To feel and call thee all his own
Ah! that were happiness too high
    For any but a God alone!

[NO TITLE]

Choose as thou wilt! the land—the main
    The court, the camp, the mart, the grove,
Power, Glory, Pleasure, Wisdom, Gain,
    Rank, Friendship, Wit, Fame, Beauty, Love—

Choose as thou wilt! since all may choose,
    And win thy choice—all *may* be won.
Their fortune none but fools accuse
    Who know not how her frowns to shun.

Choose as thou wilt!—but know whate'er
    Thy choice may be—or thy success
All are but bubbles of the air
    Deceitful forms of happiness!

[154]

Clouds that have ta'en a heavenly form
　　And heavenly hues and heavenly charms,
All that a mortal heart can warm—
　　All that escapes from mortal arms!

[NO TITLE]

I have deceived myself! . . . the dream was sweet
　　·And bitter the awaking—Let me call
My spirit up, it's destiny to meet
　　Triumph may hail, but shall not mock my fall!

Conquered, but not subdued—I scorn to yield
　　Betrayed, but yet unmoved—with steady eye
I gaze in silence on my last lost field,
　　With neither wish to live nor fear to die.

From my proud hopes of high dominion hurled
　　My transient reign of Love and Glory o'er
Dethroned—Exiled—from what I thought *my* world,
　　The Empire of the Heart exists no more!

What then is left? to bend beneath the shock
　　Tire Heaven with prayers and be of Hell the jest?
No! welcome first the vulture and the rock!
　　Prometheus-like in this, as in the rest.

I strove with Heaven for Heaven—the strife was vain—
　　The fire I stole consumes me—let it burn!—
No tyrant shall wring pleasure from my pain
　　Scorn yields such wrong it's only just return!

[NO TITLE]

Jam mihi deterior canis adspergitur aetas,
　　Jamque meos vultus ruga senilis arat:
Jam vigor, et quasso languent in corpore vives;
　　Nec juveni lusus qui placuere, placent.
Nec, si me subito videas agnoscere possis:
　　Aetabis facta est tanta ruina meae.
Confiteor facere haec annos: sed et altera caussa est,
　　Anxietas animi, continuus que labor.
　　　　　　　　　　　Ovid Epis.

[155]

My hair is gray—the flower of life is past
　　　Time flies and Death approaches. In the wave
My setting sun is sinking overcast,
　　　Hope is no more, and Peace is in the grave!

Long years of passion—grief and care have done
　　　Their work—and left their records on my brow,
My lamp is almost out—my race is run—
　　　Let the scene close!—It matters little now.

The best and worst are past—there lingers yet
　　　But a faint pulse in these poor shrunken veins,
The world and I are even, and the debt
　　　That all must pay is all that still remains.

Would it were paid!—I tire of my road—
　　　'Tis hard to live unblessing and unblest—
Forgetting and forgot—I bear a load
　　　Too far above my strength and fain would rest!

[NO TITLE]

My Sister! through how many trying scenes[25]
　　　We two have past in long long years gone by,
Even yet though half a life time intervenes
　　　I cannot think of them without a sigh.

Since thine unconscious infant lips were prest
　　　First by a brother's boyish, bashful kiss,
'Till now when he, life-weary longs for rest,
　　　And even thy hopes seek better worlds than this:

What has been done and suffered—felt and thought
　　　In this long, dismal, dark abyss of life,
Where troubled spirits toil on, overwrought,
　　　Amid temptation, sorrow, sin and strife.

How many of the loved and mourned have gone
　　　How many joys and hopes of youth have fled—
How few of all the friends who linger on
　　　Replace the lost—the changed—the cold—the dead.

Yet Hope is left! . . . One hope—the best—the last—
　　　Though we plod on o'er thorns unto the grave
However long the day, to come—or past—
　　　Our Sun at length will sleep beneath the wave.

Forever? . . . No! . . . The Ave's evening chime*
That strikes the traveller's ear as day-light dies
Although it seems to mourn departed Time
Tells too of Life Eternal in the skies!

*The Ave Maria della sera common in Catholic countries. The thought
was suggested by the well known lines of Dante:
"Era già l'ora che volge'l disio
A'naviganti, e intenerisce il cuore
Lo dì c'han detto a dolci amici addio;
E che lo nuovo peregrin d'amore
Punge se ode squilla di lontana
Che paia 'l giorno pianger, che si muore."

" 'Twas now the hour when seamen's fancies dwell
On Home—and in the traveller's heart arise
Sad thoughts of the dear friends he bade farewell:
And Love's fresh-parted pilgrim starts and sighs
Heart-stricken by the distant vesper bell
Which seems as if it mourned the day that dies!"

RUTH[26]

"And Ruth said, entreat me not to leave thee, or to return
from following after thee; for whither thou goest I will go;
and where thou lodgest I will lodge: thy people shall be my
people and thy God my God. Where thou diest I will die and
there also will I be buried."

Nay do not ask!—entreat not—no!
O! no I will not leave thy side:
Whither thou goest, I will go,
Where thou abidest, I'll abide.

Through life—in death—my soul to thine
Shall cleave as fond as first it clave—
Thy Home, thy people, shall be mine
Thy God, my God—thy grave my grave!

[NO TITLE]

If it be love, in every pulse's tide
To feel a secret pure devoted flame
And with feign'd smiles unceasing torture hide
Deep in the soul—my passion has a name!

If it be love, to live but in one thought,
To breathe but for another—weal or woe

Only to feel when from another caught
　　This, this *is* Love! . . . I feared it must be so!

If it be Love, to worship night and day
　　One object—On a fond heart's faithful shrine
All our life's hopes and fears and joys to lay
　　In silent sacrifice—such love is mine.

If it be love, our being to consume
　　In unknown, fruitless, uncomplaining tears,
And wish in bitterness an early tomb
　　Then I have cherished hopeless love for years!

[NO TITLE]

This life is but a horrid dream[27]
　　To those who squander it like me,
In wild excess and mad extreme,
　　Mock joy and sad festivity!
Rather than wake to laugh and rave,
　　Or toss in such distempered sleep,
I would that I were in my grave,
　　So there were none my fate to weep!

Yet I who wither and repine
　　Am envied by a glittering throng,
And there are hearts wrapped up in mine
　　By ties too sacred far for song.
Intense in all things—Love or Grief—
　　Rage—Pride—Joy—Hatred or Disdain,
O! not to feel were some relief
　　From this vicissitude of pain!

Yet I endure and shrink not—I
　　Have done with Hope and Joy and Fear,
The torrent of my heart is dry,
　　My burning eyes have not a tear.
Come Genius! see thy torments! come!—
　　View Fate, the tortures of thy slave!
But mark ye! his despair is dumb
　　Your power he yet can scorn and brave!

THE HERON[28]

A Fable from the French of La Fontaine

Along a glassy river's edge
Well stocked with fish and fringed with sedge
    A long-legged Heron strayed:
The day was fine the water clear
The Pike and Carp, now there—now here—
    A thousand frolics played.

The largest trouts came close to shore
As if to tempt our bird the more
    But he, unlucky wight,
Eyes them askance and steps aside
Through laziness perhaps, or pride,
    To wait for appetite.

A stated regimen he kept
At certain hours eat [*sic*] drank and slept
    As learned quacks prescribe
Full soon his appetite returns
With eager haste he strides and burns
    To thin the finny tribe.

Advancing in his former post
The nobler prey he found was lost
    Some tenches still remained
But these like Flaccus' city rat
Expecting better cheer than that
    He haughtily disdained.

"And shall I then on tenches dine?
What Heron of such parts as mine
    E'er stooped to swallow these?"
The tench refused in mighty dudgeon
He passes on, and a lone gudgeon
    Is the next fish he sees.

A gudgeon truly eh! cries he
Lord what a pretty mess for me!
    As sure as I'm a sinner,
Before I'd ope for him my bill
I'd wait (which God forbid!) until
    Tomorrow for my dinner.

Yet for far less wide gaped that bill
Since travelling farther onward still
     His legs begin to fail
No fish however small appears
Starvation much he shrewdly fears
     And gladly eats a snail.

Let us not be too hard to please
They are most wise who take with ease
     What Fate to give thinks fit.
What's near your due then ne'er refuse
Seeking too much we often lose
     And many thus are bit.

To Herons 'twere in vain to preach
Listen Mankind, 'tis you I teach
     From you my tales I draw:
A belle who like most belles you find
Was pretty vain—seemed half inclined
     In Hymen's yoke to draw.

But he whose suit she grants must be
Polite, young, handsome, well made free
     Not jealous, nor yet cold
Of fortune, wit, and birth possest,
Alas! not one man so much blest
     We in an age behold.

Some lovers of importance came,
Urged by her friends to choose, the dame
     All offers thus repels;
"Now pray don't name such fools to me
You surely rave!"—Here reader see
     A specimen of belles!

One witty was, but unrefined,
Another's nose awry inclined
     'Twas that thing, or 'twas this,
'Twas every thing—for belles discover
A thousand faults in every lover
     Whom they would fain dismiss.

Some decent matches offered then
Among the middle class of men
     But she was pleased to jeer:

[160]

These folks perhaps think I'm afraid
To lie alone—or die a maid
    But I have no such fear.

My slumbers (God be praised!) are sound
No inconvenience I have found—
    I miss not love's embrace:
Still to these notions she adhered
Age came her gallants disappeared
    Chagrin crept on apace.

A year or two in trouble past
She felt her beauty fading fast
    And every fatal day
Saw that some charm of face or air
Or form—which art could ne'er repair
    Escaped with time away.

Her mirror plainly said make haste
And wed for you've no time to waste:—
    No longer vain or cold,
She took the hint, right glad to patch
With a mean wretch a sordid match
    Though ugly cross and old.

NAPOLEON'S GRAVE[29]

Faint and sad was the moon-beam's smile,
    Sullen the moan of the dying wave,
Hoarse the wind in St. Helen's isle,
    As I stood by the side of *Napoleon's grave.*

And is it *here* that the Hero lies,
    Whose name has shaken the Earth with dread?
And is *this* all that the earth supplies,
    A stone his pillow—the turf his bed?

Is such the moral of human life?
    Are these the limits of Glory's reign?
Have oceans of blood and an age of strife,
    And a thousand battles been all in vain?

Is nothing left of his victories now
    But legions broken—a sword in rust,
A crown that cumbers a dotard's brow,
    A name and a requiem—dust to dust!

[161]

Of all the chieftains whose thrones he reared
    Was there none that kindness or faith could bind?
Of all the monarchs whose crowns he spared
    Had none one spark of his Roman mind?

Did Prussia cast no repentant glance
    Did Austria shed no remorseful tear
When England's faith, and thine honor France,
    And thy friendship Russia, were blasted here?

No!—Holy Leagues like the heathen Heaven
    Ungodlike shrunk from the giant's shock
And glorious Titan, the unforgiven,
    Was doomed to his vulture and chains and rock.

And who were the gods that decreed thy doom?
    A German Caesar—a Prussian Sage—
The Dandy Prince of a counting-room
    And a Russian Greek of Earth's darkest age.

Men called thee despot, and called thee true,
    But the laurel was earned that bound thy brow
And of all who wore it alas! how few
    Were freer from treason and guilt than thou.

Shame to thee Gaul! and thy faithless horde,
    Where was the oath which thy soldiers swore?
Fraud still lurks in the gown—but the sword
    Was never so false to its trust before.

Where was thy veteran's boast that day
    "The old guard dies, but it never yields!"
O! for one heart like the brave Dessaix
    One phalanx like those of thine early fields!

But no no, no!—it was Freedom's charm
    Gave them the courage of more than men
You broke the magic that nerv'd each arm
    Though you were invincible only then.

Yet St Jean was a deep, not a deadly blow,
    One struggle and France all her faults repairs—
But the mild Fayette and the stern Carnot
    Are dupes and ruin thy fate and theirs!

[162]

[NO TITLE]

Go! go, thou art false!—thy tears thy smiles[30]
  Thy sainted look, thy solemn vow
Thy thrilling tones, thy lovely wiles,
  All all thy charms are worthless now!

'Twas not because thy lips were sweet
  As violets bathed in heavenly dew,
I loved their melting kiss to meet
  No! 'twas because I thought them true.

Nor did I prize the trembling light
  That in thy glances warmly shone,
O no! when I believed them bright
  I thought they burned for me alone.

When thy heart changed it broke the best
  The dearest, purest, strongest, spell,
'Tis easy now to burst the rest
  How easy—thou thyself canst tell!

[NO TITLE]

Why is it then, the Earth and Sky,
  The promise of returning Spring,
And all that greets the ear and eye
  To this worn soul no joy can bring?

Has Life consumed itself?—O no!
  It is not that—its currents run
No more apart—they only flow
  Silent, intense, and deep in one.

Its source is here—what shores it laves,
  Or whither rolls the impetuous tide,
Who knows?—Who knows what kindred waves
  Claim tribute from its hope its pride?

But O! until they meet again
  (Alas! how could they ever part?)
What chance—what change can calm the brain
  What time—what thought can soothe the heart?

The Future?—Will not Hope deceive?
  The Present?—O! it must not last!

[163]

And yet alas! how vain to grieve
    Over the unreturning past!

[NO TITLE]

A sister's kiss—an infant's prayer—
    A parent's love—a vestal's vow—
The Evening Star—the morning air—
    Are not more pure than thou:
I dare not love thee—but my eyes
Have told thee whom they idolize.

I held and still I hold thee dear,
    Of more than mortal worth,
A spirit of another sphere
    Too good and fair for earth:
And I would blush to wound thine ear
With aught that Angels might not hear!

But since our pious zeal is faint
    My church must be forgiven,
If it allows at least a saint,
    To help us on to heaven:
Thou art my saint!—in every prayer
I always see thee smiling there!

TO [----------------------]

An unknown fair one designated to me only as the sixteenth letter.

Lady! the brother of my heart demands
    A hymn of praise to offer at thy shrine
But that which were Devotion at his hands,
    Becomes mere blind Idolatry in mine:
    For unrevealed to me by word or sign,
The fair Divinity I worship stands,
    Around a shadow my fond faith I twine
Like to the Gentile of far times and lands.
    They to a being whom they deemed divine
"The Unknown God—" a sacred temple raised,
    And praised his nameless name, as I do thine,
Unknowing who, or what it was they praised—
    Merely like me to murmur and repine,
That all in vain altar and incense blazed!

[164]

[NO TITLE]

A Rose between two Hearts—by moonlight given!
  What may so bright an augury forebode?
Type of the opening Spring and Star-lit Heaven
  On Grief's gray twilight all in vain bestowed!

Aye! all in vain alas!—the smiling Spring
  And the calm lustre of the starry skies
Nor Joy nor Hope nor Peace to Him can bring—
  They're but as lovely scenes to sightless eyes!

The givers and the gift can but recall
  The fading forms of long departed years
Visions of bliss all vanished—lost—all, all!
  And ev'n their memory half-effaced by tears.

Aye! that same flower!—its hue—its scent have brought
  Back on my soul a thousand nameless things
A long long train of melancholy thought
  And maddening passion's fierce and fiery stings.

Such was the gift! . . . Down busy devil!—down!
  Consume this soul in secret—if you must—
But though it's pangs no revelry can drown,
  Feast like the worm that revels on the dust!

In darkness and in silence feast! . . . No more!—
  Such thoughts should have no tongue—within their tomb
Let them bleed on, but without running o'er
  No eye should mark and shudder at their gloom.

So, to our theme again!—that it may fling
  Oblivion o'er a spirit wrung and riven,—
Farewell! sweet emblem of the blooming Spring
  Farewell! calm type of the blue starry Heaven!

On Roses, woman's words, and moon-lighted nights,
  Unnumbered, soft, sad tender memories dwell
Heart-treasured thoughts—unspeakable delights—
  And all I may not utter—Fare ye well!

[NO TITLE]

'Tis the hour when Twilight stealing
  O'er the Earth and Sea and skies

Wakes a high and holy feeling,
    And fond thoughts of Home arise:
Love's fresh-parted Pilgrim sighing,
    Starts to hear the vesper bell,
Breathing to the day-light dying
    One last wild—sweet—sad farewell!*

In this hour still and solemn
    O'er a shrine in fragments laid
Memory on a broken column
    Marks the ruin Time has made:
Well—too well alas! recalling
    Hopes and Joys forever fled. . . .
O! what burning tears are falling
    For the loved—the changed—the dead!

*Imitated from Dante's 'Era già l'ora.'

BARCAROLA[31]
Imitated from the Italian

My Gondola's waiting dearest!
    The night is well nigh to it's noon,
And the sea is the calmest and clearest
    Ever lit by a summer's moon:
O! come like a white cloud flying
    O'er the heavenly blue of the skies
And the ripple that murmurs in dying
    Will seem but to echo our sighs!

O come to my Gondola—dearest!
    And sail with me side by side
I know there are times when thou fearest
    To trust either me—or the tide:
Yet a mother her infant sleeper
    Or the moon-beams this dreaming sea
Regard with a love no deeper
    Or purer than mine for thee!

[NO TITLE]

Zoe farewell!—How much is in that word[32]
    Deep, solemn, chill and sad as Memory's knell
Recalling Joy departed—Hope deferred—

[166]

Fond dreams—dear thoughts—kind looks—lost friends—
   Farewell!

Farewell! . . . We have not known each other long
   Nor much—But what of that?—How soon and well
Fate binds by ties invisible yet strong
   All that love those we love, to us. . . . Farewell!

Since first we met some few but fatal years
   Upon my life and brow have left their spell
Love-Sorrow—Pride—Rage—Hate—Despair and Tears
   Have writ their burning annals there—Farewell!

Farewell! among my few unclouded hours
   Are those I owe unto your voice and shell
When with bright smiles, sweet words, and tuneful powers,
   You chased my evil spirit. . . . Fare ye well!

TO A LOVELY BRUNETTE
WHOM THE AUTHOR SAW AT HER LATTICE

O! darkly fair!—yet beautifully bright,
   I know not how to call thee, sweet unknown!
Whether a Tropic Day or Arctic Night
   Or the soft Twilight of a temperate Zone.

Although I have but seen thee from afar,
   And haply never may behold thee near,
Let me adore thee as a lovely star,
   Altho' my words may never reach thine ear!

No hopeless ship-wrecked mariner could watch
   Through dim, death-glazing eyes for morning's ray,
More eagerly, than I have striv'n to catch
   That movement of thy lattice, once a day!

Nor always once!—day after day has past
   And be it pride, or bashfulness, or scorn,
Thy well-named Jealousie is closed as fast,
   As though it had been of the monster born!

Did'st thou observe me? Hence is thy disdain?
   Ah! pardon I entreat, my wandering eyes!
They sought with fond Astrology to gain
   Some hint from Destiny's high star-lit skies!

[167]

Alas! oershadowed by a cloudy veil
    The skies disclose their oracles no more,
And even the beacon, I was wont to hail,
    The taper in thy window gleams no more!

Darkling I tempt my solitary fate
    Full of heart throbbing wishes, doubts and fears,
As thou may'st be a widow—maid—or mate
    So must my vision end—in bliss or tears!

And yet—if maiden, I should never win—
    If widow, both would be too wise to marry—
If wife, twere worse—to love thee were a sin—
    And I have quite as much as I can carry!

[NO TITLE]

Why should her misery o'er my own prevail?
    Hence horrid shadows! from my brain depart! . . .
It may not be!—the melancholy tale
    Rings in my ear, and weighs upon my heart!

I cannot rest!—I knew there were such woes
    But thought them singular, and did not deem,
That such again would break on my repose
    With all the tortures of a troubled dream.

Lovely and innocent and good and kind
    Young, sensitive, yet wise from early grief,
A faultless body and a spotless mind
    Supremely wretched!—'Tis beyond belief!

But truth and that which seems so are not one
    And spite of all that wisdom said of old
There still are mysteries beneath the sun
    All the hearts secrets have not yet been told!

I may not tell them! . . . There are wounds that bleed
    And must bleed inwardly, while there is breath
Yet thou may'st bear them Mary, for indeed
    Others have borne them and will bear 'till death!

But come what will!—worn out with grief and care
    Whether you totter on—or cast them down
You have one fellow sufferer in Despair
    One friend to cheer thee though the World should frown!

[NO TITLE]

You call me sad!—you err—I'm gay
    Who hath yet mark'd my spirits sink
Who hath beheld by night or day
    My lip, voice, eye, or visage shrink?

My looks? . . . Joy wrinkles just like care
    Go trace the marks that Pleasure brings
You'll find them in the face and air
    Of Charles, merriest of kings.*

You err!—you err!—I sad?—you dream
    Sorrow ne'er touched a heart like mine
Wit—Beauty—Love are still my theme
    And crown'd with Music, Flowers and Wine!

Boy bring the cup, the vase, the lyre
    Awake, awake the soul of song!
Let odours, sound, sight, taste inspire
    The pleasures that to sense belong.

What shall they say with ills opprest
    Unto their yoke I bowed my neck?
When scaffolds echo to a jest,**
    And laughter rises from the wreck:

What hearts from living bosoms torn
    Have bled with greater pangs than mine?
What ships on Ocean's bosom borne
    Held hopes like those all wrecked on thine?

Yet the dark Indian's self-control
    As soon shall leave him at the stake
As this stern, sullen, stubborn soul
    Shall ever bow or bend or break.

No, no! all, all shall deem me gay
    The sound of revelry and mirth
Shall grossly cheat these souls of clay
    Who deem me of their kindred earth.

Bring, bring the cup, the vase, the lyre!
    Wake Pleasure's maddening syren song!
Mask! quickly mask, that cursed fire,
    The torches of the Fury throng!

[169]

The song! the Dance! away! away!
Rouse Mirth 'till all Night's echoes start!
Who now shall say I am not gay?
Who shall pretend to read my heart?

*Charles the II - a sad dog as his face shews.
**'Till even the scaffold echoes with the jest.'
Rogers.

TO _____

... Farewell! and if forever . . .—still farewell!—
Howe'er it fare with me—I would not leave
One word, one thought, at which thy veins might swell
Thy temples throb—or even thy bosom heave.

Farewell!—Despite experience—prudence—pride—
My Destiny o'ertakes me once again;
I strove to shun the blow—or turn aside—
Yet I endure, and shrink not from the pain!

Farewell! farewell!—Thine be the peace I lose,
Mine be the grief I would not have thee share—
With Thee be all it was thy choice to choose—
With me the pangs I cannot choose but bear.

Farewell! Thou wilt forget me—be it so!
'Twere better far—I could not bear to dwell
In cold remembrance—every other woe
To that were nothing!—Now farewell! farewell!

[NO TITLE]

Yes! let us part, while yet we may,[33]
Ere wishes wild and warm begin,
Or Love will lead our souls astray
And we may wander into sin.

Where then would be thy spirits light,
Thy manners innocently gay?
The peaceful slumbers of the night,
The tranquil pleasures of the day?

And where would be the steady beams
That Virtue lends thine eyes of flame?

[170]

And where the blush that never gleams
    To warn us of the bosom's shame?

O! they would fly, forever fly
    To seek some purer holier shrine;
But not to light a brighter eye,
    Or warm a lovelier cheek than thine!

What then were left?—a hectic blaze
    The beacon-fire of vicious guile,
An anxious look—an eager gaze—
    A feverish sigh—a languid smile!

Thus thou would'st lose, in beauty's prime,
    The purity that won my heart,
And I should live to curse the crime
    That taught thee every wanton's art.

Or oh! if less ensnared by ill,
    Thy soul should mourn its lost repose,
Should weep our fault—yet love it still,
    That were the keenest—worst of woes!

For could I bear to hear thee sigh
    And know thy sighs were caused by me,
Or see thee weep, and feel that I
    Had wrung those bitter tears from thee?

Think'st thou, that I could witness this,
    Nor give thee tear for tear again? . . .
And is one moments guilty bliss
    Worth a whole Life of fruitless pain?

And yet one hour . . . one little hour,
    In Love's esteem far far outweighs
The richest gift in Virtue's power
    Heaven's sweetest softest note of praise!

And thou wilt hate me, if we part,
    And turn my counsel all to jest,
Scorning the cold and languid heart
    That might—and did not dare—be blest!

Then Dearest stay!—one moment yet—
    Turn, turn, those fatal eyes away

[171]

And let me, if I can forget,
  The light that leads my soul astray!

The flame that burns so brightly now
  Like other flames may yet decay;
The heart that broke a former vow
  O! will it not again betray?

Then shun, O! shun, the wild'ring fire
  Beneath whose dangerous light we range
Seek milder beams that ne'er expire
  And calmer hearts that never change!

They'll love thee with so pure a love
  With such a holy, heavenly zeal,
As sainted souls in Heaven above
  For other saints on earth might feel!

Will that suffice?—What no reply
  Nay then my pious rhetorick faints—
Thou know'st my heart—I read thine eye—
  Alas! we were not made for saints!

SONNET[34]

Thou hast thy faults *Virginia!* yet I own
I love thee still, although no son of thine,
For I have climbed thy mountains—not alone—
And made the wonders of thy vallies [*sic*] mine:
Finding from morning's dawn to days decline
Some marvel yet unmarked—some peak whose throne
Was loftier—girt with mist and crowned with pine;
Some narrow rugged glen with copse o'ergrown
The birth of some sweet fountain—or the line
Traced by some silver stream that wandered lone:
Or the dark cave* where hidden chrystals shine—
Or the wild arch** across the blue sky thrown—
Or else those traits of Nature more divine
That in some favored child of thine had shone!

*Weir's Cave
**The Natural bridge

[NO TITLE]

Oh! dearer by far than the land of our birth[35]
    Is the land where the hours of our infancy flew
And the dearest and loveliest spot upon earth
    Is the spot where our loves and affections first grew.

What home can we have but the home of the heart
    What country but that of our friends can we claim
Or where is the powerful spell that can part
    The soul from the scenes of it's hopes and it's fame?

Then tell us no more we were born far away
    Where Liberty's star never rose or has set
We were nursed where it shines and have caught from it's ray
    A warmth which our bosoms can never forget!

And dearer by far than the land of our birth
    Is the land where the hours of our infancy flew
And the dearest and loveliest spot upon earth
    Is the spot where our loves and affections first grew!

[NO TITLE]

Forget me not! or grave or gay
    Joyous or sad whate'er thy lot
Whether to sigh, or smile, or pray,
    Forget me not! forget me not!

Forget me not! O! no no no!
    I could not bear to be forgot
Whate'er I am—where'er I go
    Forget me not! forget me not!

Forget me not!—the world of me
    May say and deem—I care not what—
I ask but one fond thought from thee
    Forget me not! forget me not!

Forget me not! by night or day
    Whate'er deceit may subtly plot
To lead thy heart from mine astray
    Forget me not! forget me not!

Forget me not! O let no spell
    Remembrance from thy bosom blot

By every tone of voice and shell
    Forget me not! forget me not!

Forget me not! my dust, my fame
    May all in . . . cold obstruction rot . . .
So—thou wilt but preserve my name
    Forget me not! forget me not!

NIGHT REVERIES

O! let no skeptic's reasoning zeal
    Awake me from my dream of bliss!
There is—there is—I know—I feel—
    There must be other Worlds than this!

What are their joys or why conferr'd
    Or how—Iwill not stop to scan
Nor ask if any heavenly word
    Revealed their mysteries to Man.

I need but look on those bright orbs
    Which shine so calmly from above,
That single look my soul absorbs
    In reveries of hope and love!

I look, and as they roll and blaze
    My soul claims kindred with the skies
And they persuade me as I gaze
    There's *that* in me, which never dies!

It is divine to think that Earth,
    And earthly thoughts are cold and dim
Compared with those of Heavenly birth
    Which lift the enraptured heart to Him!

For here, from youth to age we still
    For some pure pleasure thirst and pine,
Our greatest good is mixed with ill,
    Ev'n Love is only half divine.

Either it is our cruel fate
    To see our young affections crost—
Or find a mutual heart too late,
    Only to know how much we've lost:

To languish many a dangerous hour
  Reading each other's glance and sigh—
To tremble in Temptation's power
  Yet neither dare to sin nor fly.

Or else in broken hearted grief
  O'er our first cherished passion bend
'Till Death shall come to our relief
  The wretches true and only friend!

Or worse—when all is won—to find
  Perfection's dream dissolve away—
The charm was only in our mind
  Our idol but a thing of clay.

In cold indifference or disgust,
  To drag a goading chain along,
And false ourselves,—in falsehood trust—
  An interchange of wrong for wrong—

Or when the grave has set its seal
  Upon the heart we wronged and wrung,
To find Remorse has clutch'd his steel,
  And Conscience found at last her tongue!

[NO TITLE]

In utter loneliness of heart[36]
  Mid well-known scenes and looks I roam
As I were a thing apart
  A being without friend or home.

Alone in peopled solitude,
  I gaze unconsciously around—
Alas! this seeming vacant mood,
  But marks remembrance too profound.

Yet here my boyhood rolled away,
  And here too in maturer years,
Successive passions held their sway,
  Through agonies of blood and tears.

I have outlived them all!—and now
  Though inwardly the bosom bleed
A purer heart—a calmer brow—
  A more untroubled mind succeed.

[175]

[NO TITLE]

Good-Night! good night!—those few kind words are all
 That mark our partings now. . . . It was not so
In times gone by— Why cannot I recall
 Those days with all their bliss and all their woe?

Unmarked—unhidden then, our hopes our fears,
 Were freely interchanged alone for hours;
We hid not from each other smiles or tears
 But the heart's sunshine mingled with its showers!

Now frosty welcomes usher in the morn,
 And formal partings close the lingering day
Beneath the World's keen glance like bondsmen born
 We toil through hateful tasks, as best we may.

I murmur not! . . . I know thy lofty soul
 Spurns like my own this yoke—this servile chain,
No! the World's minions let the World control,
 We only fear to give each other pain!

Good Night! good night then! . . . on thy gentle lids
 Light sweet repose, and as thou sink'st to rest
Dream it is he—thy friend—thy brother bids
 Good-night!—and whispers[,"Be] thy slumbers blest!"

ON POWER'S IDEAL HEAD OF ROGERS' GENEVRA[37]

 Each word, each thought—each single drop of ink
 That lips or pens of master-minds let fall
 Becomes a germ—to make new millions think:
 So said the noble bard*—nor is this all—
 Not only from the vasty deep they call
 Spirits that come—embodied in new forms
 But these again at pleasure we recall
 Helped by each art that into being warms
 The mind's creations.—Shakespeare's stricken deer
 Mid Cowper's holiest—Moore's most tender themes,
 In Proteus beauty charms the heart and ear:**

---

*Lord Byron
**'I was a stricken deer that left the herd'
       Cowper
'Come rest in this bosom, my own stricken deer'
       Moore

And poor Genevra's innocence which gleams
In Rogers' verse even through her fearful bier
In Power's marble now immortal beams!

[NO TITLE]

In this dull world of books and men
    Where scarcely anything's worth heeding
And not much more than one in ten
    Of men or books deserves a reading

'Tis rapture now and then to find
    A face or page, so rare in spirit—
So full of grace—so rich in mind
    That it bears heaven's own seal of merit.

And if such page be given to song
    The heart feels all its beauties nearer.
And if such lovely face belong
    To woman—O! how much 'tis dearer!

Yet when alas! we've conned it o'er
    And seen how many charms surround it,
How do we wish we'd found before,
    Or if not then, had never found it!

[NO TITLE]

Sey mir gesegnet
Hier in der ferne
Liebliche heimath!
Sey mir gesegnet
Land meiner Träume
Kries meiner Lieben
Sey mir gegrüsst!
        Körner

Farewell! my more than father land,[38]
Home of my heart and friends adieu!
Lingering beside some foreign strand
How oft shall I remember you:
How often o'er the waters blue
Send back a sigh to those I leave,
The loving and beloved few
Who grieve for me—for whom I grieve.

We part!—no matter how we part—
There are some thoughts we utter not,
Deep treasured in our inmost hearts
Never revealed and ne'er forgot—
Why murmur at the common lot?
We part!—I speak not of the pain
But when shall I each lovely spot
And each loved face behold again?

It must be months—it may be years—
It may—but no! I will not fill
Fond hearts with gloom, fond eyes with tears
Curious to shape uncertain ill:
Though humble, few and far, yet still
Those hearts and eyes are ever dear
Their's is the love no Time can chill
The truth no chance or change can sear!

All I have seen—and all I see
Only endears them more and more,
Friends cool—hopes fade—and honors flee
Affection lives when all is o'er:
Farewell my more than native shore
I do not seek or hope to find
Roam where I will what I deplore
To leave with them and thee behind!

[NO TITLE]

Lady farewell! . . . bear with thee o'er the wave[39]
   Back to the scenes we lov'd in early youth,
My wishes, hopes—aye pray'rs—if aught so grave
   From one so frivolous may seem like truth!

Farewell! . . . Thou wilt forget both them and me
   Before thy vessel cleaves the foaming main—
But of the brief—bright moments passed with thee
   I shall a deep remembrance long retain!

[NO TITLE]

In sad constrained and tedious hours
   Time lingers on—and day by day

[178]

Soul—body—hopes—affections—powers
    Sink by a slow but sure decay!

And this is life! . . . a living death,
    Whose loss I well might count a gain,
Since it is but unwilling breath,
    And sensibility to pain!

So be it! . . . In a few short years
    The burning brain's last throb is o'er,
And the heart's ashes quench'd in tears
    Emit their caustic fire no more!

So let it be! . . . in silent gloom
    I see and I abide my fate! . . .
If this is life, the closing tomb
    Will but shut out a world I hate!

LINES WRITTEN IN LADY _____'S ALBUM[40]

We all have treasures which we fondly cherish
    Precious and rare memorials of the past,
Relics of days that do not wholly perish
    At least as long as Life and Memory last.

The antiquary hoards his coin and gem
    Medal and manuscript and ancient tome:
And jewelled Krees [Kreese]—chibouque with curious stem—
    Or fish—or bird the Mariner brings home.

The artist, and enthusiast of art,
    Have sketches gather'd wheresoe'er they've been
And Nature's musing votaries do not part
    Without mementos of each favorite scene.

The traveller brings from each enchanted spot
    Something that may recall it to his view,
A leaf from Virgil's tomb—Egeria's grot—
    Fragments of Rome—a flower from Waterloo.

After his pilgrimage the Palmer keeps
    The garb, and staff, and cockle-shell he bore,
After her Lover's death the maiden weeps
    Over the ring he gave, or tress he wore.

Thus is it ever!—In the heart's affections
    In Friendship—Love and Memory we live

Life's strongest spells are wishes—recollections—
    Joys we have gained or giv'n—or hope to give!

But in the Museums of the Soul like this,
    The calmly meditative mind may see
The inborn thirst of past and present bliss,
    All we have been—and yet expect to be.

Lady! may thy collection long increase!
    Rich with the spoils of each succeeding year,
Proofs of the heart's content—the bosom's peace—
    Hope—Love and Joy, unsullied by a tear.

[NO TITLE]

They say no Love's so deep—so pure,
    As that where Death has set his seal*
It is not so!—at least I'm sure
    Death could not add to what I feel!

No! no!—descended from the skies
    And breathing Heaven upon the heart
Love—real—true Love, never dies
    The immortal soul's least mortal part!

All other passions bear a stain
    Which shews they are not from above:
Of Earth—to Earth they turn again—
    From Heaven—to Heaven returns true Love!

There may be times when his bright face
    With thoughts pale cast is sicklied o'er
Blindfold, his statue wore such trace—
    But drop the fillet—'twas no more.**

So all that Death for Love can do
    Is rend the Veil that dims his sight
Clear from the brow its pensive hue
    And on his smile pour endless light!

---

*"There is no passion so full of soft[,] tender and hallowing associations as the Love which is stamped by Death!'
                                        Bulwer

**"The Statue of Love by Praxiteles. When its eyes were bandaged the countenance seemed grave and sad: but the moment you removed the fillet, the most serene and enchanting smile diffused itself over the whole face.'
                                        W.

[NO TITLE]

Cease, cease thy song! it tells me much
    Of those whom this sad heart held dear,
'Tis heavenly sweet!—but ah! not such
    As thou should'st breathe or I must hear.

There was a time!—but no 'twere vain—
    'Twere folly to confess it all—
Thou must not breathe those notes again
    I cannot bear what they recall!

Once they were loved, and even yet
    Deep in my inmost soul they dwell:
I cannot if I would forget
    The dear, bewildering, dangerous spell.

But let them not be breathed by Thee!
    Let me not hear thy witching tone
Lest in my looks my eyes you see
    All I have felt but dare not own!

[NO TITLE]

Excepto, quòd non simul esses caetera laetus.
Hor.

Come! come to us hither! the goblet is flowing,[41]
And Wit dropping sparks like the sun-shine in showers
And warm hearts have met, and bright glances are glowing,
The moon's shining softly, the summer breeze blowing
And odours and melody round us are throwing
Their spell, 'till our souls seem all music and flowers!

O come to us hither! the moments are flying,
The longest of lives has not many such hours;
The goblet is sinking—the South wind is sighing—
The moon-beams are waning—the night flowers dying—
O come to us hither! we'll take no denying
Your pleasure is all that's now wanting to ours!

[NO TITLE]

Here all is heartless, hollow, loud
    Vain glittering shew and empty sound:
Society's a lonesome crowd,
    Pleasure, the same dull tedious round.

[181]

One heart to love—one life to press—
    One friend to trust—in some wild glen
Were less a waste, O! ten times less,
    Than this vast solitude of men.

TO ――――――――――⁴²

who lent me Taylor's Physical Theory of a future life after
reading it

Were each letter a page and a book every line
    Half my thoughts on this sheet I might hope to convey
But 'till angels shall teach us the shorthand divine
    In limits so narrow what is there to say?

If soul unto soul (with some slight corporeity)
    Could impart by mere contact, as Taylor proposes,
A soul-full of meaning in all the variety
    Of heart thrilling bliss which in Heaven he supposes

How many sweet dialogues then might I hold
    With you dear little spirit, both nightly & daily,
When no thought would have time on the lips to grow cold
    But by pressure, from heart, pass to heart, bright & gaily!

What exquisite things we should say by a touch!
    By *im*pression *ex*-pressions quintessence revealing,
Our *re*-formed existence—*in*formed overmuch
    And language exchanged for communion of feeling.

To my notion such things might have been had the Lord
    So pleased it, or else, if with due veneration,
Alphonso the Wise had but put in a word
    In behalf of us all, at the hour of creation.*

You shall hear why I venture to say so, because
    I abhor every quibbling and cavilling objection,

――――――――――

*This King is reported to have said that if God had consulted him about
making the World he could have given some good advice.

    The learned dispute whether this was said theologically or merely
as an astronomer. The Jesuit father Andrès in his admirable history of
Literature warmly defends the monarch from the charge of impiety: of
course it can't be impious to quote him.
            V. Storia d'agri Letteratura

[182]

And the very amendment proposed to the laws . . .
     Grows out of themselves, by an easy deflection.

For example on earth you no doubt have seen eyes,
     Speaking volumes on volumes to all but a dunce,
And perhaps have heard utter'd in two or three sighs,
     The whole of Love's Encyclopedia at once.

From a small hand's soft pressure, so slight as to seem
     Mere hazard of Friendship, I know there has sprung
Whole years full of thought, 'twixt a doubt & a dream
     Too subtle by far for the pen or the tongue.

So there wanted in truth, but a single link more,
     Such as Mesmer half guessed at—a magical ring
Like the one that from Solomon Chrystalline bore
     By which soul to meet soul over worlds could take wing.**

Had we such electro-magnetic attraction
     In the sweet sphere of Venus so lovely & bright
Whose air is made up of Caprice & Distraction***
     I would ask for a tête a tête meeting to-night.

TO JULIA

More than three lustres since the sportive scroll
     Retraced fair Julia now at thy command,
Avouched the honest homage of a soul
     That held thee sovereign of its fairy land.

Since then the summer-days of life have flown
     And years like ages seared my heart and brow,
Yet underneath their ashes still is strewn
     More of the past than words shall e'er avow.

All hopes, all thoughts, save of a few fond days
     Hallowed by innocence, by friendship cheered,
Whose sole memorials are those careless lays—
     All else have perished—even the most endeared.

**The Ring of Solomon is mentioned in the Arabian nights entertain-
ments, & the Lady also, as well as her extraordinary manner of acquiring
such tokens: but as it is no where said—not even in the Quatre Facardins,—
that she got one from the wise monarch the author must have drawn on
the fables of the Talmud or his own fancy for this scandal on the good
King.
***This line is unintelligible unless what the Italians sometimes call a
'capriccio' and the French a 'distraction' is intended.

These too ere long must perish!—be it so:
    Love, Friendship, Hope, Ambition, all have fled—
Then why should Memory linger?—To bestow
    Flowers on the false—the changed, the lost, the dead?

WHO KNOWS?[43]

"Die liebste unter allen Gestirnen. Wann ich Nachts von dir
gang, wie ich aus dienen Thore trat, stand er gegen mir über:
mit welcher Trunkenheit habe ich ihn oft angesehen! Oft mit
aufgehobenen Händen ihn zum Zeichen, zum heiligen Merkmaal
meiner gegenwartigen Seligheit gemacht!—und noch—"

Goethe

Some authors tell us gaily—
    I mean the most veracious—
Mankind are getting daily
    Less Pug— and less Men—dacious
And by reading Watt and Paley
    Grow virtuous and sagacious
        Good Gracious!

Our Ancestors—sad fellows!
    Loved ignorance and yawning
But such pistons pipes and bellows
    Our improving age is spawning,
As steam-engines impel us,
    That day is sooner dawning—
        So they tell us!

On rail-roads—our reliance—
    Without any tedious poking,
We shall fly through art and science,
    Hissing, fizzing, snorting, smoking;
Setting distance at defiance,
    And Time himself provoking—
        No Joking!

O'er Experience lightly glancing
    Like a steamer on the Ocean—
Our ethic speed enhancing—
    Locomotiving Devotion—
And in politics advancing,

[184]

With a double compound motion,
I've a notion—

Each day our new condition
    Will display some strange example—
Some striking proposition—
    Or extraordinary sample
Of increasing expedition
    On the road so straight and ample
        From Perdition.

For instance—maid and lover
    Being all, they were appearing
No faults will e'er discover
    By seeing or by hearing
But will find fresh Cupids hover
    By new Honey—moons so cheering—
        How endearing!

High pressure education
    Will so increase wives' worth,
That no innocent flirtation
    Jealous doubts will e'er bring forth,
But the husband's situation
    Make of bachelors a dearth
        Heaven and Earth!

No spendthrift heir will borrow
    On *Post-Obits*, whose huge growth,
If Dad should die tomorrow,
    Would wake his grief for both—
Unless to soothe his sorrow
    He could make—tho' somewhat loath
        Matrimony—Matter o'money.

Great men no more will savor
    Base flattery—but flee it—
Nor pay with gold and favor
    Vile sycophants who knee it—
And if ever they should waver
    Will have the grace to see it:
        So be it.

[185]

From one pole to the other,
      No rogue will soon be found
Like brothers with a brother
      Our neighbors all around
Will live with one another
      In peace the most profound
            Above ground!

Our jails, as they assure us,
      Will be all dilapidation,
Hang-men needless to secure us—
      Hulks in utter desolation,
Man—*scelerisque purus*
      And law one long vacation—
            O! Creation!

On state-house and state prison
      Solemn owls will soon renew—
When the full-orbed moon has risen,
      Grave questions, not a few—
Seeking falsehood to bedizen
      Too-hoo! Too-hoo! Too-hoo!
            To Who?

We shall shew on all occasions
      Frank hearts, and honest faces;
Politicians in high stations,
      Need not mask to keep their places;
Nor dear friends, and near relations
      Waste a Carnival's grimaces,
            On good graces.

All simple, all laborious—
      We shall be, without hypocrisy,
Good, great, but not vain—glorious—
      The Earth one wide Pantocracy—
Philanthropy victorious—
      And Congress no Logocracy,
            Uproarious!

With all our cares suspended,
      And a shirt and loaf of bread each—
The currency amended—
      Every trouble we shall head—reach—

No Tariffs apprehended,
　　Or taxes to distress us—
　　　　God bless us!

Our wit shall all be Attic—
　　All gold our circulation—
Melo-comic—not dramatic
　　Our addresses to the Nation
And our States so Democratic
　　Will refute Repudiation,
　　　　Degradation.

With no Bank-notes—unbankable—
　　No M O N S T E R S to affright us—
Newspapers almost frankable—
　　With Vetos to delight us—
And Presidents unthankable,
　　Serving twice before they slight us—
　　　　O Titus!

But this sweet Arcadian season—
　　This specific for all woes—
This Age of Perfect Reason,
　　And Millenium of Repose—
We hope it is no treason—
　　Are they Poets' dreams?—or Prose?
　　　　Who knows?

(1) Alluding to the fancy of the Dutch Innkeeper who upon the appearance of St. Pierres '*Universal peace*,' put up for a sign a *Church-yard* with the inscription—'à la paix universelle.'

The hint of this bagatelle was taken from *Guadagnoli's 'Chi lo sa?'*

FORCED CONTRIBUTION

levied in second hand rhyme on a worn out Author, violently suspected of plagiarism, by the most absolute command of the very worshipful and gracious Lady, Georgiana _____

　　The Saints of Scotland hold it meet
　　　　That sinners for some choice transgressions
　　Should stand, in penitential sheet
　　　　At the Kirk-door, and make confessions.

[187]

So I, between these sheets—once white,
  For rhyming in my youth must stand,
No other reason, wrong or right,
  But a most orthodox command.

Gray Journals, by my sad fate,
  Take warning, and avoid this place,
See, what men come to, soon or late,
  By flirting with a Muse—or Grace.

Yet since from this 'apparent shame'
  There's no escape by prayer or tear;
Georgie at least shall share the blame,
  I'll tell for spite, *who* brought me *here!*

TO _____⁴⁴

"It is not true! words are but air!"
  "Die Sprache aber ist unendlich, und nicht bloss in Tönen wird gesprochen. Der Taubstumme redet in Geberden, Liebende mit den Augen, der Kutscher mit der Putsche, der true Hund mit dem wedelnden Schanze, erhabne Menschen nur mit Handlungen, Gemüther mit Gesichtszügen, die Zeit mit Glockenschlägen, der Zeitgeist mit Druckerschwärze, und Sprichmörtern, Dichter, Weltweise und Künstler in Gleichnissen, Bildern und Gestalten, Engel in Lichtstrahlen und Klängen, und Gott redet in der Weltgeschichte. Aber Alle die da reden, musst die verstehen, den Missverständniss ist der Urquell des Bösen und die Schlange des Teufels."

                                          Rudolph von Fraustadt

It is not true!—'words are not air,'
  That pass and leave no trace behind
Words are the souls of things that were
  Works of the mightiest of Mankind.

Of life and empire, sword and crown
  Historians, bards, and fame bereft,
Of Egypt's monarch's high renown
  What but a hieroglyph is left?

Where now were Hector's deeds of arms
  Ulysses craft—Achilles' ire—

[188]

Where lovely Helen's fatal charms,
    But for the breath of Homer's lyre?

Pious Aeneas, where wert thou
    With all thy toils by land and wave,
But for the wreath that crowns thy brow
    Which Virgil's verse immortal gave?

Where, where were each Ausonian chief
    Whose tones through Dante's trumpet tell
Their name and story, bold and brief,
    To Purgatory, Heaven and Hell?

Geoffry the brave—the wise—the just—
    With all his Holy Wars might rot
The Knight in dust, his sword in rust
    If Tasso had not changed his lot.

A timely or untimely word
    Decides the fate of men and things
On tempests borne—in thunders heard—
    The Oracle of Realms and Kings!

'Avoid delays!'—'The Die is Cast!'
    From Curio's and from Caesar's tongue
As fell each phrase, a simoom's blast
    Its blight o'er Roman freedom flung.

When Mirabeau's tremendous bolt
    "Go slave, and tell thy master!" fell,
In tones that startled knave and dolt,
    What millions might have heard their knell?

And He—the Man of Fate—the Star—
    Lord of the Iron Soul and Crown,
Was not his word once peace or war
    Like Jove's or Destiny's his frown?

A word then shapes the fate of Man
    Makes or unmakes the great—the wise—
Even with a Word the world began
    And at a word the dead shall rise!

Tell me not then, that 'Words are air,'
    Of all things mortal they can claim

[189]

The highest and the noblest share,
　　The share of Heaven from whence they came.

For words are not in sounds alone
　　Or letters framed by Hermes' art
Nature has voices of her own
　　Their tongue the Sea—the Stars—the Heart.

And to the souls of those whose soul
　　The Universe's spirit hears
There is a language in the whole
　　Beyond the Music of the Spheres.

And he who holds its key can read
　　Far into the abyss of Time
Beyond the reach of craft or creed
　　To monsters of the Earth's first slime.

And higher than the realms of day,
　　To stars with systems still unknown,
Track to lone worlds, each wandering ray,
　　Long ages ere it reached our own.

Aye, and record for humbler skill
　　The triumph, and the fact attained,
That deeper depths—heights higher still,
　　Truth upon truth, shall yet be gained.

Then do not say that 'Words are air,'
　　Spirits they are, of mortal birth,
Wing'd messengers of Man that bear
　　To God the voices of the Earth!

And who can say that even at length
　　Mankind—the living and the dead—
The Heart—the Soul—their weakness—strength—
　　Hopes fears and mysteries may be read?

What I of others, on such page,
　　Or they of me, might now be told
'Twere vain to ask—another age
　　Must pass, before such leaves unfold.

Yet ere I die—unseen—unheard,
　　Fain would I, one dark leaf explore,

Construe one line—translate one word—
    Or guess it's meaning, if no more.

And for such knowledge, good or ill,
    I fear me much, were Eden mine,
Spite of the past—the Serpent's skill
    Its joys might tempt me to resign.

Then tell me not that words are air
    Words are the Sons of Heaven that sought
To light in Earthly bosoms fair
    The deathless flame of Heavenly Thought!

GEMMA DONATI[45]

He loves me not!—no! he has never loved me!
Yet men have called me fair, and women frown'd,
Curling their lip with well affected scorn,
Or subtler still, join'd in their gallants praise,
With earnest admiration sweetly pale,
Lauding my greatest faults. He loves me not,
And yet I am well-born—Donati's daughter
Has little need to envy rank in Florence,
Nor can the proudest Alighieri deem
Their Dante matched beneath his gentle blood.
I did not come unportioned to his bed,
Though that were nothing: gold he prizes not,
Ev'n his worst foes, in all their bitterest strife,
Have failed to soil his glory with that stain.

    But what avails it all? He loves me not,
Altho' I am the mother of his children,
Have loved, and love, and must forever love him,
Spite of his coldness, and our houses' discord,
These civil broils—the poverty and exile
He will not let me share, and last and worst,
The cherished passion of his early youth,
That has survived them all, and even the grave!
Thrice happy Beatrice!—dying young—
Beloved of Dante—in his heart embalmed,
And by his prose and verse to after years,
Perhaps to other ages handed down!

[191]

Would I were with thee gentle Portinari!
Or thou wert here, and free to share his love,
Who neither can return nor conquer mine!
But let me perish first!—I could not bear
To witness all his tenderness for Thee.
And yet thy soul can ne'er have known for him
The passionate devotion felt by mine.

Had Dante loved *me,* think'st thou all the world
Would e'er have won or forced me from his arms?
No, never! never!—far too like his own,
In Nature's sternest mould my heart was cast;
O'er ruined hopes, with silent grief and rage,
In violent desperate calm—to brood and break,
May be its destiny—but not to change!

Yes! they may call me proud and harsh and stern,
And gossips hint 'twas Dante's shrewish wife
Taught him Philosophy—of such I reck not—
But none have known, and none will ever know
How deep a love abided in my bosom,
How keen the pang to find it unreturned.

Heaven knows, that often when to them I seemed
Sullen or froward all my soul was tasked,
Far, far beyond its strength, to hide my tears.
Their blame I could endure but not their pity
Nor even his—and therefore have I hid,
In my shut breast, it's self-consuming care,
Rather than loving, seem unloved, or scorned.

O! who can tell how my whole being shook
Convulsively as if the living clay,
Like the inanimate Earth, could quake and shudder,
As the Volcano bids with trembling agony;—
O! who can tell how more than lava flames
Burned in my brain when I was first aware
That Dante loved me not, and I was doomed
To share his bed, a stranger to his heart?
Tormenting doubts reluctantly admitted
Strange phantom shapes—dream horrid and obscure,
Suspicions—hideous shadows of the Truth
Haunted me long and rose almost to phrenzy
Till the bolt fell, and crushed me, to a calm!

Strange fits of absence, reverie and gloom
Hung o'er his spirit often from the first,
Nor had I power to chase the cloud away:
He loved not question in these moods of mind,
If sportively I chid him, he repelled
My fondness gravely—Levity displeased him,
Silence and sorrow tacitly reproved.
The lion and the eagle in his blood
Made him impatient of the least restraint
And even watchful tenderness annoyed him.
At times indeed, he half-rebuked himself,
And craved my pardon for his waywardness,
Pleaded his studies—and the state of Florence—
Forese's death—and Guido's banishment,
Or else my kinsman Corso's fiery temper
Pride and vindictiveness, and civil feuds.

But yet some words half uttered in his sleep—
A name too well pronounced—tho' in a sigh
Sufficed to tell *these* were not all his griefs.
He used to sit and watch Arnolfo's labors
As if St. Reparata's wondrous pile
Wrapt him in contemplation—but the vault
Where Beatrice's relics lay was there
And Portinari's palace full in view.

When our accursed factions in their war
With fierce, blind, cruel, undiscerning fury
Condemned my Alighieri in his absence,
And when our house to pillage & the flames
Was given, and I strove to save what he
With jealous care had ever held most precious
The treasures of his mind—the hallowed page
To which he poured out all his secret soul,'
O! what a pang it was to find H E R there
The load-star of his verse—his theme—his Muse!
Since then my life has been one long disease
On which Death only can bestow a cure.

My Gabriello! were it not for thee
And Jacopo, Pietro, and thy sister,
Called by *her* name—I knew not wherefore then,
I had not lingered in the world thus long
To pine in hopeless widowhood of heart,
And leave behind a blighted memory!

[193]

STAR OF MY LOVE! I[46]

Il y a parmi ces étoiles un amour eternel qui peut seul suffire
à l'immensité de nos voeux.

De Stael

Star of my Love! how brightly burns
Thy mild, pure, tranquil flame, tonight,
Though thousands from their chrystal urns
Are pouring floods of silver light,
In thine alone I take delight,
For one who in my absence mourns
Gazes upon thee in thy flight
And every look I give returns
And therefore dost thou seem so bright
Star of my Love!

Star of my Love! while thus on high
The heavenly host their vigils keep
Careering through the dark blue sky,
And earth seems sunk in slumbers deep,
There yet are those who do not sleep
But gaze upon thee with a sigh,
And eyes that long, yet scorn to weep,
While gloomy clouds across thee fly
Like thoughts that o'er our fancies sweep
Star of my Love!

Star of my Love! I see thee shine
Even now as when thou met'st the gaze
Of one, whose hand was clasped in mine
When last we saw thy glories blaze:
Then as we marked thy beauteous rays
With spirits soft and pure as thine
We asked thine aid in thorny ways
And bowed our hearts before thy shrine
With souls all gratitude and praise
Star of my Love!

STAR OF MY LOVE II

Stern der Liebe! . . . der freundlichste der Sterne
Körner

[194]

Star of my Love! I hail again
  Thy light on Nights calm, dark, blue, stream,
An absence grief and care and pain
    Are as a half forgotten dream:
    For she is here whose glances seem
To purify the earth from stain
    And lend a more celestial beam
To Heaven and all it's glorious train—
    O how our souls with rapture teem!
                    Star of my Love!

Star of my Love! the holiest shrine
    On which fond hearts were ever laid
Thou art, thou must be all divine,
    And thou hast heard the vows I made,
    When with heart-broken grief I prayed
Benignant Star, one favoring sign,
    O! thou hast not denied thine aid
And Heaven has heard my prayers and thine:
    Thus then to Thee my thanks are paid
                    Star of my Love!

Star of my Love! most lovely star
    Of all in heaven's high temple hung!
Though wandering now asunder far
    Thou hast for us an angel's tongue
    Thou saw'st the parting pang that wrung
Our bosoms from thy silvery car
    For us thy golden Lyre was strung
To *Him* that made us what we are—
    And thus to thee our hymn we sung
                    Star of my Love!

STAR OF MY LOVE III

Stern meines Lebens,
Schmacht' ich vergebens
Nach deinem Licht?
Du zeigst dich nicht!
. . . .
Stern, willst du dich nicht zeigen?
            Körner

[195]

Star of my Love! unmarked of late,
    Again on thee my eyes I bend
Celestial messenger of Fate
    What thoughts on thy bright path attend!
    Evil or Good dost thou portend?
Pleasure or Pain? or Love or Hate?
    Alas! how fondly do we blend
Our Earthly with thy heavenly state
    What hopes what fears to thee ascend
                    Star of my Love!

Star of my Love! I gaze on thee
    As though upon thy sparkling brow
I saw what thou alone canst see
    The look of Her, who even now
    Recalls the sad and solemn vow
Long since breathed for—though not to me,
    I need not utter when or how. . . .
Thou didst receive it silently—
    As thus to Thee my heart I bow
                    Star of my Love!

STAR OF MY LOVE IV

Dum loquor, et flemus; coelo nitidissimus alto
    Stella gravis nobis, Lucifer ortus erat.
                    Ovid Trist.

Star of my Love! most faithless star
    That e'er on mortal misery shone!
Years pass—and still thy votaries are
    Apart—self-exiled—sad—alone—
    And can it be our woes are known
To Heaven, and we still doomed to feel
    Pangs which though seraphs breasts were stone
Might stroke upon their hearts like steel,
                    Star of my Love!

Star of my Love! my years decline,
    My spirits sink, my hopes decay,
In moody wretchedness I pine
    And perish slowly day by day,

[196]

Ages of pain have rolled away
Since first with mingled love and awe
I gazed upon thy silver ray
Murmuring at Fate's resistless law
Star of my Love!

Star of my Love! I ask no more
Omen or sign or aid from thee:
Cast up a wreck, beside the shore
Of dark despair's cold calm dead sea,
All that has been—all that shall be—
Are now unchangeably the same:
Blasted by one accurst decree
Sic Hope,—Love,—Joy,—Ambition,—Fame—
Star of my Love!

Star of my Love! I've proved thy power,
It has no strength to help or save!
Star of my Love! I wait the hour
When God shall claim the breath he gave:
I cannot be denied a grave—
And this is all I hope or ask
He whose kind hand redeems the slave
Will end at length my weary task
Star of my Love!

STAR OF MY LOVE V

'S war ein Stern! Jetzt ist er zwar versunken
Körner

Star of my Love! upon the deep
Struggling through Night's dim misty veil
Whilst low winds o'er the waters creep
Still heaving from the by-gone gale,
And solitary sea-birds wail—
Though all below are sunk in sleep—
Beneath the lazy flapping sail,
My lonely midnight watch I keep,
Thy holy light once more to hail
Star of my Love!

Star of my Love! too well!—too well!—

[197]

Those sights and sounds past years recall!
O'er Memory's deep with sullen swell
    As troubled passions rise and fall
    Though Mystery in her sable pall
Shrouds the dark caverns where they dwell,
    What shades—what voices hear her call
And come obedient to her spell!
    Alas! for them—for *Her*—for all!
                    Star of my Love!

Star of my Love! since that marked hour
    Worn ever on my heart and brow,
Which gave thee o'er my thoughts the power
    No orb in Heaven can claim but thou,
    Through every chance and change 'till now
When Fate's most dismal shadows lower,
    And to Despair my spirits bow
Blessings or curses may'st thou shower
    As I have kept, or broke my vow,
                    Star of my Love!

Star of my Love! with grief and pain
    I've numbered many an hour of years
O'er days that never come again
    Outpouring all my soul in tears:
    Consuming life in doubts and fears
And wearing out my heart and brain
    And now what hope my bosom cheers
What soothes me for my long borne chain?
    Who loves me now or marks or hears?
                    Star of my Love!

Star of my Love! I did not deem
    For me this hour could e'er arrive!
Star of my Love! my cherished dream
    Is gone, and I am yet alive!
    Why is it that I still survive?
Suspended o'er the ocean stream
    I need but loose my hold to drive
My thoughts forever from this theme! . . .
    And yet, to see her *once* I strive
                    Star of my Love!

TO MISS _____

Fair daughter of the West! whose cloudless skies
    And gorgeous suns I may no more behold,
How have they tinged thy ringlets and thine eyes
    Celestial azure hung with molten gold!

Likeness to things of more than mortal birth
    We trace—not merely in thy charms alone—
An emanation thou from Heaven to Earth,
    The wandering spirit of some starry zone.

So purely, sweetly, innocently bright,
    Embodied Hope & Joy, and Peace & Love,
Seeming to others as the Day to Night
    Or to this wretched world the realms above.

So wise, so good, so fair, so kind, so just,
    Thou beam'st an Angel on this vale of tears
And I bow down before thee in the dust
    Stained with the pilgrimage of long long years.

O! I am sick of Earth and all its harms
    Its care, pain, woe, fear, hate, strife, guilt & shame,
Come! spread thy wings then, clasp me in thine arms
    And bear me to the skies from whence ye came!
5 Jany 1838

[NO TITLE]

Why is that gaze? Canst thou not tell—
    Is it not written on my brow—
By whom—on whom was wrought this spell?
    Art thou not conscious when—and how?

V

The Italian Lyric Poets

In the Library of Congress is a long work by Wilde, in two volumes, consisting of a number of translations from Italian poets with introductory biographical sketches. The work, catalogued as *The Italian Lyric Poets*, was never completed. William Cumming Wilde worked on it, preparing it for the press; but it was never published.[1]

The son, who numbered the pages of this work, had a total of 415 pages in the first part and 538 pages in the second part; many of the pages, however, consist of the poems in their original Italian.

Of the biographical introductions written by Richard Henry Wilde, the longest are on Petrarch, which begins on I, 193, and goes to I, 326; on Boccaccio, which begins on I, 357, and ends on I, 405; and on Tasso, which begins on II, 170, and ends on II, 206. The other introductions by Wilde are short, some of them consisting of no more than a page or two.

Although no "First Preface" exists, there is a "Second Preface" by William Cumming Wilde, which shows that the son completed the biographical introductions. This preface neglects to mention the translations from the poems of Cino da Pistoia and the translations from anonymous poems.

All of the poems by Tasso and by Guarini, which had been published in the *Conjectures and Researches Concerning the Love, Madness, and Imprisonment of Torquato Tasso* (1842), were included in this work.

An important study of Italian literature by an American is *Dante in America* by Theodore Koch. Commenting on Wilde's description of his first entrance into the Florentine archives, Koch writes:

Here one already sees the mark of the dilettante. Wilde never reached the point of trained scholarship and discrimination so necessary to the investigator and historian. He had a great fund of enthusiasm, and, as Washington Irving said of him, he went about his work with all the "patience and accuracy of a case hunter." In fact, he shows himself the advocate by the eagerness with which he supports his favorite theories in the case of certain vexed questions. Not that he was a biased investigator, nor that he was unwilling to give up a cherished tradition, once overthrown; but until disproved, the pleasing figments of time had for him the usual attraction they hold alike for the poet and dilettante, and Wilde was somewhat of both.

Writing in 1896, Koch unfortunately used the word *dilettante*, which today has, for many people, the unflattering connotation of superficiality. If Koch were writing now, he probably would substitute the word *amateur* instead.

Furthermore at one place Koch states:

The systematic searching which has been going on during recent years has brought to light all that Wilde was able to turn up, and a great deal more. The indefatigable Del Lungo has it nearly all in his masterpiece of scholarly editing and annotation, "La Cronica di Dino Compagni."[2]

Such a comment, though it may be seeking to discredit Wilde's achievements, nevertheless, does imply that Wilde was able to make certain discoveries about Dante.

Koch in his short work treats seven people in the following order—Lorenzo da Ponte, George Ticknor, Richard Henry Wilde, Henry Wadsworth Longfellow, Thomas William Parsons, James Russell Lowell, and Charles Eliot Norton.

When Lorenzo da Ponte, remembered today for being the librettist of *Don Giovanni* and *Il Nozze di Figaro*, came to America in 1809 at the age of sixty, he found but one book written in Italian, an old *Decameron*. Becoming a private tutor at Columbia University, he succeeded in bringing to that institution many Italian works. He sold a collection to the New York Society Library, and the Library of Congress secured through him a fine edition of Dante as well as some other works.

George Ticknor, who traveled widely in Europe and knew Wilde, occupied the chair of modern languages at Harvard from 1819 until 1835. He stressed Dante in his lectures and made many notes on the *Divine Comedy*, generally dealing with linguistics.

At the same time that Wilde was writing the life of Dante, Longfellow was translating some of Dante's poetry. Longfellow's translations, however, were published after Wilde's death.

Although it is true that Koch in his work devotes more pages to Wilde than to any other person, he does not suggest that Wilde is the most significant person treated. Rather Koch had access to Wilde's unpublished works on Dante and *The Italian Lyric Poets,* and he wanted to quote freely from them.

A review in the *New York Times Book Magazine* stated that Richard Henry Wilde and Thomas W. Parsons "were much better known in Italy than here."[3] Yet all the seven men treated by Koch were pioneers in Italian literature in America.

There is no title page to *The Italian Lyric Poets*. The following pages contain William Cumming Wilde's "Second Preface" and the translations, all by Richard Henry Wilde, just as they are arranged in the work. Of these translations, Koch states: "Wilde was at his best in dealing with the sonnet form; with the canzone he did not succeed so well." In addition, the first line of the original has been given, followed in parentheses by the title of the poem if there is one in the manuscript.

On the death of a beloved parent all of his writings fell into my hands. Among these was a work containing translations from the lyrics of Folcacchiero dei Folcacchieri, Piero delle Vigne, King Enzo, Guido Guinicelli, Mazzeo Ricco, Onesto Bolognese, Fra Guittone, Brunetto Latini, Guido Cavalcanti, Boccacio, Petrarch, and Tasso with biographical sketches of these poets attached. There were also translations for which no lives had been written—from Dante, Antonio Pucci, Bojardo, Ariosto, Lorenzo de Medici, Machiavelli, Michael Angelo Buonarotti, Guarini, Giovanni della Casa, Marino, Redi, Maggi, Francesco da Lemene, Filicaja, Orsi, Gigli, Pedrochi, Zappi, Recanati, Metastasio, and Alfieri.

The last I determined to attempt, in the few moments of leisure allowed by a very absorbing business. My labors were twice seriously interrupted; once by the complete destruction of an exceedingly valuable library of 2000 printed books, and manuscripts, which obliged me to begin my collection anew. But, my lives at last, are presented. May I cherish the hope that they do not utterly disgrace the poems to which their destinies have been united.

N. O. May 10 1867   W. C. W.

Folcacchiero dei Folcacchieri
"Tutto lo mondo vive senza guerra."

War on the earth is o'er,
Yet I no peace can find.
O God! where shall I flee?
How bear the world once more?
Odious I seem to all mankind,
And savage they to me.
For me no more the flowers
Bloom as in former days,
Nor the birds' notes in leafy bowers
Seem but of love and praise.

When I behold the other knights
Bear arms or talk of Love,
All bitterly I grieve:
For turned to cares are my delights,
And I men's wonder move,

Such change do they perceive.
Myself I do not know,
Nor what may be my doom,
But all my days are woe,
And joy is turned to gloom.

Life soon must wear away,
Nay, it begins to sink;
No words may speak my pain;
My garb no more is brave and gay;
Tasteless are food and drink;
Tortures alone remain.
I know not where to fly,
Nor on whose help to call;
Yet I must bear without a sigh,
Aye! and dissemble all!

And this is love I ween,
No God but he, alone,
So cruel could be found,
Because his power is seen
In heart and mind, alike his throne,
Who frees whom he has bound?
Even I, although I mourn my chain,
Yet would not have it break,
And were it broke, would bind again
For my dear Lady's sake.

Sweet lady! then, if I should die,
To serve thee to thy mind
None will be found so true—
I sought not—Seek—nor e'er will I,
Save in thy love, a pleasure find,
Yielding thee homage due.
Then Lady, pity me I pray,
And save me from despair,
So shall my flame now hid from day
Blaze glorious forth to air!

Piero delle Vigne
"Peroch'Amore non si può vedere."

Because in human breasts *Love* lurks, unseen,
To the dim sight of the corporeal eye,
Mortals, so scant of Wisdom there have been,
As *Love's* existence wholly to deny:
Yet, since invisibly, despite his screen
He lords it o'er men's hearts, with rule so high,
If such his power, when barriers intervene,
May it not thought, as well as sight defy?
The virtue of the *Magnet* all allow
Which to itself attracts the subject steel,
Nor is it the less true though none know how:
And hence, most firmly, I believe and feel
That *Love* exists,—a faith which I avow,
And others, too, will soon confess and kneel!

King Enzo[4]
"Tempo viene a chi sale ed a ch' scende."

There is a time to rise, and to descend—
A time for everything—to speak, and cease,
To wait, and to adventure, strive, and bend,
A time to threaten, punish, bind, release;
A time to hear when others reprehend,
A time to lavish wealth, and to increase,
Time for revenge on all who may offend,
And time to feign and shut your eyes for peace.
Prudent I do account him then, and wise,
Who chooses a fit time for every aim;
Knowing discreetly how to temporize,
And win by courtesy a goodly name;
So shall he find whatever the emprize
He undertake, there will be few to blame.

Guido Guinicelli
"Fra l'altre pene maggior credo sia."

Of all the pains of life there's nothing worse
Than to hold freedom at another's will;
Therefore the wise before he shapes his course
Bethinks him of what rocks the way may fill.
He who depends is his not in his own ward;
Howe'er he rage he must obey at length
Because when once ensnared the prison'd bird,
By constant struggling but exhausts its strength.

Then guilty endure your servile state,
If you would please your Lord, and turn your back
Upon all thoughts of Freedom soon or late.
For you who serve, sirs, this is the right track;
Remember the wise saw of ancient date:
"The willing knave rich guerdon shall not lack."

Mazzeo Ricco
"Chi conoscesse si la sua fallanza."

Of his own failings were but man aware
As perfectly as of his neighbours faults,
Of all ill-speaking he would have a care
Because of his own conscience-stricken thoughts.
But wicked custom hath become so bold
That every one of his own honor vaunteth
While in contempt each doth the other hold
And even the most despised his fellow taunteth.
Therefore I would it had been ordered so
That everyone might see his proper fame,
And his true honor and dishonor know
As well and clearly as his neighbor's shame,
For conscious worth slighteth all outward shew
And seeketh not it's praise in other's blame.

Onesto Bolognese
"Ragione e vedimento d'avere."

Wisdom and Prudence should united be
In whosoe'er are judges among men,
And patience, and sagacity to see
Whom justly to absolve, and whom condemn:
Their hands the balance should so firmly hold
And justly balance too, that none should deem,
In balancing, it was the weight of gold,
Or favor or affection turn'd the beam.
Therefore, Signors, be provident and trust
In Providence—and let not fear or love
Corrupt your judgments—no, nor wealth nor lust;
For if ye screen the sinner, or approve
The sin—, unjustly sentencing the just—
Ye shame yourselves, and anger God above.

Fra Guittone d'Arezzo
"Homo fallito, pien di van pensieri."

Dost thou not, fallen man, thy state perceive?
Thus wasting in vain thoughts thy Life away?
Dost thou not know—Riches—Power deceive
And the world's pleasures tempt but to betray?
A Pilgrim here—o'er *Times* quick flight dost grieve
Yet blindly wander amid snares astray?
Though dying old, scarce born—doomed all to leave
Yet where thou goest know not—nor thy stay.
Bethink thee of thyself! 'tis not too late
O'er the next moment thou hast no controul;
Weigh transient joy, 'gainst endless pain and hate,—
Let not Life's precious hours in folly roll—
Remember! every day is full of fate—
To gain the whole world, would'st thou lose thy soul?

Brunetto Latini
"Sed io havessi ardir quant io ho voglia."

If I had daring equal to my will,
Into thine ear to pour out all my mind,
And tell thee how my love torments me still
Some respite though no cure my pain might find:
But in thy sight such fears my bosom fill
That shaking like a leaf which feels the wind
All—all my forethought, courage, voice and skill
By eager trembling passions left behind.
And hence to *Love* my Lord I do resort
To pray he'll reason with you on my part
And my fond passion faithfully report
Telling you all that's passing in my heart,
And Lady, when he comes to pay his Court,
Entreat him not with cold discourteous art.

Guido Cavalcanti[5]
"Chi è questa che ven, ch'ogni uom la mira."

Who is it comes, to fascinate all eyes
And fill with tenderness the trembling air
Leading Love captive?—Before whom none dare
To breathe a word, though everybody sighs?
Heavens! at her sight what ecstasies arise—

Describe them Love, for they defy my art;
Yet her looks beam such gentleness of heart
That others' pride and fierceness strike surprise.
Her matchless loveliness surpasses speech,
To her with reverence every Virtue bends
And Beauty hails her Goddess. In the mind
No human power, nor heavenly grace we find,
That of her worth a just conception lends—
So far is her perfection past it's reach.

Dante Alighieri
"O patria degna di trionfal fama."   (Canzone IV)

My Country! worthy of triumphal fame,[6]
Mother of many a chief,
Above thy very sister thou mayest claim
Preeminence in grief;
And even he who honored most thy name,
Hearing how base, and vile, and like a thief,
Thy deeds have grown, blushes with rage and shame.
Alas! how oft thy wicked sons endeavor
To band themselves together for thy death;
False lights for true, to eyes distorted ever,
Shewing thy mob, who change with every breath.
Raise up thy fallen of heart!—Kindle their blood!—
Smite traitors with the sword of Justice keen!—
So shall thy grace and thy return to good,
Making that praise, which was reproach, be seen.

In good old times how happy was thy fate;
Thy breast with honor glowed;
The virtues then were pillars of thy state;
For thee the founts of health and glory flowed;
Pure Faith was at thy gate,
And the Seven Virgins all with thee abode.
Thy spotless robe, now tattered and defiled,
Is changed for filthy rags of vice and woe,
Fabricius and the loyal are exiled,
And vile yet proud thou art—of Peace the foe!
Shame on thee! Faction's mirror!—Mars' ally—
To Antenora thou would'st send the true
Who from thy stained and widowed lily fly,

Because by thee and thy degenerate crew
Who loves thee best, is the first doomed to die.

Serene and glorious, with kind influence blest
By every star in Heaven,
Thus acting, honored shalt thou reign and rest,
Thy name of *Flowery*—now a bitter jest—
Then seeming fitly given.
Soon as affection consecrates thy worth,
Happy the soul that owes to thee his days;
For thine thenceforth shall be all power and praise—
A model thou for Earth.
But if thou change not those that rule thy state,
Worse storms with fatal death may yet be thine
And then, bewailing thine all-evil fate
Mid grief and lamentation, shalt thou pine.
Choose freely now,—fraternal peace again,
Or wolf and wolf-like ever to remain.

Root out the evil weeds that waste thy soil!
No pity shew to those
Who make thy noble flower a filthy spoil;
And let the Virtues triumph o'er their foes,
Until Fidelity rewards thy toil
And Justice, sword in hand guards thy repose.
Mark well the beacon-lights Justinian gave,
Correcting thine unjust and fiery laws
With wisdom high and grave—
Securing thus, from Earth and Heaven applause.
To honors then, and power and riches call
The sons who love thee well:
Nor let thy gifts on the unworthy fall
So Prudence and the Seven Sisters all
In harmony with thee once more shall dwell.

Go forth my Song! thy bold demeanor keep;
Love is thy guide.
Enter my native land whose state I weep,
Some good men there abide
Whose light shines not—they and their virtues deep
Down-trodden in the mire or thrust aside.
Cry out arise! for you my trump I sound—

To arms! to arms! raise up your abject state,
Which scarcely breathes of late—
By Crassus, Capaneus, the false Greek—
And Magus and Aglaura, spoiled and bound,
While Pharaoh and Jugurtha vengeance wreak
And blind Mahomet fiercely raves around.
Turn to her just!—So may they hear thy prayer—
And She Imperial honors ever wear!

    Dante Alighieri
    "Guido, vorrei che tu e Lappo io."
      (To Guido Cavalcanti)

Guido I would that Lapo thou and I[7]
Were by some kind enchantment borne away
In a brave ship that o'er the sea should fly
And spite of wind and tide our will obey;
So that ne'er fickle Fortune nor foul weather
Should interrupt our course or mar our peace
And living free and happily together
The wish to live so ever, might increase.
Vanna and Beatrice should be there
With her who o'er the thirty reigns supreme
That too should be the good enchanter's care
And Love should be our everlasting theme
As much contented they our lot to share
As we our fate to blend with their's I deem!

    Dante Alighieri
    "Io maledico il dì ch'io vidi imprima."

I curse the day on which I first beheld
The treacherous light of those deceitful eyes;
I curse the hour, when from her throne expelled
Reason gave up my captive soul your prize.
I curse my own poetic art that swelled
Your praise in choral numbers to the skies,
Making immortal—boundless—unexcelled
Charms soon to perish, had I been but wise.
Aye! and I execrate my stubborn mind,
That clings perversely to its proper ill,
In its false idol's witcheries to find
What love still swears by, and is perjured still;

A jest to him becoming, and mankind,
For trusting Fortune's Wheel, and Woman's Will!

Antonio Pucci
"Amè, Comun, come conciar ti veggio."

(On Florence From Fraticelli's Dante)

Unhappy Commonwealth! how art thou torn
At once by neighbors and transalpine foes,
But more by sons in thine own bosom borne
Who should promote thine honor and repose.
Worst used by him, most bound to be thy friend,
Thou hast not left one unperverted law,
And something for himself from thee to rend,
Each plies a vultures talent—beak and claw.
There's not a soul who thinks thy good his care,
One takes thy staff—one makes thy shoes his prize—
Others thy garments part and leave thee bare,
Of every sin on thee the burthen lies
And while thy sorrows there are none to share
By thine abasement all attempt to rise!

Antonio Pucci
"Se nel mio ben ciascun fosse leale."

If all were honest and to serve me strove,
With half the zeal that all to rob me try,
Rome when her rulers best deserved her love
In Majesty could not with *Florence* vie.
But be assured the Spoiler soon or late
Signal and just revenge shall yet pursue,
Since whosoe'er he be that wrongs the State
Must answer ev'n with life the forfeit due.
Once the flood-tide of Power and Fortune swelled
For one that wrong'd and plunder'd me as now
Whose vacant seat I afterwards beheld—
And thou who mounted when he fell, mark thou
My words!—and at the cost of the expell'd
Learn Wisdom by rememb'ring *why* and *how*.
Justice you see of Vengeance gives full measure
Beware then how you traffic with my treasure!

Cino da Pistoia
"Voi che per nuova vista di ferezza."

[211]

O thou, who seek'st in vain by looks of scorn
To check the love that in my bosom first,
Of thine own beauty, and my daring born,
By absence and despair is only nurst;
Know that my heart would rather bear the worst,
If worse there be, than that already borne,
And loving, perish of its own fond thirst,
Than have thine image from its memory torn.
Cease Lady! then, to hope I can forget,
Long as I breathe, to love and think of thee,
Thy rigor can but hasten nature's debt;
Nor say I this to move thy sympathy,
Knowing thy cold disdain on triumph set
Makes thee, fair Savage, pitiless to me!

Cino da Pistoia
"Io fui 'n su l'alto e'n sul beato monte."

Upon the high and holy mount I stood[8]
And reverently kissed the sacred stone
Where She had laid her head—the fair, the good—
And threw myself upon it, sad and lone.
On every virtue's fount the marble closed
That day the lady of my heart alas!
From all Earth's utmost excellence deposed
Through bitter death, to heavenly life did pass.
And there I called on Love—O God! you know
How wearisome this world thenceforth became.
Take, take me then to her who sleeps below!—
None heard!—I listened—gazed—'twas all the same—
So I arose, passing the Alps with woe
And calling on my lost Selvaggia's name.

Francesco Petrarca
"Zefiro torna, e'l bel tempo rimena."

Zephyr the lovely season brings again,
With all her family of herbs and flowers
Progne's [Procne's] soft notes, sad Philomela's strain
And Nature's balmy breath and rosy hours.
The meadows smile, the days are warm and bright,
His children's happiness rejoices Jove
In loving every creature seeks delight,

[212]

And Heaven and Earth and Ocean teem with Love.
To me alas! return but deep drawn sighs
Wrung from a heart that hope no longer warms,
For Her who bore its treasures to the skies,
And birds, flowers, spring—the world with all its swarms
Of life—the brave—the beautiful—the wise—
To me are desart [desert] wilds and savage forms!

Petrarch
"S'io avessi pensato, che sì care."

If I could e'er have thought that after-times
Would hold the music of my sighs so dear
I might perhaps have framed more idle rhymes
And striven to make them sweeter to the ear:
But she is gone forever who should hear
The mistress of my love, and lyre, and heart
Who made my crude harsh numbers smooth and clear,
And I in losing her have lost the art.
She was my inspiration, and I strove
To pour my soul and sorrows out to her,
For then it was not fame I sought, but love,
And now alas! it is too late to stir
Ambition's fire, when Laura from above
Beckons, my flight to hasten, not defer.

Petrarch
"Se lamentar augelli, o verdi fronde."

When plaintive birds lament, and gently bend
To Summer's balmy breath the verdant bowers,
And softly murmuring chrystal waters wend
Their winding way through banks of fragrant flowers,
Oft as I sit and frame my pensive lay,
She who has set on Earth, in Heaven to rise,
I see and hear—for still though far away
She lives, and marks and answers to my sighs.
"Why prematurely thus consume thy years?"
She asks with tender voice.—"And wherefore claim
From eyes long sad, more streams of burning tears?
Weep not for me! for dying I became
Immortal—closing earthly eyes and ears
To wake in bliss—full, endless, and the same! ["]

[213]

Petrarch
"I'vo piangendo i miei passati tempi."

I mourn with bitter tears my wasted days
When my whole soul on earthly love intent
Its useless wings towards Heaven never bent
To seek by brighter example lofty praise.
O! while thine eye my wretched state surveys
Invisible eternal King of Heaven!
Unto my frail and sinful soul be given
The grace to mend the error of its ways.
So that a life in war and tempest flying
Closed by a peaceful death in port may be,
And living vainly cured by holy dying.
In the few years that yet remain to me
Be with me still.—On thee O Lord! relying,
In life and death I have no hope but thee!

Petrarch
"Vago augelletto, che cantando vai."

Thou sweet sad warbler! in thine airy flight
Sing'st thou of Love and Summer's vanished hours
When coming Winter now, and falling Night
Sadden the day and strip the fading bowers?
Since thus thy little heart, by ills opprest,
Its sorrow speaks, my kindred grief it knows,
Come then! and sheltered in this lonely breast
Together let us tell our mutual woes.
I know not whether our hard fate's the same,
She thou bewail'st perhaps still lingers here,
Heaven's will I mourn, and Death's unerring aim—
While fading twilight and the dying year
So many sweet and bitter memories claim
That song for song I give thee, tear for tear!

Petrarch
"La vita fugge, e non s'arresta un'ora."

Life hurries on, nor lingers for an hour,
And day by day Death follows close behind
The Present and the Past with equal power
Strive with the Future in my weary mind:

[214]

And Hope and Memory by turns assail
With such fierce warfare my unhappy breast
That did not pity for itself prevail
This troubled spirit had long since sought rest.
Lost Joys redouble every Grief I mourn
Like lightnings o'er the gloom of midnight sent
While Fortune smiles in port, all tempest worn
Onward my poor bark drives—her sails are rent—
Her Pilot tired—mast broke and rigging torn
And bright familiar lights in darkness spent.

Petrarch
"Solo e pensoso i più deserti campi."

Alone and sad, through some deserted scene
Loitering I roam, with slow and measured pace
My eyes intent to shun the slightest trace
That marks where any human foot has been.
Alas! I find no other resting place
From the keen gaze of crowds, which in the shew
Of Joys gone by, would read upon my face
The ravage of the flame that burns below:
And thus at length, the mountain and the plain,
River and dell, and fount and forest know
What others know not—all my life of pain;
And Love as through wild solitudes I go
Comes whispering in my ear some tender strain,
Or listening to my sorrows as they flow.

Petrarch
"Rapido fiume, che d'alpestra vena."

Swift *Rhone!* that from the Alpine glaciers' mine
Thy name and waters gathering, boundest free
Descending gaily night and day with me,
Love my sole guide, and Nature only, thine:
Roll on! roll on!—thy blue stream's arrowy flight
Nor sleep nor weariness can e'er detain
But ere thou pay'st thy tribute to the main
Seek where the Earth's most green, the skies most bright,
So made, by our sweet living sun, whose beam
Gladdens with flowers thy left bank where it plays:
Should she (sweet hope!) too slow my footsteps deem,

While her fair feet and hands thy current stays,
Kiss them, and say in murmurs from thy stream,
"The weary flesh the willing soul delays."

Petrarch
"Io amai sempre, ed amo forta ancora."

I ever prized, and prize much more than ever,
And every day must cherish more and more,
The spot oft seen, and without weeping never,
Where my full heart with its deep love ran o'er.
And ever must I bless the day and hour,
That placed me past all low base thoughts' controul
And more than all transcendant beauty's power
Which virtue by example taught my soul.
But how could I have ever dreamt to find
So many dear sweet enemies conspire
To wage a fearful conflict in my mind?
Love! thou consum'st me with so fierce a fire
That were not gentle *Hope* with thee combined
I should seek *Death* when *Life* I most desire!

Petrarch
"S'Amor non è, che dunque è quel ch'i'sento?"

If 'tis not Love, what is it then I feel?
But if 'tis love, Great God what passion's this?
If good—why does it wound like mortal steel?
If ill—why are its torments so like bliss?
If willingly I burn—I grieve amiss;—
And if unwillingly, 'tis vain lamenting—
O! living death! O! torturing happiness!
How canst thou sway me thus, I not consenting?
And if I do consent,—I mourn in vain:—
Thus my frail, helmless bark, at random turning
Her course, with winds in conflict—o'er the main
Drives, error-laden, on—all wisdom spurning;
Nor what I wish, can I myself explain,
Trembling in summer, and in winter burning!

Petrarch
"Rotta è l'alta colonna e'l verde lauro."

Fallen is the stately column and fair tree
That spread their shadow o'er my weary mind

[216]

And my lost bliss from Spain to India's sea
From North to South, I ne'er may hope to find.
Death! thou hast spoiled me of the twofold prize
That gave life zest, and thought, and purpose high,
Nor gold nor gems—the wisdom of the wise
Nor Earthly power can win it from the sky.
Since Destiny for me has wrought such woe
How can my soul but sink in gloomy fears?
My head but bow with grief—my tears but flow?
O Life! that to our hopes so bright appears,
How instantly Fate robs thee at a blow
Of all so dearly won through long, long years!

Petrarch
"Padre del Ciel, dopo i perduti giorni."

Father of Heaven! after many days,
And many wasted nights in sorrow spent,
Musing on charms for my misfortune sent,
To light the flame that on my bosom preys;
Vouchsafe at length my thoughts tow'rd thee to raise,
That I henceforth, on better purpose bent
May foil my adversary's fell intent
Escaping from the thousand snares he lays.
For see O Lord! 'tis now eleven years
Since first my neck unto that yoke I bowed
Whose humblest slaves are scorned with greatest pride;
Take pity then, on my unworthy tears,
And chasing hence the idle thoughts that crowd
Remind me, thou this day wert crucified!

Petrarch
"Voi, che ascoltate in rime sparse il suono."

O! ye, into whose kind and gentle ears
My rhymes shall pour the sighs that rent my heart,
In the first error of my youthful years
That kept me from myself so long apart;
The varied style in which the Poet's art
Recounts the lover's hopes, and doubts, and fears,
If you have ever felt the poisoned dart
May move your pity, and perhaps your tears:
Perhaps your scorn—for well I see that long

[217]

Unto my fellows I have been a jest,
But if I blush for many an idle song
At least Shame brings Repentance as her guest
Since Reason late reclaimed from years of wrong
Holds Life and all its pleasures dreams at best!

Petrarch
"Cesare, poi che'l traditor d'Egitto."

Great Caesar when the Egyptian traitor brought
The cruel gift of Pompey's honored head,
Wept outward from the eyes—as it is said,
Hiding his inward joyfulness of thought.
And Hannibal, when adverse fortune wrought
The ruin of the band his brother led,
Smiled bitterly though every hope had fled,
Masking the grief with which his soul was fraught.
And thus the heart, to hide it's real feeling,
Feigns grief in joy, and joy in grief agen,
By falsehood oftentimes the truth revealing;
And thus it is, that I, like other men,
In careless smiles, a ceaseless care concealing
Dissemble woes untold by tongue or pen.

Petrarch
"Son'animali al mondo di si altera."

Creatures there are of Earth that soar to Heaven
And gaze undazzled on the noon-day sun
Others that never stir abroad 'till even
Because their eyes too weak his glories shun:
And others that with foolish fondness run
Into the flame they love, because 'tis bright
But find when there it burns—and I am one
Of those alas! attracted by a light
I cannot bear to lose or look upon,
For in its absence all to me is night;
Spell bound, though warned—incapable of flight
I see my folly but Fate drives me on,
Infirm of purpose, I avert my sight,
And rush to Death, though *Reason* cries, "Begone!"

Giovanni Boccaccio
"Dante Alighieri son, Minerva oscura."

[218]

Dante am I—the oracle obscure[9]
Of Wisdom and of Art, divinely sung,
Who formed the accents of my mother-tongue
To eloquence Laconic, bold and pure.
My fancy high, prompt, daring, and secure,
Passed Tartarus, and up to Heaven sprung,
And o'er the story of my journey flung,
A beauty destined ever to endure.
Florence my glorious mother was—to me,
More like a step-dame—though her loving child—
The fault of civil strife and calumny.
Ravenna gave me shelter when exiled,
And keeps my dust—my soul to God on high
Rose from it's earthly prison undefiled.

Giovanni Boccaccio
"C'è chi s'aspetta con piacere i fiori."

There are, who hail with joy returning Spring[10]
To mark the fields their verdant hue resume,
To hear the birds their amorous ditties sing
And see the trees and flowers renew their bloom:
I am not one of those—It is my doom,
When vernal breezes and fair days return,
Those outward pleasures inwardly to mourn
Shrouding my anxious heart in tenfold gloom.
And of my sorrow *Baiae* is the cause
That with false joys my Lady hence invites,
And she with her all my soul's quiet draws.
Me therefore every season more delights
Than this; For she, whose pleasure gives me laws,
My presence there forbids—and anguish slights.

Giovanni Boccaccio
"Se Dante piange, dove ch'el si sia."

If Dante's ire, where'er he be, is moved,
To see conceits, by his high soul designed,
Laid open to the base and unrefined,
Wherewith thou hast my lectures' fault reproved;
'Twill grieve me much—nor e'er can be amoved.
From my own heart remorse and self-disdain—

[219]

And yet one thought might well-nigh soothe my pain—
The folly others, and not I, approved.
Besides vain hope, and poverty too true,
And partial friends, with judgment fondly blind
By prayers wrought on me, what I did, to do.
But little taste for wares of such a kind
Have the mechanical and envious crew
Who hate or scorn the loftiest works of mind.

Giovanni Boccaccio
"Or sei salito, caro signor mio." (On the Death of
      Petrarch)

Now thou hast joined, dear Lord, the blessed choir,
In those bright realms above, which the elect
All seek to reach, and humbly all expect,
When leaving this low world of grief and ire:
Now thou art there, where often thy desire
Of Laura's presence made thee long to be
And my fair Fiammetta thou may'st see
Seated with her, where pleasures never tire.
With Cino, Dante, and Senuccio thou
Enjoyest calm, eternal, pure repose,
Beholding wonders never dreamt 'till now.
Oh! if thou lov'dst me in this world of woes
Take me to thee and Her *who* love's first vow
Won from me, and will keep 'till life's last close!

Matteo Maria Boiardo
"Oggi ritorna l'infelice giorno."

Again returns the sad, ill-omened day,
On which my endless misery began;
The grass springs forth anew, the flowers are gay,
And all rejoices,—Heaven, and Earth, and man:
I, only, grieve—and my complaints renew
Of Nature, and the Stars, and my hard fate
And my own heart—whereon love fed and grew
Despite neglect, indifference, and hate.
Aye! Time returns the same—suns set and rise—
Night follows day—Day night—moons wax and wane—
The woods are green—cloudless and pure the skies—
But I am changed—anger, and grief and pain,

[220]

Have done their work, and to my own surprize
I know the day, but not myself again.

Ludovico Ariosto
"Benchè'l martir sia periglioso, e grave."

Though dire my martyrdom because I wear
Your image in a breast too fond and true,
Without a murmur every pang I bear,
Blessing whate'er it be that comes from you!
Yet I confess it grieves me to percieve [*sic*]
In spite of all my pains, do what I will,
That you refuse my passion to believe,
Scorning all proofs, a stubborn skeptic still.
If words persuade you not—nor tears—nor sighs—
And if you will not hear or heed my strain,
Nor trust my acts, no nor believe your eyes,
What is there left but death to prove my pain?
And then alas! it were too late to prize
The truth that never could be shewn again!

Lorenzo de' Medici
"Spesso mi torna a mente, anzi giammai." (The First
    Meeting)

Oft to mind returns—or rather never
From my fond memory parts, the scene, the day,
The look—the time—the place—beloved forever,
When on my sight thine eyes first flashed their ray.
What thou didst seem, the star-lit hours that sever,
Yet blend, the beauties both of night and day
To Love may tell—who is beside thee ever—
None else can paint or fancy—much less say.
Upon thy spotless robe in golden flow,
The rich luxuriant tresses streaming fell,
Like setting sun-beams upon mountain snow;
But when, or where we met, I need not tell,
'Tis light when Phoebus shines, as all men know,
And it is Paradise where angels dwell!

Niccolò Macchiavelli
"Chi sei tu, che non par donna mortale?" (Opportunity)

O! who art thou of more than mortal birth
With grace and beauty heaven-adorned and crowned?

[221]

And why those winged feet that scorn the Earth?
["]My name is *Opportunity*—renowned,
Yet known to few—and my perpetual flight
Poises me on this wheel's incessant round:
As swift as thought it flies—swifter than light
My wings glance on, to dazzle and confound.
Over my face and bosom falling low,
My scattered locks, in front entwining meet,
Behind no long luxuriant tresses flow,
And thus scarce any know me when they greet,
Or knowing, see whether I come or go". . . .
Who follows thee with brow so overcast?
"It is *Repentance!* mark!—the weak or slow
Who seize *me* not, by *her* are grappled fast.
And Thou who in vain words hath wasted so,
The moments full of fate, which never last,
Dost thou not see I've fled? Dost thou not know
That none can overtake 'Occasion past!'["]

    Michael Angelo Buonarotti
    "Per molti, donna, anzi per mille amanti." (On Florence
        under the tyranny of Duke Alexander de'Medici, in
        the form of a dialogue)

Michael Angelo.
Thousands and thousands loved thine angel charms[11]
Avouching heart in hand an honest flame;
And do the Heavens sleep when, in the arms
Of one sole Ravisher thou sink'st to shame?
Light of our eyes! let fond complaints reclaim
Their loved lost fair, to those who mourn her harms,
And curse their Life, since it survived her Fame.

Florence.
Nay hide kind hearts! your holy grief within,
The spoiler's crime brought him not Joy but Pain,
For guilty Fear poisons enormous Sin:
The happiest Lovers are not those who drain
Passions' unshared excess—but those who win
High Hopes from Misery that bears no stain!

    Michael Angelo Buonarotti
    "Grato m'è'l sonno, e più l'esser di sasso."

Epigram of
Giovanni Strozzi

On the Night of Michael Angelo

The *Night* you see wrapt in such calm repose[12]
An Angels chisel did in marble seek:
Even in her sleep the signs of life she shews,
If you believe not—wake her—she will speak!

Reply of
Michael Angelo

'Tis well to sleep—and better to be stone,
When all around alas! is shame and woe;
Therefore no wish to hear or feel I own,
And that you may not wake me, pray speak low!

Michael Angelo Buonarotti
"Dal mondo scese a i cicchi abissi, e poi." (On Dante)

He from our World descending into Hell[13]
And Purgatory, thence to Heaven arose,
And to the living back returned to tell
Of endless glory, and Eternal woes,
In verse divine,—each thought, each word a spell—
Lighting the deepest mysteries they disclose
To man's blind wonder, starlike. Earth full well
Shewed him the gratitude she always shows.
Ill did his thankless countrymen repay
Dante's high mind—a doom the good and great
Have often met before and since his day.
Yet give me still his genius and his fate!
With virtuous fame in exile to grow gray
Is more than worth the world's most prosperous state!

Torquato Tasso
"Tre gran Donne vid'io ch'in esser belle."

Three high-born dames it was my lot to see,[14]
Not all alike in beauty, yet so fair,
And so alike in act and look and air
That Nature seemed to say—"Sisters are we!"
I praised them all—but one of all the three
So charmed me that I loved her, and became
Her bard and sung my passion and her name,
'Till to the stars they soared past rivalry.

She only I adored—and if my gaze
Was turned elsewhere, it was but to admire
Of her high beauty some few scattered rays
And worship her in idols—fond desire
False incense hid—Yet I repent my praise
As rank idolatry 'gainst Love's true fire.

Torquato Tasso
"Or che L'Aura mia dolce altrove spira."

'Till *L'aura* comes who now alas! elsewhere
Breathes amid fields and forests, hard of heart,
Bereft of joy I stray, from crowds apart
In this dark vale, 'mid grief and ire's foul air,
Where there is nothing left of bright or fair
Since Love has gone a rustic to the plough,
Or feeds his flocks—or in the summer now
Handles the rake—now plies the scythe with care.
Happy the mead and valley, hill and wood,
Where man and beast, and almost tree and stone
Seem by her look with sense and joy endued:
What is not changed on which her eyes e'er shone?
The country courteous grows, the city rude
Even from her presence or her loss alone!

Torquato Tasso
"In quell'etate in cui mal si difende."

While of the age in which the heart but ill
Defends itself—and in thy native land,
Love and thine eyes unable to withstand
They won me, and though distant dazzle still.
Hither I came, intent my mind to fill,
With Wisdom, study—gathered from on high,
But loathed to part, so that to stay or fly
Kept, and still keep sore struggle in my will.
And now all careless of the heat and cold
With ceaseless vigils *Laura,* night and day,
That thou a worthier lover may'st behold
For thee to Fame I strive to win my way:
Then love me still and let me be consoled
With hope until I meet thine eyes, bright ray.

[224]

Torquato Tasso
"Amor, colei, che verginella amai."

She, who a maiden, taught me[,] Love, thy woes,[15]
Tomorrow I shall see a new made bride,
Like, if I err not, a fresh-gather'd rose
Opening her bosom to the sun with pride.
But Him, for whom thus flush'd with joy it blows
Whene'er I see, my blood will scarcely glide,
Perhaps with *Jealousy* it would have froze
Had not a ray of *Pity* thawed its tide:
Thou only know'st—And now alas! I haste
Where I must see that snowy neck and breast
By envied fingers played with and embraced;
How shall I live, or how find peace or rest
If one kind look on me, thou wilt not waste
To hint not vain my sighs nor all unblest?

Torquato Tasso
"Dell'arboscel c'ha sì famoso nome."

With the fair tree so famous, Hymen now
His hallowed sacrificial torch is feeding
And with its verdant garlands crowns his brow
Thy grief O Love! and thy despair not heeding:
And thou that oftimes around it hover
Like a starved bird after it's loved food greeding,
In its sweet shade no more shalt find a cover
Peace, Love, is gone, and thou tow'rd scorn art speeding.

Torquato Tasso
"Arsi mentre a voi piacque." (Madrigal)

I burned whilst thou wert true,
And to affection kind
Paid of my sighs the tribute due,
But since thy fickle mind
To other love is turned,
Quenched is my early flame
And burning where it burned
Are rage and grief and shame
For my fond offering scorned.
With *Laurel* wreaths I crowned thy name
Thus were they seared and spurned!

[225]

Torquato Tasso
"Fummo felici un tempo."

Some happy days we proved
While thou my heart possest,
I loving thee and loved,
Thou blessing me and blest.
When thou becam'st a foe
Disdain replaced desire,
With disdain I tell thee so,
While mingled shame and ire
From my gift neglected, flow,
As I strip the leaves now faded
From the *Laurel* wreaths I braided.

Torquato Tasso
"Era la notte, e sotto il manto adorno."

'Twas Night, underneath her starry vest[16]
The prattling loves were hidden, and their arts
Practised so cunningly upon our hearts,
That never felt they sweeter scorn and jest:
Thousands of amorous thefts their skill attest
All kindly hidden by the gloom from day;
A thousand visions in each trembling ray
Flitted around in bright false splendor drest:
The clear pure moon rolled on her azure way
Without a cloud to dim her silver light
And high-born beauty made our revels gay
Reflecting back on Heaven beams as bright,
Which even with the dawn fled not away—
When chased the Sun such lovely ghosts from night?

Torquato Tasso
"Voi volete ch'io v'ami." (Madrigal)

You would have me love
Yet repress my sighs,
What new tortures must I prove
Kindling from those eyes,
While my fond lips dare not move
Nor my heart's flame rise?
If my love you prize,
I to prove it strove—
Cruel! why the proof despise?

Torquato Tasso
"Sdegno, debil guerrier, campione audace."

Anger a champion bold but warrior weak,
Led me with feeble armour to the field,
Against Love's bow and shafts blunt arms to wield
And Freedom or Revenge in battle seek.
Fool that I was! what human arms avail
In conflict with that torch of heavenly fire
Whose light alone turns anger to desire?—
Peace I implore—and own me rash and frail:
Mercy I beg—and my weak hands extend—
And kneel and bow and bare my humble breast—
If fight I must—Pity her aid shall lend
And win the palm for me or death and rest!
If with my blood some tears of her's should blend
Defeat is triumph and I perish blest!

Torquato Tasso
"Duo donne in un di vidi, illustri, e rare."

I saw two ladies once—illustrious—rare—[17]
One a sad sun, her beauties at mid-day
In clouds concealed—the other bright and gay
Gladdened Aurora-like, Earth Sea and Air:
One hid her light, lest men should call her fair,
And of her praises no reflected ray
Suffered to cross her own celestial way—
To charm and to be charmed, the others care:
Yet this her loveliness veiled not so well
But forth it broke—nor could the other shew
All her's—which wearied mirrors did not tell:
Nor of *this* one could I be silent, though
Bidden in ire—Nor *that* one's triumph swell
Since my tired verse o'ertasked refused to flow!

      Torquato Tasso
      "Non son scemo di fede." (Madrigal)

      I am not faithless! no, oh no!
      But with too fond belief
      And heart too humble and too low
      False I appear—with grief.
      Pity me Lady!—and because

My stars will have me now
But the mere ghost of what I was,
To my poor shade allow
Another's by each outward sign
To *seem*—yet *be* more truly thine!

Torquato Tasso
"Arsi, e alsi a mia voglia." (Madrigal)

Yes! at my will I freeze or glow
Loyal—not lost to shame—
A lover and no foe—
Thy light thoughts may disclaim
Alike my fire and snow,—
But scorned by love and hate and fame,
Thy senseless proud works go!

Torquato Tasso
"Questi, ch'ai core altrui cantando spira." (Sonnet
　　against Giovanni Battista Guarini)

He who thus sighs and sings his amorous pain
Moving all hearts with his enchanted lyre,
And asking love and pity in a strain
That softens hatred and appeases ire—
Who would believe it? turns and turns again,
Like sand before the desert wind of fire—
No faith—no love—no truth—he does but feign
Affection—torment—rapture—and desire—
Seeming at once to worship and despise
Fond hearts insidiously he wins to wear,
From female spoils his impious trophies rise;—
But Love will never yield the high-born fair
Who all reward to a true heart denies,
A victim to the faithless spoiler's snare.

Torquato Tasso
"Più non potea stral di Fortuna, o dente." (Sonnet to an
　　ungrateful friend)

Fortune's worst shafts could ne'er have reached me more
Nor envy's poison'd fangs—By both assailed
In innocence of soul completely mailed
I scorned the hate whose power to wound was o'er:

When *Thou*—whom in my heart of hearts I wore,
And as my rock of refuge often sought—
Turned on myself the very arms I wrought
And Heaven beheld—and suffered what I bore!
O holy Faith! O Love! how all thy laws
Are mocked and scorned—I throw my shield away
Conquered by fraud. . . . Go! seek thy feat's applause
Traitor!—yet still half-mourned with fond delay. . . .
The hand not blow is of my tears the cause,
And more thy guilt than my own pain I weigh!

Torquato Tasso
"Falsa è la lingua, onde deriva e esce." (Sonnet Against
    a Calumny)

False is the tale by envious Rumour spread![18]
False are the hearts wherein it sprung and grew!
And false the tongues that first its poison shed
And others to believe their malice drew!
But that the Furies lent it gall is true—
And true it is that Megara supplies
Its thousand slanders, heaping old on new
And grieving still she cannot add more lies.
O! were they ever to be reached by steel
Shorn from her bust on earth should writhe and trail
Her slimy snake-like folds—thus taught to feel:
But thou *Lamberto* the detested tale,
Will banish from men's minds with friendly zeal
And Falsehoods overthrow fair Truth shall hail!

Torquato Tasso
"Io pure al nome tuo dolce rischiaro." (Sonnet to Duke
    Alphonso of Ferrara)

At thy loved name my voice grows loud and clear
Fluent my tongue, as thou art wise and strong,
And soaring far above the clouds my song:
But soon it droops, languid and faint to hear,
And if thou conquerest not my fate, I fear
Invincible Alphonso, Fate ere long
Will conquer me—freezing in death my song,
And closing eyes now opened with a tear.
Nor dying merely grieves me, let me own,

[229]

But to die thus—with faith of dubious sound,
And buried name, to future times unknown.
In pyramid, mausoleum, brass, or stone,
For this no consolation could be found
My monument I sought in verse alone!

Torquato Tasso
"Un Inferno angoscioso è'la mia vita." (Sonnet)

A hell of torment is this life of mine
My sighs are as the Furies breathing flame,
Desires around my heart like serpents twine
A bold fierce throng, no skill nor art may tame;
As the lost race to whom hope never came
So am I now—for me all hope is o'er—
My tears are Styx—and my complaints and shame
The fires of Phlegethon but stir the more.
My voice is that of Cereberus, whose bark
Fills the abyss and echoes frightfully
Over the stream, dull as my mind and dark:
In this alone, less hard my fate may be,
That there poor ghosts are of foul fiends the mark
While here an earthly goddess tortures me!

Torquato Tasso
"Me novello Ission rapida aggira." (Sonnet to the Duke
    Alphonso asking to be liberated)

Like a new Ixion on Fortune's wheel
Whether I sink profound, or rise sublime,
One never ceasing martyrdom I feel,
The same in woe, though changing all the time.
I wept above, where sun-beams sport, and climb
The vines—and through their foliage sighs the breeze,
I burned and froze, languished and prayed in rhyme
Nor could your ire, nor my own grief appease.
Now in my prison deep and dim, have grown
My torments greater still and sharper far—
As if all sharpened on the dungeon-stone:
Magnanimous Alphonso! burst the bar,
Changing my fate and not my cell alone
And let my Fortune wheel me where you are!

[230]

Torquato Tasso
"Suore del grand Alfonso, il terzo giro." (Sonnet to the
    Princesses of Ferrara)

Sisters of great Alphonso! to the west
Three times have sped the coursers of the Sun
Since sick and outraged, I became a jest
And sighed o'er all that cruel Fate had done.
Wretched and vile whatever meets my eye
Without me—wheresoe'er I gaze around,
Within indeed, my former virtues lie
Though shame and torment's the reward they've found.
Aye! in my Soul are Truth and Honor still
Such as if seen the world were proud to own,
And your sweet images my bosom fill;
But lovely idols ne'er content alone
True hearts—and mine, though mocked and scorned at will,
Is still your temple, altar, shrine and throne.

> Torquato Tasso
> "Ardo sì, ma' non t'amo." (Madrigal)

I burn, but love thee not,
False one! and cruel too—
More worthy far to be forgot,
Than loved by one so true.
No more my grief thy boast shall prove
Nor my heart bleed anew.
I burn—but 'tis with Rage not Love!

Torquato Tasso
"Scipio, o pietade è morta, od è bandita." (Sonnet to
    Scipio Gonzaga)

Sure Pity, Scipio! on Earth has fled[19]
From Royal breasts to seek abode in heaven,
For if she were not banished, scorned, or dead,
Would not some ear to my complaints be given?
Is noble faith at pleasure to be riven?
Though freely pledged that I had nought to dread,
And I by endless outrage to be driven
To worse than Death—the death-like life I've led?
For this is of the quick a grave—and here
Am I a living breathing corpse interred

To go not forth 'till prisoned in my bier—
O Earth! O Heaven! if Love and Truth are heard,
Or Honor, Fame and Virtue worth a tear
Let not my prayers be fruitless or deferred!

Torquato Tasso
"O figlie di Renata." (Canzone To the Princesses of
Ferrara)

Fair daughters of René my song[20]
Is not of pride or ire
Fraternal discord, hate and wrong
Burning in life and death so strong.
From rule's accurst desire
That even the flames divided long
Upon their funeral pyre.
But you I sing, of royal birth,
Nurst on one breast like them
Two flowers both lovely blooming forth
From the same parent stem,
Cherished by Heaven beloved by Earth,
Of each a treasured gem.

Sisters of Great Alphonso! ye
Whose native charms and lofty fate
With Goddesses' might likened be,
Or their's of Egypt's royal state,
When *Berenice's* tresses flew
A votive offering to the skies—
If all the gifts of Heaven to you
To Heaven again like her's should rise,
Not kindly into stars alone
Their flight the planets would outrun,
And make the constellations own
With envy pale their light outshone
By those new rivals of the Sun.

To you I speak, in whom we see
With wondrous concord blend,
Sense, worth, fame, beauty, modesty,—
Imploring you to lend
Compassion to the misery
And sufferings of your friend.

[232]

The memory of years gone by
O! let me in your hearts renew—
The scenes, the thoughts o'er which I sigh,
The happy days I spent with you—
And what I ask—and where am I—
And what I was—and why secluded—
Whom did I trust? and who deluded?

Daughters of Heroes and of Kings,
Allow me to recall
These, and a thousand other things
Sad sweet and mournful all!
From me few words—more tears, Grief wrings,
Tears burning as they fall.
For royal halls and festive bowers
Where nobly serving I,
Shared and beguiled your private hours,
Studies and sports I sigh:
And lyre and trump and wreathed flowers—
Nay more—for Freedom—Health—Applause
And even Humanity's lost laws!

Why am I chased from human kind?
What Circe in the lair
Of brutes thus keeps me, spell-confined?
Nests have the birds of air—
The very beasts in caverns find
Shelter and rest and share
At least kind nature's gifts and laws,
For each his food and water draws
From wood and fountain, where,
Wholesome, and pure, and safe, it was
Furnished by Heaven's own care:
And all is bright and blest, because
Freedom and Health are there!

I merit punishment, I own,
I erred I must confess it—yet
The fault was in the tongue alone,
The heart is true—Forgive!—forget!
I beg for mercy, and my woes,
May claim with pity to be heard;
If to my prayers your ears you close

Where can I hope for one kind word
In my extremity of ill?
And if the pang of hope deferred
Arise from discord in your will,
To me must be received again
The fate of Metius [Metis] and the pain.

I pray ye then, renew for me
The charm that made you doubly fair,
In sweet and virtuous harmony
Urging resistlessly my prayer
With him, for whose loved sake I swear,
I more lament my fault than pains
Strange and unheard of, as they are.
And hence his victories and his fame,
Though glorious both in peace and war,
Another trophy yet may claim
Greater than all and nobler far
A pardoned wrong—which I deplore
Who loved him once—and now adore.

Go! Canzon, where the Virtues bide
Fortune, to me resorts no more,
So *Faith* alone must be your guide!

Torquato Tasso
"Quando sarà che d'Eleonora mia."

O when shall I with my own *Lenore*[21]
Love's dear delight in liberty renew?
Has pitying Fate indeed such joy in store?
Laurels, and lyre, and bashfulness adieu!

Torquato Tasso
"Quel labbro, che le rose han colorito."

Sweet pouting lip! whose colour mocks the rose[22]
Rich ripe and teeming with the dew of bliss,
The flower of Love's forbidden fruit which grows
Insidiously to tempt us with a kiss!
Lovers take heed! shun the deceiver's art—
Mark between leaf and leaf the dangerous snare
Where serpent-like he lurks to sting the heart—
His fell intent I see, and cry, beware!

[234]

In other days his victim—well I know
The wiles that cost me many a pang and sigh,
Fond thoughtless youths! take warning from my woe—
Apples of Tantalus—those buds on high
From the parch'd lips they court, retiring go:
Love's flames and poison only, do not fly!

Torquato Tasso
"Giaceva esposto il peregrino Ulisse."

Wandering Ulysses on the storm-vexed shore[23]
Lay amid wrecks upon the sand scarce dry
Naked and sad: hunger and thirst he bore
And hopeless gazed upon the sea and sky.
When there appeared—(so willed the Fates on high)
A royal dame to terminate his woe;
Sweet fruits she said, sun-tinged with every dye
My father's garden boasts—Would'st taste them? Go!
For me alas! though shivering in the blast
I perish—a more cruel shipwreck mine—
Who from the beach, where famishing I'm cast
Will point to royal roofs for which I pine?
If 'tis not *Thou*! moved by my prayers at last—
What shall I call thee? Goddess! by each sign.

Torquato Tasso
"Giurai Signore, ma il giuramento mio." (To the most
    illustrious and most serene Lord Duke Alphonso)

I swore my Lord! but my unworthy oath,[24]
Was a base sacrilege, which cannot bind,
Since God alone, directs and governs both,
The quality of his works—the human mind.
Reason I hold from Him—Who would not loathe
Such gift a pledge in power's vile hands to find?
Do not forget my Lord, that even the sway
Of sovereign Kings has bounds at which it ends;
Past them, they rule not—nor should we obey,
He who to any mortal being bends
One step beyond, sins 'gainst the light of day:
Thus then, my soul her servile shackles rends!
And my sound mind shall henceforth none obey
But *Him* whose reign o'er Kings and worlds extends!

[235]

Torquato Tasso
"Tacciono i boschi e i fiumi." (Madrigal)

Silent was man and brute,
And the Heavens and Earth and Sea,
The very winds in their caves were mute,
And the Moon watched silently.
Shrouded by Night in her sable vest
Love's vigils alone we kept
The world was all but ourselves at rest
And mutely we sighed and kissed and pressed
For with us even language slept.

Torquato Tasso
"Magnanimo signor, se mai trascorse." (Sonnet To the
Duke Alphonso)

My Gracious Lord! if you indeed complain
Of the rude license of my angry tongue,
Not from my heart believe me, sprang the wrong
It honored you, and feels itself the pain:
Nor should a few rash, daring words and vain,
Weigh against praises well-matured and long
By Love and study woven into song
Which neither ire nor avarice can stain.
Why tedious suffering then for transient crime?
And brief reward for ever-during fame?
Such was not Royal guerdon in old time!
Yet my right reasoning is perhaps to blame,
Honor you gave, not borrowed from my rhyme
Which far below your merit always came!

Torquato Tasso
"Tormi potrei, alto Signor, la vita." (To Duke Alphonso)

Of life you may deprive me, mighty Lord,[25]
Such right from monarch's usurpation springs,
But *Reason*—gift of the Eternal word—
To take from Man, because of love he sings,
Of love—by Heaven and nature taught—absurd!
Nay worse, a crime—the worst of crimes in Kings.
Pardon I craved—it is denied—Adieu
My penitence I do repent anew.

[236]

Giovanni Battista Guarini
"Ardi e gela à tua voglia." (Madrigal)

Burn thou! or freeze at will—
Man without faith or shame!
Now lover and now foe, and still
In fickleness the same!
Little I prize thine ice or fire
If vain thine amorous flame
Vainer will prove thy senseless ire!

Giovanni Battista Guarini
"Questi, che indarno ad alta meta aspira." (Sonnet
 against Torquato Tasso)

He who attempts his own high mark in vain
Still seeks by falsehood to work others ill:
See! how his fangs turn on himself again,
While he would wound me without cause or skill.
Mark his own poison in his own veins burn,
And his rash weapons his own bosom strike,
Whilst into mirrors all his falsehoods turn
To shew himself most hideous when most like.
A double flame he boasts—and bursts and binds
Full often the same tie—and by those arts
(Who would believe it?) into favor winds
Even with the Gods; But Cupid versed in hearts
Yields not such beauty to such snares, and finds
My purer flame more fit to point his darts.

Giovanni della Casa
"O sonno, O della cheta, umida, ombrosa." (Sleep)

'Tired Nature's sweet restorer!' child of Night![26]
Happy oblivion of all mortal woes—
The mourner's comforter—the poor's delight—
Friend of the sick and wretched—Calm Repose!
Come to me *Sleep!* my burning eye-lids close,
And to my heart and brain some respite lend;
Quiet my tortured limbs, and still those throes,
Whose agonies to every nerve extend.
Come to me Sleep! with healing on thy wings,
Come Darkness Peace and Silence too with thee,

And the bright dream that from light slumber springs
Giving fresh spirits to the 'fancy-free'. . . .
Alas! my prayer no rest or pity brings
To my hard couch—O! weary night for me!

Giovanni della Casa
"Questi palazzi e queste logge, or colte." (Venice)

City and Port—Church—Palace—Square and Tower
With gold, and gems, and marble, rich and gay—
What wert thou *Venice*—and whence rose thy power?
Bare isles—poor huts—shoals and a fisher's bay—
But men immovable in danger's hour,
Scorning all chains, and of no vice the prey,
Espoused thee—Liberty thine only dower—
Whence *Glory*—and then *Wealth*—and then *Decay!*
No lust of Conquest and of Gold no thirst,
Thy glorious founders . . . noble hearts possest
Freedom they loved—Falsehood they spurned and curst
Like Fear unworthy of a generous breast:
Would that thou hadst their Virtues always nurst!
And not been first corrupted—then opprest!

Giovanni Battista Marino
"Gire, restarsi, e nel restar partire." (Absence)

To go, yet stay—and staying to depart—
Quieting ourselves, with some one else to fly—
To languish and complain, we know not why,
And dying, live, with grief, a life apart:
With Hope to struggle, and with Fear to start,
Fond memories with bitter tears bedew,
And separate a single soul in two,
Falling from Heaven through martyrdom of heart:
In solitude or crowds alone to dwell
Deeming mute nature mourns because we grieve,
Renouncing truth, to nurse suspicions fell,
And every hour Eternity believe,
This is the living Death—the Earthly Hell
Called Absence—whether we are left or leave.

Francesco Maria Redi
"Lunga è l'arte d'Amor, la vita è breve." (The School
of Love)

Life short—the art of Love too long we find—
Dangerous the road—the summit hard to climb—
Our Reason weak and swifter than the wind
The flight of *Opportunity* and *Time*.
High-throned the rigid *Master* sits sublime,
Grasping his scourge on cruel thoughts intent—
Each pupil's fault he tortures like a crime,
Slow in reward—but quick in punishment.
Even his rewards as punishments are meant—
And when he mixes them, his bitter rules
Seem but contrived his scholars to torment
And yet how flourishes this worst of schools!
Dulards are there, with age already bent,
Still striving to become much greater *Fools*!

Carlo Maria Maggi
"Scioglie Eurilla dal lido lo corso, e molto." (Parting)

Eurilla leaves the coast; I run and rave,
And madly tidings of the main demand:
"I met the Goddess first" exclaimed a wave
"And grateful kist her footsteps on the sand."
"I bore her vessel swan-like from the strand"
Added another. "Was she gay or Grave?"
I asked a third. "She smiled and waved her hand
And *Earth* and *Heaven* returned the smile she gave."
Then came a fourth—and told me as she flew
Tritons her galley o'er the surges bore
And pale with Jealousy the sea-nymphs grew—
"And said she naught of me?—Back to this shore
Did she not bid you bear me one adieu?". . . .
Onward the rude wave past—but spoke no more!

Francesco da Lemene[27]
"Io voglio amarti, ma . . . ma che? ma che?" (Dialogue.
    Tirsis. Phillis.)

Phillis. I'd love you Tirsis, but—
Tirsis.   —speak out! but what?
Phillis. I must not tell you that!—
Tirsis.   —Dearest! why not?
Phillis. Perhaps you'll laugh at me—
Tirsis.   —Indeed I sha'nt!

Phillis.	You won't? I'll tell you then! O no! I can't!
Tirsis.	Tell me at once you plague! don't teize me so!
Phillis.	Well then—I'd love you Tirsis—but I know—
Tirsis.	Know what?—
Phillis.	—You're vowed to Chloris—a'nt it true?
Tirsis.	And what of that? I'll vow myself to you.
Phillis.	What love us both? D'ye take me for a fool?
Tirsis.	'Love those that love you'—is not that the rule?
Phillis.	Then we must love each other—Yes, we must!
Tirsis.	Swear to love those that love you!—a'nt it just?

Francesco da Lemene
"Stravaganza d'un sogno! A me parea."

I had a dream—a strange fantastic dream,[28]
To Hell I had been doomed by wrath divine,
And she I love was there, because 'twould seem,
Heaven meant to punish both her fault and mine.
Pride was my sin—since I had dared to pine
For one whom all might well an angel deem;
And Cruelty was her's—who loved to shine
In chilling beauty like a frozen stream.
Scarce had we felt our agony and awe
Before methought, we had been damned in vain.
So willed, O Lady! Love's almighty law,
Hell turned to Heaven—and into rapture, pain,
For me—because thy lovely face I saw—
For thee—because thou saw'st my pangs again!

Francesco da Lemene
"Sento, che l'età mi da primavera."

The Spring—the Summer of my days is gone!
And even the Autumn now is fleeting past,
Of my eighth lustre—slow while speeding on,
But oh! how swift when fled—this year's the last:
The half of man's appointed time is past,
When from its weight relieved, the spirit's flame
Soars to the stars, returning whence it came,
Unless its eve ere night is overcast,
Yet still doth love torment me—and, O shame!
In all my youthful errors I grow old,
To my last hour bearing my first fault's blame

Though of my folly need I not be told:
Hopes false, and fears too true, I well might name,
Which my short life with one long grief controled!

Francesco da Lemene
"O che bel pomo d'or mi mostri, Amore!" (Dialogue. Cupid—
Phillis and afterwards Venus.)

Phillis.   O! what a splendid golden apple, Love![29]
          Where did you get it?
Cupid.   'Twas my mother's prize;
      The shepherd gave it her in Ida's grove
      When rival goddesses to mortal eyes
      Unveiled, and for the palm of beauty strove.
Phillis.   'Tis beautiful!
Cupid.   Wilt have it Phillis?
Phillis.   No!
      No! no,—I must not! What would Venus say?
      See she is coming!
Cupid.   —Take it!—O how slow!—
      Then hide it for me!—in thy bosom—Pray!
Phillis.   For thy sake—in my bosom—So?—well so!
Venus.   Ha! have I found you run away! Come here!
      Where is my golden apple?
Cupid.   I . . . don't . . . know!
Venus.   Come, come, you took it—tell the truth—don't fear!
Cupid.   Mother, if I have got it may I die!
Venus.   Take that! you wicked imp—What tell a lie!
                      (strikes him)
Cupid.   O me! O me! —pray don't—O don't my mother!
Venus.   Well tell me then!—
Cupid.   What shall I do?—
Venus.   So won't[?]
      Then for your obstinacy here's another!
                   (strikes him again)
Cupid.   O dear! O dear!—
Phillis.   —Sweet Venus! don't oh don't!
      Here is your apple!—
Venus.   —So you had it eh?
      He gave it you?—
Phillis.   —I thought it was his own
      Forgive him Venus! and me too I pray!

Venus. O Cupid! what a liar you have grown!
        Why did you steal from me to give to her?
        Tell me this moment!—See you tell me true!
        Hush! 'till you tell me why, you shall not stir!
Cupid. Because . . . I thought her . . . handsomer . . . than
        you . . .

                               (Phillis departs)

Venus. Phillis indeed!—So Phillis is your belle!
        And you think Phillis handsomer than me?
        Why do you think her prettier?
Cupid.   —I shan't tell!
Venus. Speak! what are you afraid of?
Cupid.   —Don't I see
      You're angry still? and my ears smart—I shan't—
Venus. Don't be afraid! Speak out! Say why is she
        More beautiful than I am?—
Cupid.   —Nay, I can't!—
Venus. Speak! or—you've felt my hand—you know it's strong—
Cupid. Well Ma! She's not more beautiful than thee,
        But then . . . thou hast been beautiful . . . so long! . . .

Vincenzo da Filicaja
"Dov'è Italia, il tuo braccio? e a chi ti servi."

Where's thine own arm Italia? What avails thee
That scourge, a stranger's sword?—the worst of woes.
Alike the slave that guards thee, and assails thee,
Both were thy servants once—both *are* thy foes!
Shame on thee! is it thus that thou deservest
Thine ancient glory and imperial crown?
Shame on thee! if so little thou preservest
Hereditary courage—faith—renown!
Go! and repudiate Honor, and espouse thee
'Mid tears and groans and blood with recreant Sloth—
Go! Sleep, adultress vile! if fear allows thee,
In infamy's embraces—nothing loath,
'Till the avenging steel at length arouse thee
And in thy minion's arms destroys ye both!

Giovanni Giuseppe Orsi.
"Uom ch'al remo è dannato, egro e dolente."

Hourly, the wretch condemned a galley slave,
Chains on his feet—the hard oar in his hand—

[242]

While his wing'd prison tosses on the wave—
Sighs, but in vain, for Liberty and land.
And yet if freed, unable to withstand
Inveterate habit, for his oar again
He longs, while loitering listless on the strand,
And sells himself to his accustomed chain.
Cynthia! that wretch am I—though thy deceit
My heart and vows asunder often clave,
Unto thy chains I offer still my feet
Returning like that abject foolish knave.
Nay, worse than him—for no reward I meet;
He sold his liberty—but mine I gave!

Girolamo Gigli
"Fortuna, io dissi, e volo e mano arresta."

Stay, Fortune! stay for once, thy hand and flight!
Why, faithless, why, thy changeful wings still wave?
The man thou crown'st at morn, thou spoil'st at night,
And he who sleeps a monarch, wakes a slave.
"Death" she replied "is quick—greedy the grave—
And good so rare—the gaping crowd so great,
That one alone must have what many crave,
Or some must lose, while others win, or wait."
Then said I to the lady of my fate:
"But thou at least wilt not like Fortune rove."
She answered: "Constancy was dull—the date
Of beauty short—for smiles so many strove
That some would be too sad—some too elate,
If all were not allowed to hope and love.["]

Giovanni Battista Felice Zappi
"Stassi in Cipro in su la praggia amena."

I stood in Cyprus on the flowery plains[30]
Where mighty Love has fixed his royal seat,
And laying my petition at his feet
Implored his mercy in heart-moving strains:
"Dread Sire" the writing said—"your slave complains
Of his hard servitude and cruel tasks.
Pity him, Sire! freedom he humbly asks;
Six lustres he has worn his servile chains.["]

From my extended hand the scroll he took
As if to read—but not a word could see,
Then threw it from him with disdainful look
Like one who had been scorned—Begone! said he,
Such idle mockery I do not brook,
Give it to Death,—he'll speak to you for me.

Giovanni Battista Felice Zappi
"In quell'età ch'io misurar solea."

While with my goat I measured heights, and he—[31]
Was somewhat, of the two, the taller deemed,
Chloris I loved, who from that hour to me
A wonder, not a woman, always seemed. . . .
One day I lisped—"I love thee!"—it could be
Less from my lips than heart the accents teemed—
She smiled and kissed me,—"Innocent!" said she
["]Thou know'st not what love is, thou hast not dreamed."
She loved another, and he her—Time flew
And I grew up to manhood's burning years
With them alas! my fatal passion grew;
But she disdains, or spurns me, or scarce hears,
Forgetful of the past—while I bedew
The memory of that kiss and smile with tears!

Giovanni Battista Felice Zappi
"Amor s'asside alla mia Filli accanto."

When Phillis sleeps beside her couch Love lies,
When Phillis wakes, Love follows where she roves,
Love's in her words, her silence, and her sighs,
And her whole life and all her power are Love's.
Gesture and song he taught her—and his doves
Instructed her to murmur. Even in ire
Love makes her lovelier—and with grief improves
Charms which he only, could with tears inspire.
If through the mazy dance all grace she moves,
Her fairy feet Love tunes to music's lyre,
And wings o'er flowers, like Zephyr through the groves:
Love makes her brow his throne—her voice his choir,
In tresses, eyes, and lips, his sway he proves
Her icy heart alone defies his fire.

[244]

Orazio Pedrocchi.
"Io chiesi al Tempo. Ed a chi surse il grunde."

"Whose were those wond'rous ruins, *Time*," I said,
"That seem the mightiest of all human things? ["]
He answered not—nor paused—but shook his head,
Clearing the air, with swift untiring wings;
I turned to *Fame*: "O thou! from whom there springs
Life to all glorious deeds—say whose these were?"
Silent and sad she stood with downcast air,
Like one whose bosom shame and sorrow wings,
I gazed once more—and was about to go,
But saw *Oblivion* seated on a stone
That crumbled to destruction, sure, though slow,
And would have asked of him:—Pray is it known?
Peace! cried a deep sepulchral voice and low,
What matters whose they *were*? they *are* my own!

Giovanni Battista Recanati
"Un dì gli spiriti, a cui forse dovea."

A Seraph once, committed to whose care,
The glorious stars of upper Heaven had been,
Desirous in creation's work to share
Stole of celestial fire one spark unseen.
Hoping at once his daring theft to screen,
And with a miracle, his fault repair,
Earth, purest, holiest, loveliest shrine—between
Thy bosom's orbs, he sought—and placed it there.
But as no clouds the Sun's resplendent light
No Earthly veil the soul's can wholly dim,
So in thine eyes the sacred flame burnt bright
And shone through every word, look, tone, and limb,
'Till thou becam'st an angel to the sight
And told the tale to Heaven—alas! for him!

Pietro Metastasio
"L'onda dal mar divisa."

Water from Ocean divided
Bathing the Valley and Mountain,
Whether flying
In the river
Or imprisoned

[245]

In the fountain
Flows ever murmuring and sighing
Until it returns to the sea:
To the sea whence at first it arose,
Where its cares and its murmurings cease,
To the sea, where it hopes to repose
From all it's long wanderings in peace!

Pietro Metastasio
"Ecco quel fiero instante."

The fatal moments come and fly[32]
Farewell my life! my soul, my heart!
Nice 'twere easier far to die
Than thus from love and thee to part:
Where can I hope to find repose?
Where from my own sad thoughts be free?
And thou—who knows—alas! who knows?
If thou wilt thus remember me!

My memory's poor troubled ghost
Unseen, and yet forever nigh,
Amid gay crowds, when courted most,
Will sometimes haunt thee with a sigh:
Far as Earth spreads—Long as time flows,
Where'er thou art, that shade will be,
And yet who knows—alas! who knows?
If thou wilt thus remember me!

I, on the distant shore you leave,
Must wander by the rocks and strand,
To listen to their moan and grieve
And tidings from the main demand:
From morning's dawn 'till evenings close
Calling thy name to Earth and Sea
But thou—who knows—alas! who knows
If thou wilt thus remember me!

How can I see each much lov'd spot
So happy once—when thou hast flown?
How bear to be, where thou art not?
How pass the hours—once thine—alone?
From pleasures lost, grief deeper grows,

[246]

Through memory's bitter alchemy
And yet who knows—alas! who knows?
If thou wilt still remember me!

'Twas here—beside this fountain's edge . . .—
Thus will I think—. . . her high disdain
Flash'd forth—and here, her hand in pledge
Of peace she gave me once again.
Here, in my bosom, hope first rose—
Here love was whispered first to thee—
And thou—who knows—alas! who knows
If thou wilt thus remember me!

Dearest! farewell—farewell!—we part—
In the new home henceforward thine,
Faith, vows, and incense, many a heart
Will haste to offer at thy shrine:
Among their prayers—O heaven!—suppose,
Not all unwelcome, some should be,
Nice, who knows—alas! who knows—
If thou wilt then remember me?

And yet, bethink thee love, how dear
How pure the flame thou leav'st behind,
Remember every hope and fear
And doubt that lingers in my mind:
Remember all our joys and woes—
All we have been—and yet might be—
Remember love! but ah! who knows?
If thou wilt still remember me!

Vittorio Alfieri
"Ai Fiorentini il pregio del bel dire." (Sonnet. The
    people of Italy.)

The Florentines—well-spoken smooth-tongued varlets;
The Romans—skilled in every kind of knavery;
The Neapolitans—buffoons and harlots;
The Genoese—who patient starve in slavery;
The Turinese—to other's faults quick-sighted;
The lazy, careless, let alone Venetians;
The honest Milanese, with feasts delighted;
And the Lucchese who bore one like Patricians:
In idleness and vice alone agreeing,

[247]

Such are thy heterogenous sons and daughters,
All, all, a shame to her, who gave them being
Whilst thou, Italia! sport of foreign slaughters,
Lie spoiled and scorned—thy wretchedness not seeing,
Forgotten, sunk, and lost in Lethe's waters.

Vittorio Alfieri
"Vuota insalubre region, che stato." (Sonnet. On Rome)

Poor sickly waste! that call'st thyself a State,
And art but desolation—fields untilled,
Peopled with spectres whose gaunt looks are filled
With want—guilt—cowardice and blood-stained hate;
A Senate's ghost—to act not—nor debate—
Mean paltry craft, in gold and purple drest—
Rich, noble fools—the richest always best—
And a priest-king through others' folly great!
A city citizenless—Temples grand,
But no Religion—Law of crime the nurse
Forever changing, always for the worse—
And Keys that let Heaven's gate wide open stand
For all the wickedness earth ever planned—
Art thou not Rome the seat of every curse?

Vittorio Alfieri
"Prezioso diaspro, agata e oro."

Jasper and Gems and Gold were more than due[33]
And less than worthy of this noble shrine:
No! let the Earthly great in tombs renew
Their pageantry—With precious stones may shine
The barren dust whence Laurels never grew—
For thee—thy Monument's a name Divine.

Anonymous
"Odi d'un uom che muore."

Listen! a few short hours[34]
My soul's dark veil will lift;
Take then these fading flowers,
Prize and preserve the gift!

How they were prized when mine,
How wretched from where they dwelt,
When my parch'd lip pressed thine
Who knows, but I that felt?

[248]

Pledges of rapture then!
The symbols now of grief—
Take to thy breast agen
These flow'rs, than life less brief.

And if that breast have sense
Of Love or of Despair,
Think how I snatched them thence,
And how returned them there!

Anonymous
"O se tu fossi meco." (The Wish)

O! wert thou but with me,[35]
In yon dark vessel free,
That o'er the moon-lit sea
Cleaves her way:
O were it only mine
From scenes in which we pine
To bear thee o'er the brine
Far away!

On ocean's ample breast
Beneath Night's starry vest
All else but us at rest,
Thou and I,
Of every mutual pain
Together might complain,
And unbetrayed remain,
No one by.

Thus lifting Memory's pall
From this dark life, all, all,
The past we should recall
With it's woes.
And then what could we crave,
Of Heaven and the wave
But a harbour or a grave
To repose.

[249]

VI

Other Poems

THIS section contains twelve poems that Wilde did not include in *Poems: Fugitive and Occasional* or *The Italian Lyric Poets*. Several of them were written after he made these two collections.

ON MY BIRTHDAY[1]

Another of my wasted years has gone
    And brought me nearer—nothing but the grave
And thus they wax and wane; and one by one
    Leave—as they found me—Melancholy's slave.

Each stamps it's wrinkles deeper on my brow
    Each sheds it's frost upon my scattered hair
And those who knew me once, and see me now
    Speak of me as among "the things that were."

I've watched thro' night 'till dawn—the lingering sun
    It is my Fortieth Sun—at length appears!
And seems to question me[:] "What hast thou done
    Thro' this long waste of miserable years?"

Ere his Eighth lustre gallant Surrey died
    But dying left behind a deathless name.
And hast thou then no honorable pride?
    No noble aspirations after fame?

Horace & Virgil Scipio Caesar lit
    With Glory ere thy years their sword or page,
And even while thou livedst Napoleon Byron writ
    Their brief and burning annals on the age

"And thou"—Enough!—I know it all—'tis true!
    Wasting my head and heart on love and rhyme
While the irrevocable moments flew. . . .
    I perish and bequeath no name to Time.

SONNET
SENT TO CARLO BOTTA
ON READING HIS HISTORY OF ITALY[2]

Botta! the Muse of History with thy pen
Sheds beauty, light, and wisdom on her pages,
Reviving thus, even in our days again,
Part of the Roman, Greek and Tuscan sages;
Their love of freedom, and their skill in men—
Hatred of force and fraud—the lore of ages—
With style's best virtue graced—most lovely when
Truth scorns both Demagogue's and Tyrant's wages.
There is a fascination in thy story
Beyond mere music from a Syren's tongue,
As though exulting in her ancient glory
Above the tale entranced, Ausonia hung,
Demanding back from Time now faint and hoary,
Days worthy of the land where Dante sung!

[NO TITLE]

Daughter of Grecian Genius! from whose soul[3]
    Pure—English—womanly high thought and feeling
Their heart-sprung Poetry's rich treasures roll
    Ev'n critic taste and reason's wonder stealing,
As hurrying tow'rd impassion'd meaning's goal,
    Expression under Fancy's torrent reeling,
Thy spirit seems to burst from Earth's control
    Its Heav'n-born Myths in music's breath revealing!
How sweet, how bright, how lovely, how sublime,
    Majestic and exhaustless is the stream,
Pour'd forth by Nature, thus enrich'd by Time,
    Shaming the golden tides that poets dream—
The ever-glorious Sea of deathless rhyme
    Wherein [sun], sky, and stars reflected gleam!

      Anonymous (Italian)
      "Qui giace un Cardinale."

      Here lies a cardinal far famed[4]
      For doing works of good and evil;
      He did his bad work very well,
      But spoiled his good work like the devil.

[251]

Juan Meléndez Valdés
ANACREONTIC[5]

I applied myself to science,
To be free from care and strife,
Thinking Wisdom bade defiance
To all the ills of life
Alas! what silly fancies!
I could not nurse them long;
Give me music back, and dances,
Love, friendship, wine, and song!

Has life so few vexations,
That we increase our store?
Or so many recreations,
We need not wish for more?
Fill the cup! let's drain a measure
To my own Dorilla's eyes;
Till Wisdom teaches pleasure,
'Tis no pleasure to be wise.

What heed I if the sun
Be a fixed star or no?
What time the planets run
Their course, why need I know?
Is the moon peopled, land and flood?
What millions may be there?
They never did us harm or good—
About them need we care?

Away with each historian!
And the chiefs whose deeds they tell;
Roman or Macedonian—
What matter where they fell?
While our sportive lambs may wander
In this green valley free,
What's Caesar, Alexander—
King or Khan, to you and me?

The land protects our fold—
I speak the word with awe;
If it's safe, need I be told
Of the "wisdom of the law"?

[252]

The men who study, suffer
Trouble, and toil, and care;
Each mid-night taper-snuffer
Has a sad and solemn air.

What gains the sallow student?
To doubt his studies tend;
Doubt makes new studies prudent—
In doubts new studies end.
So passes life away
In jealousy and strife,
Disputing night and day—
O enviable life!

Bring wine! my girl, bring wine!
With Love, and Song, and Jest,
While there are eyes like thine,
A fig for all the rest!

LINES WRITTEN BY THOMAS CHATTERTON WHILE MEDITATING SUICIDE IN THE AUTUMN OF 1770[6]

I love to see the fading leaf
    I joy to note the withering tree
For cold neglect and scorn and grief
        Have wasted me.

I love to hear the sullen wind,
    I love to watch the rising wave
Beneath whose swell I soon shall find
        A peaceful grave!

I love to see the surges beat
    Around this insulated rock
That spurns them proudly from his feet
        Nor feels the shock

Here will I watch the gathering storm
    And listen to the sea-birds cry
'Till night envelopes every form
        From mortal eye

Then shall my spirit take it's flight
    To that unknown mysterious shore
Where thousands every day alight
        But quit no more.

Forgive me heaven! if rash the dead
    I cannot beg; I dare not steal:
Even man's obdurate heart might bleed
        At what I feel.

Would I could pray! . . . it is too late,
    Despair has stiffened every limb!. . . .
Pray for me father! . . . mercy's gate
        Is free to him.

Bend haughty soul! unbent before
    Bow to thy maker stubborn knee!
'Tis done! the last great trial's o'er
    Angels of mercy pray for me!

LINES FOR THE MUSIC OF WEBER'S LAST WALTZ[7]

    See! the Sun is sinking
        Day is closing fast
    Twilight's pensive-thinking
        Hours will soon be past:
    Love's first Pilgrim sighing
        Starts to hear the bell
    Which to day-light dying
        Tolls a last farewell:
    Vesper's hymn is stealing
        O'er the charmed air
    Every form is kneeling
        Every sound is prayer.

    Thus 'mid all that's dearest
        Would I sink to rest
    Like that bright Star nearest
        To the drooping West:
    Let not Love bewail me,
        'Twould but wound my ear
    When my senses fail me
        Be thou only near;
    While my eyes are glazing
        Take thy hand in mine
    And be sure while gazing
        Life's last thought is thine!

ON THE DEATH OF A YOUNG LADY[8]

Soft and sweet be thy deathly sleep
   Bright and glad be thy heavenly waking
O do not dream that thou seest us weep
   Feel not thou, that our hearts are breaking!

Ne'er oh ne'er mayst thou hear us sigh
   Known to thee may our griefs be never
But if thou look'st from the starry sky
   Think that thou seest us happy as ever.

And we, when we press the holy ground
   That covers thy grave at the hour of even
Will fancy thy Spirit is hovering round
   And smiling points to it's native heaven.

Full oft when the moon of night is near
   And our wearied eye lids have sunk in slumber
We'll dream that thy golden lyre we hear
   Softly touched to its sweetest number.

And oh! we'll deem when our bosoms thrill
   With the pulse of joy or the pang of sorrow
Our good thou sharest—but not our ill
   And Patience or bliss from the thought we'll borrow

And at last, when the hour of death is near
   Around our couch thy Spirit shall hover
To whisper Hope in our dying ear
   And waft us to peace when life is over.

ON GREENOUGH'S WASHINGTON[9]

Such was the Man!—Simple—Austere—sublime—
By every fortune tried—in all unmoved—
Hero—Sage—Patriot—great without a crime
Who conquered freedom for the land he loved:—
And for himself—took nothing—but a Name
That None 'till then—& no one since has won:
Does not the very marble speak his name?
Who dare thus point to Heaven but WASHINGTON[?]

Guido Guinicelli (Italian)

When steel and lodestone touch they cleave[10]
As if in rapturous trance they hung,
Severed—each others clasp they leave
As though to life and love they clung.

Thus too the heart!—but ah beware!
When over the subtle flame has past
Both must its power forever share
And each, to each, be first—and last—

Absent or present, heart and steel
Become as if by lightning riven:
Thenceforth they only know and feel
One spell on Earth—one Star in Heaven!

[NO TITLE]

Whilst busy Memory fondly strays[11]
    O'er griefs and joys of other times
And many a much loved form pourtrays
And many a beauteous scene displays
    Of former years and distant climes.

The burning blush will sometimes rise
    For youths first wild romantic schemes
Which now, when Time hath made me wise
Appear if viewed by Reasons eyes
    But idle and fantastic dreams.

For I have sought the silent wood
    And many a live long summer day
Wrapt in enthusiastic mood
Supremely wise divinely good
    Within it's deepest covert lay.

There formed vain schemes of happiness
    For life's gay morn or cloudless even,
Encouraged worth relieved distress
Heard every tongue my virtues bless
    And smiled mid a domestic heaven!

But tho' these follies flush my cheek
    Whene'er the past is called to view
Yet still—(I dare my thoughts to speak)
Though knaves or fools should call me weak
    I mourn them false yet love them too!

This honest truth I tell full free,
    What—if the heartless crowd condemn?
Let not that steal one sigh from thee
They only *strive* to laugh at me,
    While I, sincerely *pity* them!

TO THE MOCKING BIRD[12]

Winged mimic of the woods! thou motley fool, ·
Who shall thy gay buffonery describe?
Thine ever-ready notes of ridicule
Pursue thy fellows still with jest and jibe.
Wit—sophist—songster—Yorick of thy tribe,
Thou sportive satirist of nature's school,
To thee the palm of scoffing we ascribe,
Arch scoffer and mad Abbot of misrule!
For such thou art by day—but all night long
Thou pourest a soft, sweet, pensive, solemn strain,
As if thou didst in this, thy moonlight song,
Like to the melancholy Jacques, complain,
Musing on falsehood, violence and wrong,
And sighing for thy motley coat again.

Notes

In these notes, the following abbreviations are used: RHW—Richard Henry Wilde; JWW—John Walker Wilde, the poet's brother; CAW—Catherine Ann Wilde, the poet's sister; WCW—William Cumming Wilde, the poet's son; JPW—John Patterson Wilde, the poet's son.

"RHW to Harmanus Bleecker" means a "letter from Richard Henry Wilde to Bleecker": the location of the letter appears in the bibliography.

PART ONE: LIFE

CHAPTER I

1. RHW to Harmanus Bleecker, Oct. 19, 1840; Bleecker to RHW, Mar. 8, 1841. Oscar Wilde, born in Dublin, Ireland, seven years after RHW's death, also came from the Dutch family of De Wilde; but Vyvyan Holland, the son of Oscar Wilde and the author of *Son of Oscar Wilde* (New York, 1954), wrote me on Mar. 5, 1957, that if there were any direct relationship between RHW and Oscar Wilde, he did not know what it was.

Whenever the single name *Wilde* appears in this work, it refers to RHW.

2. Unless otherwise stated, the information on Richard and Mary Wilde and their families before they came to America is taken from the following sources: "Index to Act/or Grant Books, Dublin Diocese," in *Appendix to 26th Report of the Deputy Keeper of Public Records in Ireland* (1895), p. 639; *Wilson's Dublin Directory*, 1761 to 1800; *Roll of Freemen, City of Dublin*, National Library of Ireland Ms. 78 f 177; *Freeman's Journal Newspaper*, July 7-11, 1767; Vicars, *Index to Prerogative Wills of Ireland*, p. 348; and letter, JPW to William Gilmore Simms, Apr. 4, 1855.

Mrs. Emily Newitt Pournelle White of Augusta, Georgia, a great-granddaughter of Mary Newitt Wilde, has in her possession a large silver tankard with J. N. on one side (for Jonathan Newitt) and the coat of arms of the family on the other. Recently Mrs. White has been contributing many of her possessions to the public library in Augusta.

3. Mrs. Kathleen Wilde Viscarra of Los Angeles, California, a great-

great-granddaughter of JWW, has in her possession a notebook with the names of the children. The following information is copied exactly:

Michael Wilde	Born May 31, 1784–Died Sept. 11, 1810
Mary Wilde	Born June 29, 1785
John Wilde	Born July 2, 1786–Died 1787
James Wilde	Born Sept. 22, 1787–Died July 1788
Ann Wilde	Born Sept. 4, 1788–Died 1789
Richard Wilde	Born Sept. 24, 1789
Elizibeth [*sic*] Wilde	Born April 12, 1791–Died Sept. 1791
James Wilde	Born July 3, 1792
Catherine Wilde	Born Sept. 21, 1793
Ann Wilde	Born Nov. 16, 1795–Died April 25, 1797
John Wilde	Born March 20, 1798
Ann Wilde	Born May 5, 1800

4. Baltimore *Federal Gazette*, Sept. 12, 1796.

5. JWP to W. G. Simms, Apr. 4, 1855. This letter makes no reference to Richard Wilde's being in America before Jan., 1797.

6. This non-Catholic information was furnished by Mrs. White of Augusta. It seems logical, for one of the Newitts ran for political office in Dublin (an honor denied Catholics).

7. JPW to Simms, Apr. 4, 1855; city directories of Baltimore for those years.

8. The name *Ann* was given to three of the children; the first two died, but the last one lived many years. Baltimore *Federal Gazette*, July 23, 1802; Mary's married name is sometimes spelled *Paisley* or *Parsley*.

9. JPW to Stephen Miller, Nov. 12, 1851.

10. *Life and Times of Dante* (unpublished), "The Author to the Reader," pp. ii-iii.

11. JPW to Miller, Nov. 12, 1851; JPW to Simms, Apr. 4, 1855; RHW to JPW, May 21, 1842.

12. (Boston, 1867), Canto II, Stanza LXVII.

13. *Ibid.*, Stanza LXVIII. See also the note on p. 270.

14. *Ibid.*, p. 270; JPW to Miller, Nov. 12, 1851.

15. Mrs. Viscarra's notebook has the date of his death; *Hesperia*, Canto II, Stanza LXVII.

16. *Baltimore County Inventories*, Liber 22, Folios 380-382.

17. *Baltimore County Administration Bonds*, Liber 9, Folio 182.

CHAPTER II

1. *Hesperia*, Canto I, Stanza V; a poem beginning "Oh! dearer by far than the land of our birth."

2. C. C. Jones, *Life, Literary Labors, and Neglected Grave of RHW*, p. 4, mentions Cormick. Obituary for Cormick, Augusta *Chronicle*, June 7, 1826.

3. Advertisements in Augusta *Chronicle*: Nov. 15, 1806; Aug. 29, 1801; Jan. 16, 1802; May 19, 1804; Jan. 28, 1804; Apr. 21, 1804.

4. Rufus Griswold, *Prose Writers of America* (Philadelphia, 1847), p. 258; Augusta *Herald*, Apr. 10, 1806; Augusta *Chronicle*, Jan. 3, 1807.

5. Advertisements in Augusta *Chronicle*: Nov. 7, 1807; Jan. 31, 1807; Dec. 3, 1808. Census returns in Augusta *Chronicle*, Jan. 12, 1811. A poem beginning "My task of life is almost ended."

6. JPW to Simms, Apr. 4, 1855; Cary to RHW, Nov. 27, 1831. Cary (1789-1843), a native of Maryland, settled in Columbia County, Georgia, and served in the U. S. House of Representatives from 1823 to 1827.

[259]

7. RHW to "My dear Marchioness," undated; RHW to JPW, May 21, 1842.

8. Augusta *Chronicle*, Nov. 9, 1805.

9. JPW to Simms, Apr. 4, 1855; Augusta *Chronicle*, Jan. 3, 1807.

10. Augusta *Chronicle*, Aug. 2, 1806. *Historical Collections of the Georgia Chapters DAR*, "Richmond County," ed. Mrs. G. G. Davidson (Athens, 1929), II, 29; this will shows that Mary Pasley did not remain long in Baltimore after her marriage.

11. Augusta *Chronicle*, Oct. 3, 1807.

12. Augusta *Chronicle*, Apr. 9, 1808; Jones, *Life*, p. 5.

13. JPW to Miller, Nov. 12, 1851. For information on the theatrical venture see Berry Fleming, *199 Years of Augusta's Library* (Athens, 1949), pp. 8-10; C. C. Jones and Salem Dutcher, *Memorial History of Augusta, Georgia* (Syracuse, New York, 1890), p. 291; *Acts of the General Assembly of Georgia*, 1808, 48.

14. Augusta *Chronicle*, Mar. 5, 1808, and Feb. 19, 1809.

15. JPW to Miller, Nov. 12, 1851; E. A. and G. L. Duyckinck, *Cyclopaedia of American Literature* (New York, 1855), II, 106.

16. Augusta *Chronicle*, Sept. 9, 1809. For a while the office of the Augusta *Chronicle* was between "Mr. Nesbit's new brick building and Messrs. Hutchinson & Wilde's Law Office," according to the Augusta *Chronicle*, Dec. 8, 1810.

17. Augusta *Chronicle*, Nov. 15, 1811. The dates can be proved by reference to almanacs of the period. See Miller, *Bench and Bar*, II, 369-379, and notice that when he gives the solicitor-generals for the middle circuit, he uses the term "attorney-generals." See J. E. Ward to Henry Clinch, Jan. 13, 1855, with reference to *Senate Journal* (of Georgia) for Nov. 9, 1811. Augusta *Chronicle*, Mar. 19, 1813. A manuscript document signed "R H Wilde, Attorney General, April Term, 1812," at the University of Georgia, deals with the State of Georgia against Jonathan Kittell, the latter being accused of "corrupt . . . Prying."

18. Augusta *Chronicle*, Feb. 26, 1817.

19. Miller, *Bench and Bar*, II, 366; *A Compilation of the Laws of the State of Georgia Passed by the Legislature, 1810-1819*, Lucius Q. C. Lamar, ed. (Augusta, 1821), pp. 554-563.

20. Augusta *Chronicle*, Dec. 2, 1814; Jones, *Life*, p. 7; a newspaper advertisement of the work is in Augusta *Chronicle*, Aug. 19, 1814.

21. RHW to ?, Nov. 24, 1814; Canto I, Stanza XCVII.

22. JPW to Simms, Mar. 20, 1855; a poem beginning "Beneath thy friendly roof dear Few."

23. *Arguments on the Unconstitutionality of the Alleviating Act*, pp. iv-v.

24. Augusta *Chronicle*, June 14, 1816. An advertisement describing vacancies, signed by RHW in Augusta *Chronicle*, Nov. 8, 1817; a letter signed "cashier" is RHW to A. W. McGill, Jan. 8, 1818.

25. Augusta *Chronicle*, Jan. 5, 1816, and Nov. 25, 1814.

26. *Letters from Alabama* (Washington, 1830), p. 187.

27. RHW to Dr. Alex Cunningham, Apr. 1, 1816; RHW to President and Board of Directors of Bank of U. S. in Augusta, May 18, 1818; Augusta *Chronicle*, Aug. 13, 1823; RHW to Verplanck, Dec. 16, 1833.

28. Augusta *Chronicle*, Sept. 15, 1810. The "Master Bernard Wilde," who died at the age of twelve, according to Augusta *Herald*, Sept. 16, 1817, was probably Michael's son.

29. The bill involved was entitled "An Act to Authorize the Settlement of the Account of James Wilde." See *Annals of Congress, Register*

of Debates, and *House Journal* for the following dates: Dec. 2, Dec. 11, and Dec. 30 in 1818; Jan. 13, 1823. See letters from R. R. Reid to RHW, Apr. 22, 1822; Jan. 21 and Feb. 26, 1823.

30. Obituaries, Augusta *Chronicle,* July 28 and Aug. 17, 1815. The latter incorrectly spells her father's name of Newitt as "Nesbitt."

31. RHW to JWW, Apr. 26, 1816.

32. The epistles begin "Beneath thy friendly roof dear Few" and "Dear George, tho' no more in the morn of our youth."

33. A poem beginning "Beneath thy friendly roof dear Few"; RHW to Mrs. Rebecca T. Somerville, Jan. 31, 1842.

34. Wilde's letters owned by Mrs. Crockett are full of references to members of the Weyman family of New York City. Wilde was always on friendly terms with the family and frequently stayed at 35 Howard Street, the Weyman home, while in the city. His children corresponded with and visited their cousins. City directories of New York for 1841-1845 give the addresses of the Weyman family. See also the following sources for references to marriages in the family: Walter Barrett, *Scoville's Old Merchants of New York City* (New York, 1885), III, 74-75; New York *Evening Post* for Feb. 28 and Oct. 25 of 1826 and July 3, 1833.

35. The record of the marriage is at Christ Church Episcopal, New York City. There is some confusion of initials for Buckle. Christ Church has him listed as William B. Buckle; the New York *Weekly Museum* of Mar. 27, 1802, which reported the marriage, lists him as William J. Buckle; the Augusta *Chronicle* for Oct. 22, 1808, and July 22, 1809, gives John W. Buckle (the only references to anyone named Buckle in Augusta). I am convinced that William B. Buckle, William J. Buckle, and John W. Buckle are the same man.

36. Augusta *Chronicle,* Oct. 2, 1812, and Dec. 6, 1816.

37. RHW to JWW, Apr. 19, 1816; Augusta *Chronicle,* Nov. 11, 1818.

38. The license bond reads as follows: "GEORGIA, Richmond County. Know all men by These Presents, That we R. H. Wilde & A. Cunningham are held and firmly bound unto the Court of Ordinary of Richmond County, in the sum of Eight Hundred Fifty Seven Dollars and Fourteen Cents, to which payment well and truly to be made we bind ourselves, our heirs, executors and administrators, jointly and severally, firmly by these presents, sealed with our seals and dated this Sixth day of February A. D. 1819. The condition of the above Obligation is such, That Whereas there is a Marriage intended to be Solemnized between the above named R. H. Wilde and C. J. Buckle—now if there be no lawful cause to obstruct the same, then this obligation to be void, else to remain in full force and virtue. Signed, Sealed and acknowledged, in the Presence of Isaac Herbert Clerk, C. O. R. H. Wilde (Seal) A. Cunningham (Seal)."

The record of the marriage is in St. Patrick's Catholic Church, Augusta.

39. The birth record of the oldest child and the baptismal records of all three children are in St. Paul's Episcopal Church, Augusta. The parents then were married in a Catholic ceremony and the children were baptized in an Episcopal Church. Throughout the biography of RHW and his descendants, there is the mingling of these two creeds. A son of RHW wrote to C. C. Jones, Oct. 9, 1885, that he wanted his father, though a Catholic, to be buried at "St. Paul's—and a simple tablet be placed in the church which he always attended."

Augusta *Chronicle,* June 13 and June 24, 1822.

40. Lawton Evans, "Historic Spots in Georgia," *Georgia Historical Quarterly,* I (Mar., 1917), 138.

41. Wilde wrote on June 6, 1835, a poem to his son, beginning "This is your birthday, Will."

William Cumming, for whom the town of Cumming, Georgia, was named, was the eldest son of the first intendant of Augusta, Thomas Cumming. After resigning from the army, he later on declined the commission of brigadier general offered by President Andrew Jackson and the commission of major general offered by President James Polk. See L. L. Knight, *Georgia Landmarks, Memorials and Legends* (Atlanta, 1913), II, 29, 317.

42. John Patterson (1783-1851) lived for most of his life at his country residence "Atamasco" in Maryland. There were many Pattersons living in Augusta, and John Patterson inherited some land there. There was a long controversy about his attempt to obtain the land, and Richard Henry Wilde was one of the lawyers he employed. As a result, the two men became good friends.

43. Augusta *Chronicle*, Jan. 27, 1827.

44. "Closed are the labours of the day," dated June 5, 1828. RHW to Berrien, Feb. 1827 (?); RHW to John Patterson, May 22. 1827.

45. The record of the marriage is at St. Paul's Church. RHW to JWW, May 4 and May 23, 1831; RHW to JWW, Dec. 6, 1832; Augusta *Chronicle*, Nov. 30, 1839.

46. Inscription on Mary's tomb as given in M. L. Reese, *Cemetery Records, mainly from Richmond County, Georgia* (Augusta, 1948,) I, 70-71. *DAR Yearbook* (1932), "Bible Records"; for a while Dr. Anthony (1805-1854), the son of Sarah Menzies and Anselm Anthony, lived at Raytown (Taliaferro County), Georgia. Dr. Anthony was a cousin of Dr. Milton Anthony, founder of the Medical College of Georgia. The name is also spelled *Antony*.

47. For detailed information on John Walker Wilde, see Edward L. Tucker, "John Walker Wilde," *Georgia Historical Quarterly*, XLV (June, 1961), 120-127.

48. Augusta *Chronicle*, July 12, 1821; RHW to JWW, June 4, 1827.

49. Augusta *Constitutionalist*, Jan. 3, 1826.

50. Jones, *Life of RHW*, p. 5. Charles C. Jones, Jr. (1831-1893), a native of Savannah, settled in Augusta. Since he was sixteen at the time of RHW's death, he probably saw the poet and heard direct reports of him.

Berrien to RHW, Dec. 10, 1826; RHW to JWW, Aug. 30, 1827; RHW to CAW and Ann Wilde, Dec. 1, 1828; RHW to JWW, Apr. 6, 1832; RHW to JWW, Sept. 25, 1832.

51. RHW to JWW, May 23, 1831; RHW to JWW, Aug. 21, 1832; RHW to CAW and Ann Wilde, Dec. 1, 1828; RHW to JWW, Aug. 25, 1830.

52. Augusta *Chronicle*, Apr. 18, 1822; Lamar, *Trustees of Richmond Academy*, p. 3; Augusta *Chronicle*, Oct. 26, 1833.

53. Augusta *Chronicle*, Dec. 6, 1821; Milledgeville *Georgia Journal*, Dec. 13, 1821; Jones and Dutcher, *Memorial History*, p. 238; Augusta *Chronicle*, Apr. 1, 1822. R. Reid wrote to RHW on Apr. 22, 1822, saying he regretted the recent change in the mayoralty.

54. Miller, *Bench and Bar*, II, 296, 317.

55. *Biographical Directory of the American Congress, 1774-1927* (Washington, 1928).

56. James Barnett Adair, ed. (Los Angeles, 1924), pp. 75-87. Athens, Georgia, *Southern Banner*, June 29, 1833.

57. RHW to JWW, Aug. 2, 1827.

58. RHW to Berrien, May 22, 1827. RHW to JWW, Apr. 20, 1829; RHW to JWW, July 20, 1827; RHW to JWW, Nov. 17, 1828.

59. RHW to JWW, Nov. 17, 1828; RHW to JWW, Apr. 20, 1829. The interesting controversy about the slaves, which was listed in the *Register of Debates in Congress* for 1828 as "The Case of Richard H. Wilde," forms the background of some letters from RHW to Berrien for 1825 and 1827.

60. RHW to JWW, c. July 19, 1829; RHW to JWW, Aug. 6, 1829.

61. RHW to JWW, Jan. 17, 1829; RHW to JWW, c. July 19, 1829; RHW to JWW, Aug. 18, 1829; RHW to JWW, Oct. 29, 1835; Ellen White to RHW, Feb. 6, 1841.

In three places authors have linked the names of Ellen Adair White and RHW together, in each case in connection with his most famous poem beginning "My Life is like the Summer Rose." E. C. Stedman in the Stedman-Hutchinson *Library of American Literature*, V, 1841: "Stanzas—Inscribed to Ellen Adair—Mrs. White-Beatty—Daughter of Gen. John Adair of Kentucky"; Louise Manly, *Southern Literature* (Richmond, 1895), p. 179: "The verses were inspired by Mrs. White-Beatty, daughter of Gen. John Adair, of Ky., the beautiful 'Florida White' of 'Casa Bianca' "; Caroline Mays Brevard, *A History of Florida* (Deland, 1924), p. 197: "It was Colonel White's beautiful wife, known outside the territory as Mrs. Florida White, who inspired Richard Henry Wilde's well known lyric."

Hesperia is dedicated to a fictitious Marchesa Manfredina di Cosenza. Aubrey H. Starke, "The Dedication of Richard Henry Wilde's *Hesperia*," *American Book Collector*, VI (May and June, 1935), 204-209, has shown that the Marchesa was Ellen Adair White. This article contains much detailed information about Mrs. White-Beatty. For instance, the Whites returned to America before RHW did; on Oct. 1, 1839, they arrived in St. Louis, Missouri, where Colonel White died on Oct. 19, 1839. She returned to Florida and married Dr. Theophilus Beatty, a physician of New Orleans. Of this marriage, RHW wrote to JWW on Feb. 25, 1842: "I fear she has not done well, but according to my maxim you know that is the business of the parties concerned." After the death of Dr. Beatty, she helped in various projects such as substantially aiding a Presbyterian Church in Washington; she spent her last years with relatives and finally died Nov. 22, 1884, at Oxford, Mississippi.

62. RHW to JWW, Oct. 23, 1841; RHW to JWW, Sept. 14, 1828; RHW to JWW, June 15, 1831; RHW to JWW, May 23, 1831.

63. RHW to JWW, Aug. 15, 1831.

64. For a detailed account of this duel, see Joseph B. Cumming, "The Cumming-McDuffie Duels," *Georgia Historical Quarterly*, XLIV (Mar., 1960), 1-23; Edward Tucker, "The Cumming-McDuffie Duel and Richard Henry Wilde," *Georgia Review*, XIII (Winter, 1959), 409-417. See *Recollections of the Life of John Binns* (Philadelphia, 1854).

CHAPTER III

1. RHW to John Forsyth, Dec. 12, 1833; RHW to JWW, Oct. 26, 1828.

2. Augusta *Chronicle*, Nov. 19 and 26, 1813.

3. Augusta *Chronicle*, Aug. 19, 1814.

The returns, often incomplete, used for the different elections come from the following Georgia newspapers:

Fourteenth Congress, Milledgeville *Georgia Journal*, Oct. 12, 1814; Fifteenth Congress, *Georgia Journal*, Oct. 23, 1816; Sixteenth Congress, Augusta *Chronicle*, Oct. 24, 1818; Eighteenth Congress vacancy, *Georgia Journal*, Dec. 21, 1824; Twentieth Congress vacancy, *Georgia Journal*, Oct. 22, 1827; Twenty-first Congress, *Georgia Journal*, Oct. 27, 1828; Twenty-second Congress, *Georgia Journal*, Oct. 23, 1830; Twenty-third Congress, *Georgia Journal*, Oct. 25, 1832; Twenty-fourth Congress, *Georgia Journal*, Oct. 29, 1834.

4. *Register of Debates*, Twenty-second Congress, first session, VIII (part III), 3495; *Annals of Congress*, Fourteenth Congress, second session, p. 598. Most speeches are in the third person.

5. *Register of Debates*, Twenty-second Congress, first session, VIII (part III), 3495-3496. Rufus Griswold in *The Prose Writers of America* (Philadelphia, 1847), p. 262, published RHW's descriptions of the six men under the title "Stars of the XIVth Congress."

6. *Register of Debates*, Twenty-third Congress, first session, X (part III), 3042.

7. *Hesperia*, Canto II, Stanza XLIV. Benjamin Watkins Leigh (1781-1849) was a senator from Virginia; Littleton Waller Tazewell (1774-1860) was also a senator from Virginia.

8. *Ibid.*, Canto IV, Stanza LXXI.

9. RHW to Mary Pasley, Mar. 27, 1816.

10. *Annals of Congress*, Fourteenth Congress, first session, pp. 623-631.

11. *Ibid.*, pp. 376, 1063-1064. The members of the various Congressional committees can be easily found in the first few entries for each session of Congress, as given in *Annals of Congress, Register of Debates in the Congress of the United States*, and the *House Journal*, printed by Duff Green and Gales and Seaton.

12. A letter to the Milledgeville *Georgia Journal* of Aug. 14, 1816, wished to know: "Why did not our representatives speak on the subject? Why did they take the money?" Augusta *Chronicle*, Aug. 30, 1816.

13. Augusta *Chronicle*, Nov. 27, 1824.

14. The *Biographical Directory of the American Congress* (1928) is in error when it states that RHW was a candidate for these two Congresses. See the candidates as given in the *Georgia Journal*, Oct. 12, 1824, and the Augusta *Chronicle*, Sept. 30, 1826. Augusta *Constitutionalist*, Sept. 25, 1827.

15. Augusta *Constitutionalist*, Apr. 20 and June 4, 1830; *Register of Debates*, Twentieth Congress, second session, V, 117. RHW was interested in squash (Josiah Meigs to RHW, Oct. 11, 1819), peach orchards, cherry trees, and Guinea grass (RHW to JWW, Oct. 4, 1829).

16. Horace Binney to WCW, June 11, 1852.

17. RHW to Gulian C. Verplanck, Nov. 21, 1833. The other men are the following: Richard M. Johnson (1781-1850) of Kentucky, who became Vice-President of the United States (1837-1841); James M. Wayne (1790-1867) of Georgia; Andrew Stevenson (1836-1841) of Virginia; Joel B. Sutherland (1792-1861) of Pennsylvania.

18. Verplanck (1786-1870) of New York became one of Wilde's closest literary friends; thirteen letters from RHW to Verplanck, now at the New York Historical Society, consitute some of the poet's most interesting correspondence. RHW to JWW, July 2, 1832.

19. See the lists for the different tickets in the Milledgeville *Georgia Journal*, Sept. 27, 1832.

20. Hayne to C. C. Jones, Sept. 29, 1885; Augusta *Chronicle*, Sept. 3, 1842.

21. *Register of Debates*, Twenty-first Congress, first session, VI (part II), 1079-1103.

22. Augusta *Chronicle*, July 7, 1832, as reprinted from the New York *American*.

23. RHW to Griswold, Mar. 7, 1845. RHW to JWW, July 22, 1832: "I send you a corrected copy of the speech upon which my hope of a statesman's muddy immortality must rest." *Narrative of a Tour in North America* (London, 1834), II, 447-448.

24. RHW to JWW, Aug. 21, 1832.

25. Augusta *Chronicle*, Sept. 16, 1833.

26. *Register of Debates*, Twenty-third Congress, first session, X (part IV), 4370-4373. The Milledgeville *Georgia Journal*, Mar. 31, 1835, reprinted the following news item from the Richmond *Whig*: " 'Anti-White and Anti-Van' in the Virginia Herald, nominates Richard Henry Wilde of Georgia for President and John Davis of Mass. for Vice-president. They are excellent men, but want the indispensable quality in a Whig candidacy for the Presidency—a capacity for being elected."

27. RHW to Editor of the New Yark *Star*, June 1, 1835; Augusta *Chronicle*, Mar. 28. 1829.

28. Augusta *Constitutionalist*, Mar. 15, 1833. The writer of this editorial said he could not believe that Wilde was "guilty of the duplicity insinuated in the remarks" made in the Washington *Globe*.

29. John Forsyth to RHW, Dec. 10 and Dec. 14, 1833; RHW to Forsyth, Dec. 12, 1833.

30. Augusta *Constitutionalist*, Dec. 17, 1833.

31. RHW to State Rights Committee, Jan. 27, 1834.

32. The two tickets are listed in the Augusta *Chronicle*, July 26, 1834.

33. RHW to Edward Everett, Oct. 17, 1834.

34. Milledgeville *Georgia Journal*, Dec. 30, 1834, as reprinted from the Boston *Atlas*.

35. RHW to a committee of fifty-six citizens, Nov. 11, 1834.

36. RHW to David Blackshear, Feb. 20, 1825; RHW to JWW, Feb. 7, 1830.

37. RHW to JWW, Apr. 26, 1831.

38. RHW to JWW, Dec. 2, 1844; RHW to Alex Cunningham, Dec. 15, 1815.

39. Jackson to Joel R. Poinsett, Jan. 24, 1833. Jackson to Van Buren, Jan. 25, 1833: "Mr. Wild of Georgia night before last, threw a firebrand into the House which will defeat the passage of the Tarriff—it is said by many that it was done with this view. [H]e is *wielded by Calhoun*. Last night the ire raged, it is said, beyond every thing ever heard before." These two letters are in J. S. Bassett, ed., *Correspondence of Andrew Jackson*, V, 12-13.

40. RHW to JWW, Sept. 22, 1841.

41. Canto IV, Stanza LXX.

42. Augusta *Chronicle*, June 13, 1835.

43. RHW to JWW for the following dates: Sept 22, 1841; Sept. 12, 1835; Nov. 18, 1835.

CHAPTER IV

1. RHW to JWW for Dec. 18 and July, 1836, and Oct. 7, 1835.

2. JWW to RHW, Aug. 25, 1835; RHW to John Patterson, May 22, 1827; RHW to JWW, Apr. 6, 1832; RHW to Verplanck, May 1, 1834.

3. RHW to JWW, Apr. 6, 1832; RHW to a State Rights Committee, Jan. 27, 1834; RHW to JWW, July, 1836.

4. Augusta *Chronicle*, Nov. 21, 1821, reprinted in *Southern Literary Messenger*, December, 1834. The poems by Zappi are dated Oct. 11, 1829, and Mar. 30, 1830; those by Francesco da Lemene, Apr. 1, 1830, Mar. 27, 1833, and Aug. 29, 1834. RHW to JWW, June 15, 1831.

5. RHW to Verplanck, May 15, 1835; RHW to Ann Wilde, May 29, 1835; RHW to JWW, June 2 and June 25, 1835.

6. RHW to JWW for the following in 1835: June 27, June 29, July 10, July 15, July 25.

7. RHW to JWW, Sept. 17, 1835; RHW to CAW, Aug. 12, 1835.

8. RHW to JWW. Sept. 25, 1835.

9. Greenough to RHW, c. Nov. 1835; RHW to JWW, Dec. 3, 1835; Greenough to RHW, c. Sept. 1840.

10. RHW to JWW, Nov. 18, 1835, and Aug. 11, 1837.

11. RHW to JWW, Mar. 24, 1839; RHW to Greene for the following: Apr. 18, 1838; Nov. 4, 1837; Sept. 9, 1836.

12. RHW to JWW, July 13 and Nov. 18, 1838; JWW to RHW, Feb. 2, 1839.

13. RHW to JWW, Nov. 25, 1835; RHW to CAW, Sept. 9, 1836.

14. In 1934 and 1935 Aubrey H. Starke was working on an article entitled "The Dedication of Wilde's *Hesperia*," in which he centered his attention on Mrs. White-Beatty. He had access to a letter from Mrs. Kate Adair Hine of Athens, Alabama, a relative of Mrs. White-Beatty; it contained a letter written May 16, 1838, from Paris, by a niece of Mrs. White, which stated that Wilde was about "to be married to a lady, young, rich and titled, I forget the name, in Florence, where he is." Colonel and Mrs. White, together with their niece, saw Wilde when all of them were in Paris in 1838. Nowhere else does RHW (or anyone else) mention such an engagement.

RHW does mention Mary Bartolommei in the following letters to Powers: Mar. 15, 1846; Sept. 26, 1846. The Biblioteca Nazionale Centrale of Florence in a letter of Feb. 11, 1957, sent me the following information: she was Mary Robbins before her marriage and was of an English background. Born July 11, 1806, the daughter of Thomas Robbins and the granddaughter of Ralph Robbins, she, on Feb. 19, 1824, secretly married the Marquis Lorenzo Bartolommei of Florence, who had been born May 27, 1802; by the marriage she became a marchesa. Her husband died on July 1, 1836, about a year after RHW left for Europe. While RHW was in Florence in 1838, she was thirty-two and he was forty-nine. If she is the titled lady mentioned by the niece, RHW never married her. The Marchesa Mary Bartolommei died July 9, 1869, and left as her heir her brother, the Rev. George Robbins. The latter, educated at Oxford, took orders in the Anglican Church, served congregations at Pisa, the Baths of Lucca, Florence, and finally at Courteenhall in Northamptonshire, England. He is buried in Florence. See Catherine D. Tassinari, *History of the English Church in Florence* (Florence and London, 1905), p. 198.

15. All the information on Nouvel comes from Nathalia Wright, "The Italian Son of Richard Henry Wilde," *Georgia Historical Quarterly*, XLIII (Dec., 1959), 419-427. My attempts to prove that this son was not Wilde's have been unsuccessful. Powers endorsed two of the six letters: "Wilde's son." I have been unable to find another Wilde who could have been the father. Hamilton Wilde, an artist living in Florence, who knew Powers and who painted a famous portrait of the child of Elizabeth and Robert Browning, did not die until 1884.

16. RHW to JPW, Feb. 17, 1844.

17. RHW to Greene for Aug. 20 and Feb. 24, 1838; RHW to JWW, May 28 and Sept. 24 of 1836, and Dec. 31 of 1835.

18. RHW to JWW, Sept. 23, 1836; RHW to CAW and boys, Nov. 4, 1836; RHW to JWW, Oct. 2, 1835; RHW to JWW, Nov. 5, 1835; RHW to a friend in Washington, Feb. 26, 1836.
The poem begins "Such was the Man!—Simple!—Austere—sublime." RHW also has the phrase "Greenough's fame" in a description of Massachusetts in *Hesperia*, Canto III, Stanza CIII.

19. RHW to Greene, Dec. 14, 1837; RHW to Sumner, Nov. 24, 1839; Canto IV, Stanza XCVIII (the note is on p. 328).

20. RHW to Greene, Nov. 26, 1839. Pierce, *Memoir of Sumner*, I, 142. WCW to Sumner, May 11, 1852.
RHW to Sumner, Sept. 15, 1839: "Enquiries to be made by Mr. Sumner for R. H. Wilde. In Ferrara & Padua. To ask what has become of the Library & especially the MSS that belonged to *Aqostero Faustini*, the Historian of Ferrara? If they have passed into any Public or private library, I should like to know which and where? . . . In Venice. Besides enquiring as before for the MSS of the Discorso, I wish to know if the MSS of Lionardo Aretino the Florentine historian are still preserved in Venice?"

21. Everett to WCW, June 3, 1852.

22. The *Frances Appleton Journal* is in the Longfellow House, Cambridge, Massachusetts (also known as Craigie House). See Volume I, pp. 72, 168, 173, 179, 181, 106, 135; and Volume II, pp. 8, 49. In 1843 Frances Appleton married Longfellow. On October 2, 1845, Wilde visited Mr. and Mrs. Longfellow at the Craigie House. Longfellow made the following entry in his journal: "Thursday 2—Wilde from New Orleans called, with his floating white locks. Says he has entirely given up poetry, and all literature save that of law. . . ."

23. RHW first mentioned the MSS. in a letter to JWW, Jan. 26, 1836. RHW to JWW, Apr. 2, 1836; RHW to CAW, Apr. 13, 1836.

24. *F.A. Journal*, I, 135.

25. RHW to J. K. Paulding, Apr. 20, 1836, pub. in *Knickerbocker*, VIII (Oct., 1836), 447-454; RHW to his sons, Jan. 21, 1837; RHW to Greene, Sept. 9, 1836; RHW to JWW, June 17, 1837.

26. Greene to RHW, May 31, 1838; RHW to John Murray, Nov. 22, 1837; RHW to JWW, Jan. 29, 1840; Cogswell to RHW, Apr. 20, 1841; Sidney Brooks to RHW, July 29, 1841; RHW to Powers, Sept. 22, 1841.

27. RHW to JWW, Oct. 23 and Nov. 20, 1841.

28. *Life and Times of Dante*, "The Author to the Reader," p. ii.

29. *North American Review*, LIV (April, 1842), 501-504; *Graham's Magazine* (Mar., 1843), p. 203. Browning's review, called "Tasso and Chatterton" and later reprinted as *Essay on Chatterton*, first appeared in *Foreign Quarterly Review*, XXIX (July, 1842), 466-467. The reviewer in the *Orion* of May, 1842, stated that this work was the first impartial and complete biography of Tasso. He further added: "The minute investigation, the careful, circumstantial scrutiny which, in these volumes, are brought to bear upon the subject, are worthy of all praise, and exhibit astonishing industry and patience, in connection with powers of analysis and elucidation which we are sure no common mind could have exercised."

30. RHW to JWW, Aug. 11, 1837.

31. These descriptive passages of Wilde's literary activities are taken from the preface to the unfinished *Life and Times of Dante*. See also RHW to William Mann, Mar. 31, 1840.

32. RHW to JWW, Jan. 29, 1840.

33. RHW to Powers, Aug. 11, 1842; Pierce, II, 174.
Southern and Western Monthly Magazine (also called *Simms' Monthly*), (August, 1845), p. 144: "We are pleased to learn that the Life of Dante by Richard Henry Wilde, of New-Orleans, is in rapid preparation for the press. Mr. Wilde has had this work in hands for a considerable length of time. He has bestowed the utmost pains upon it, as well in regard to the acquisition and analysis of his material, as in the careful finish of his style. We have had the pleasure of hearing portions of the work read, by the accomplished writer himself, and we feel quite safe in making these assurances. Mr. Wilde has enjoyed many advantages for the preparation of this biography—has spent several years in Italy, is a master of the language, and has been an industrious explorer among its ancient records. . . ." Simms dedicated a novel *Castle Dismal* (New York, 1844) to Wilde. Wilde also knew well two other Southern novelists—John Pendleton Kennedy and William Alexander Caruthers.

34. RHW to Sumner, Aug. 4, 1841; RHW to Powers, Aug. 11, 1842; Simms to E. A. Duyckinck, Dec. 12, 1845, in Simms' *Letters*, II, 123; RHW to Griswold, Feb. 6, 1843.

35. Augusta *Chronicle*, Feb. 25, 1836. When the Library of Congress did not buy the collection, RHW wrote to the governors of various states, trying to encourage some one to purchase it; see RHW to Governor of Georgia, Oct. 23, 1836. For a background see David C. Mearns, "The Story Up to Now," *Annual Report of the Librarian of Congress, June 30, 1946* (Washington, 1947), pp. 55-61. According to Mearns, when these books and MSS. which had belonged to the late Graf Dimitrii Petrovich Buturlin, who died in Florence, Nov. 7, 1829, were declined, "a singular opportunity was lost, an opportunity which might have advanced incalculably the intellectual resources of the Nation."

36. Sources used for discussion of the portrait of Dante are as follows: Irving, "American Researches in Italy; Life of Tasso, Recovery of a Lost Portrait of Dante," *Knickerbocker*, XVIII (Oct., 1841), 319-322; an article by Bezzi, London *Athenaeum* (Feb. 5, 1848), p. 146; letter by Kirkup, *Spectator*, XXIII (May 11, 1850), 452; letter by Bezzi, *Spectator*, XXIII (May 25, 1850), 493-494; R. T. Holbrook, *Portraits of Dante from Giotto to Raphael* (New York, 1911), pp. 73-150; RHW to Powers, Aug. 11, 1842.

Suggestions have been made that the work is not by Giotto but by the "School of Giotto." See A. Wherry, *Stories of the Tuscan Artists* (London, 1910), p. 32; New York *Times Book Section*, Feb. 13, 1921. The articles on Dante in *Enciclopedia Italiana Di Scienze, Lettere, ed Arti* (1950) and *Encyclopaedia Britannica* (1956) say that Giotto is the artist.

37. RHW to JWW, Jan. 29, 1840; Nathalia Wright, "Richard Henry Wilde's Italian Order of Nobility," *Georgia Historical Quarterly*, XLIII (June, 1959), 211-213, based on a letter, WCW to Powers, undated; letter to me from Mrs. Virginia Crockett, Feb. 5, 1958.

38. *Hesperia*, Canto IV, Stanza XII; Canto I, Stanza VII; Canto IV, Stanza XXIX. RHW to Powers for the following: Jan. 23 and Sept. 22, 1841; Aug. 10, 1845; Mar. 27, 1847. The word for *money* is generally spelled *quattrini*.

CHAPTER V

1. RHW to JWW, Feb. 2, 1836.

2. The first line of the poem published in the *Orion* of January, 1843,

is "Farewell, fair Florence! Not, I hope, forever"; RHW to Powers, Jan. 23, 1841; Greene to RHW, July 26, 1841; Columbus *Enquirer*, Feb. 3, 1841.

3. RHW to Emily Wilde, Feb. 3, 1841; Irving put his praise into an article entitled "American Researches in Italy; Life of Tasso; Recovery of a Lost Portrait of Dante," *Knickerbocker* (Oct., 1841), XVIII, 319-322; the poems appeared in Augusta *Chronicle*, Mar. 4, 1841, and Columbus *Enquirer*, Apr. 14, 1841, the latter being reprinted from the Milledgeville *Recorder*.

4. RHW to Powers, Jan. 23 and Mar. 11, 1841; Ellen White to RHW, Feb. 6, 1841.

5. RHW to Powers, Mar. 11, 1841, and Aug. 11, 1842.

6. RHW to Powers, Aug. 11, 1842; RHW to JPW, Oct. 8, 1842; RHW to Mary Pleasants, June 10, 1843.

7. Records at Georgetown University dated Aug. 31, 1841, and Feb. 28, 1842.

8. RHW to JPW, Aug. 8, 1842.

9. RHW to JPW, Oct. 8, 1842.

10. Records at Georgetown. RHW to John Nicholson, May 5, 1843.

11. Sumner to RHW, July 28, 1841; RHW to Sumner, Aug. 4, 1841; RHW to Powers, Aug. 11, 1842; RHW to Griswold, Feb. 6, 1843; James L. Petigru to RHW, Dec. 20, 1843.

12. RHW to JWW, Nov. 20, 1841.

13. RHW to Emily Wilde, May 25, 1841.

14. RHW to Powers, Aug. 11, 1842; Augusta *Chronicle*, June 16, 1842.

15. Milledgeville *Southern Recorder*, June 21, 1842.

16. RHW to Powers, Aug. 11, 1842; *Southern Recorder*, June 21, 1842.

17. Augusta *Chronicle*, Sept. 3, 1842.

18. Milledgeville *Southern Recorder*, Aug. 16, 1842.

19. The complete returns are in the Milledgeville *Federal Union*, Oct. 25, 1842; Wilde came in twelfth in a total of sixteen candidates. Augusta *Chronicle*, Dec. 31, 1842, and Oct. 24, 1843.

CHAPTER VI

1. An important article is Aubrey H. Starke, "Richard Henry Wilde in New Orleans and the Establishment of the University of Louisiana," *Louisiana Historical Quarterly*, XVII (October, 1934), 605-624. RHW to JPW, c. Feb., 1844; RHW to CAW, Apr. 7, 1844; RHW to Mary Parmelee, Mar. 21, 1847.

2. RHW to Griswold, Feb. 6, 1843; RHW to JWW, Mar. 26, 1843.

3. RHW to JWW, Feb. 24, 1843; RHW to CAW, Mar. 7, 1843; RHW to JWW, Mar. 12, 1843; RHW to JWW, Mar. 22, 1843; RHW to Franklin Society of Augusta, Aug. 19, 1843.

4. MH (Maria Hopkins?) to RHW, May 31, 1835; RHW to JWW, Jan. 20, 1844.

5. Augusta *Chronicle*, Nov. 27, 1843, lists the slaves; J. H. Hammond to RHW, Dec. 17, 1843; RHW to JWW, Jan. 18, 1844.

6. RHW to JWW, Jan. 20, 1844; Micou to Wilde, Oct. 4, 1843.

7. RHW to JPW, Feb. 4 and May 31, 1844; Micou to RHW, Oct. 4, 1843; RHW to JPW, Mar. 17, 1844.

8. RHW to JPW, Apr. 10 and May 26, 1844.

9. RHW to Powers, Aug. 24, 1844; RHW to JPW, Sept. 3, Sept. 9, Aug. 24, and Oct. 24, 1844.

10. RHW to CAW, Aug. 16, 1844; RHW to JPW, Aug. 9, 1844.

11. RHW to JPW, Sept. 3, 1844.

12. RHW to JPW, May 31, 1844; RHW to JWW, Dec. 21, 1845.

13. RHW to JPW, Feb. 17, Aug. 14, and Oct. 4, 1844.

14. RHW to JWW for the following: Dec. 21, 1845; Sept. 20, 1844; June 8, 1845.

15. RHW to JWW, Sept. 20, 1844; RHW to S. R. Plummer, Oct. 20, 1845; RHW to JPW, May 31, 1844; RHW to CAW, Nov. 16, 1844; RHW to JPW, Feb. 17 and Mar. 10, 1844.

16. RHW to JPW, Oct. 24, 1844; RHW to JWW, Dec. 21, 1845.

17. RHW to JWW, Sept. 20, 1844; RHW to JPW, Oct. 4, 1844; RHW to CAW, Jan. 15, 1847; RHW to JWW, Mar. 31, 1846; Miller, *Bench and Bar*, II, 367.

18. RHW to JWW, c. Feb. 1844; RHW to CAW, Nov. 3, 1844; RHW to JPW, Mar. 17, 1844.

19. RHW to JPW, June 9, May 26, Aug. 9, and Feb. 17, 1844; RHW to JWW, June 19 and June, 1845; RHW to Powers, Aug. 10, 1845.

20. RHW to JPW, Feb. 17 and Mar. 3, 1844; RHW to Cara Stanford, Mar. 25 and May 12, 1845.

21. RHW to JPW, Apr. 10, 1844.

22. RHW to S. R. Plummer, Aug. 20, 1845; RHW to Mary Parmelee, Mar. 21, 1847.

23. RHW to CAW, Mar. 7, 1845; RHW to Maria H. Walker, c. Apr., 1846.

24. RHW to JPW, June 12, 1846.

25. RHW to W. A. Mosley, Jan. 8, 1846, and Feb. 6, 1845; RHW to Mary Parmelee, Mar. 31, 1846; RHW to Maria Hopkins Walker, c. Mar., 1846, and c. Apr., 1846.

26. RHW to CAW, Mar. 7, 1845.

27. RHW to JWW, Mar. 2, 1846.

28. RHW to JPW, May 6, 1846.

29. RHW to JPW, Mar. 17, 1844; RHW to Caroline Stanford, Mar. 25, May 12, and Aug. 28, 1845.

30. *A Second Visit to the United States* (London, 1850), II, 98-129. RHW described Lyell in a letter to Powers, Mar. 15, 1846.

31. RHW to Powers, May 3, 1844; RHW to Francis Lieber, 1847; RHW to Maria Hopkins Walker, Apr. 9, 1847.

32. RHW to Powers, Aug. 24, 1844; RHW to JPW, May 4 and Apr. 22, 1844; a committee from New Orleans to Powers, undated; *New Orleans City Guide*, WPA (Federal Works Project), (Boston, 1938), pp. 319-320.

33. RHW to JPW, Oct. 4, 1844; RHW to CAW, Nov. 3, 1844; RHW to JPW, Dec. 24, 1844; RHW to CAW, Mar. 26, 1845; RHW to WCW, Mar. 8, 1845; RHW to JWW, Apr. 12, 1845; RHW to CAW, May 8, 1845; RHW to JWW, Apr. 14, 1845.

34. RHW to JPW, Apr. 27 and May 11, 1844; RHW to JPW, Apr. 14, 1846; RHW to JPW, June 19, 1845; RHW to CAW, Mar. 7 and Aug. 7, 1845.

35. RHW to JPW, Oct. 24, 1844; RHW to WCW, Oct. 10, 1845; RHW to CAW, July 22, 1845; RHW to Powers, Mar. 27, 1847; RHW to JWW, Feb. 14, 1846; RHW to CAW, c. Dec. 15, 1846; RHW to JWW, Apr. 27, 1847.

36. RHW to CAW, Jan., 1847; RHW to JPW, June 12, 1846.

37. RHW to JPW, May 4, 1844; Augusta *Chronicle*, Sept. 30, 1843, as reprinted from the New Orleans *Picayune*, and Augusta *Chronicle*, Oct. 4, 1843, as reprinted from the New Orleans *Tropic*; RHW to JPW, Feb. 4, 1844.

38. RHW to JPW, Apr. 22 and Apr. 27, 1844.

39. RHW to JWW, June 19, 1845; RHW to JPW, June 16, 1844.

40. *The Manhattaner in New Orleans* (New York, 1851), p. 83.

41. For a background of the law school, see Dora J. Bonquois, "The Career of Henry Adams Bullard," *Louisiana Historical Quarterly*, XXIII (Oct., 1940), 999-1106.

42. New Orleans *Delta*, May 17, 1847; the catalogue of Tulane University states that the Law Department was organized on May 4, 1847; Augusta *Chronicle*, Sept. 17, 1847, as reprinted from the New Orleans *Bee;* RHW to Francis Lieber, 1847; RHW to JWW, June 16, 1847.

43. RHW to Lieber, 1847. *The Biographical Directory of the American Congress* (1928) is apparently in error when it states that Wilde was "professor of law in the University of Louisiana at Alexandria"; the Alexandria school—Louisiana State University and Agricultural and Mechanical College—was originally called the Louisiana State Seminary, but it was created under an act of the Louisiana legislature of 1852 and physically established in 1859. Obituary, Augusta *Chronicle*, Sept. 17, 1846, as reprinted from the New Orleans *Bee*: "It was while ardently prosecuting the studies necessary to prepare him for the Course of Lectures to take place in November that this child of genius was stricken down."

44. RHW to JWW, Feb. 14, 1846; RHW to JWW, Jan. 4, 1847; RHW to JPW, Apr. 14, 1846; RHW to JWW, c. Nov. 30, 1846; RHW to CAW, Feb. 21 and Jan. 15, 1847.

45. RHW to CAW, June 3, 1845; RHW to JWW, Aug. 4, 1847.

46. RHW to JWW, Jan. 4, 1847; RHW to CAW, Mar. 18, 1847.

47. RHW to CAW, Jan. 13, 1847; RHW to JWW, Aug. 4, 1847.

48. RHW to JWW, Aug. 4, 1847.

49. RHW to JWW, Aug. 24 and Aug. 4, 1847.

50. RHW to JWW, Sept. 4, 1847; Micou to JWW, Sept. 11, 1847. A year after Wilde's death, Micou named his new-born son Richard Wilde Micou (1848-1912); Micou became the law partner of the famous Judah Philip Benjamin from 1846 until 1856; and in 1853, he was a nominee to fill a vacancy on the Supreme Court, though he was not confirmed. See Louis Gruss, "Judah Philip Benjamin," *Louisiana Historical Quarterly*, XIX (Oct., 1936), 985. Also the Micou genealogy in *The Abridged Compendium of American Genealogy*, ed. Virkus and Marquis (Chicago, 1925), I, 726-727.

51. Athens, Georgia, *Southern Whig*, Sept. 16, 1847, as reprinted from the New Orleans *Delta;* Augusta *Chronicle*, Sept. 11, 1847, as reprinted from the New Orleans *Delta*, Sept. 4, 1847; Augusta *Chronicle*, Sept. 18, 1847, as reprinted from the New Orleans *Delta*, Sept. 12, 1847.

52. See JPW to Powers, Dec. 23, 1848, printed in Nathalia Wright, "The Death of Richard Henry Wilde," *Georgia Historical Quarterly*, XLI (Dec., 1957), 431-434.

53. Augusta *Chronicle*, Sept. 17, 1847, reprinted the obituaries from the New Orleans *Picayune*, Sept. 11, 1847; the New Orleans *Delta*, Sept. 13, 1847; the New Orleans *Bee;* and the New Orleans *National*. In general, Georgia newspapers reprinted one of the New Orleans obituaries and did not write their own. The Augusta *Chronicle*, Sept. 16, 1847, however, did have its own tribute.

Other obituaries were in the following works: *Knickerbocker*, XXX (Oct., 1847), 377; *Southern Literary Messenger*, XIII (Oct., 1847), 637-638; *Archivio Storico Italiano*, VI (Florence, 1848), 454-457.

Three poems in honor of him were the following: John Tomlin, "Lines on the Death of the Hon. Richard Henry Wilde," *Holden's Dollar Magazine* (Mar., 1848), p. 138; A. Oakey Hall, an untitled poem beginning "Th' envenomed whirlwind o'er the city passed," *The Manhattaner in New Orleans*, pp. 85-86; A. B. Meek, "The Death of Richard Henry Wilde," *Southern Literary Messenger*, XIV (Jan., 1848), 26-27.

The Bar of New Orleans held a called meeting on Sept. 18, 1847, and resolutions were passed about the death of the poet. The New Orleans *Picayune*, Sept. 19, 1847, which printed the resolutions, commented: "Had the pestilence which wasteth us cost but the life of this gentleman, it would still be deplorable."

The following is the will of Richard Henry Wilde, filed in both Augusta and New Orleans:

"I, Richard Henry Wilde of the City of Augusta in the State of Georgia, do make and ordain this my last will and Testament, Hereby revoking all wills previously made. I give devise and bequeath all my law Library to my beloved brother John W. Wilde. Having heretofore as far as my ability extended provided for my sisters, and having advanced my step daughter Caroline Jane Buckle afterwards Ringold & now Matthews, at the time of the first Marriage an equal share of my own and her mothers estate:

"I do now give devise and bequeath, the residue of my Estate, Real and personal, Lands, Tenements and Hereditaments Goods and Chattels, and all and every other species of property, Whatsoever the same may be or wheresoever lying, Which I, now have or at my death, & may be possessed of or entitled to including Lands acquired if any after the date of this Will, to my Sons William C. and John P. Wilde, to be equally divided between them share and share alike to them and each of them and their Heirs in fee Simple forever:

"I hereby nominate and appoint my brother John W. Wilde Esqr. and my said sons William C. and John P. Wilde as soon as they respectively shall attain the age of Twenty-one Years, Executors of this my last Will and Testament, Hereby releasing my said Brother from all sums and dues of money heretofore paid by me as Surety or endorsed for him or Torance and Wilde and from all notes Bonds or Mortgages given in account thereof;

"In witness whereof, I have hereunto set my hand and seal this First day of January in the year of our Lord Eighteen hundred and forty-two (Signed) Rd. Hy Wilde

"Signed sealed Published and declared to be his last Will and Testament by Richard H. Wilde in our presence who have attested the same in his presence; and in the presence of each other B. H. Warren H. Bowdre Michl. T. Bosclair."

There are a number of documents on file which show that the sons did not get their inheritance immediately.

The original will has apparently been lost. A copy of it and the documents mentioned above exist in a group of papers entitled "The Succession of Richard Henry Wilde, No. 1132" of the docket of the late Second District Court of New Orleans.

54. These replies to Jones are at Duke University.

55. John M. Graham to Aubrey Starke, Oct. 5, 1933.

CHAPTER VII

1. Much of the information in this chapter is based on letters written to me by Mrs. Emily P. White of Augusta, the granddaughter of Ann Wilde Anthony; by Mrs. Arthur T. Loving of New Orleans, the granddaughter of the sister of Virginia Wilkinson of Augusta; by Mrs. Kathleen Wilde Viscarra of Los Angeles, the great-great-granddaughter of John Walker Wilde; and by Mrs. Virginia Giraud Crockett, the great-granddaughter of Richard Henry Wilde.

2. One letter by CAW still exists—to Mrs. Hiram Powers, June 13, 1852.

3. See minutes of the Georgia Railroad and Banking Company of Augusta and the obituary of John Walker Wilde, San Francisco *Bulletin,* Aug. 4, 1862. He and Emily Wilde had nine children. One son, John Richard, married Ann Whitehead, the daughter of Amos Whitehead and Elizabeth McKinne and as a result became a part of the well-known McKinne family of Augusta. A direct descendant of John Richard and Ann Whitehead Wilde is Mrs. Kathleen Wilde Viscarra of Los Angeles, who has in her possession many important family documents.

4. One daughter, Miss Martha Wilde Pournelle, who for many years was principal of the John S. Davidson School in Augusta, helped in preparing the biographical sketch of Richard Henry Wilde in the *Biographical Directory of the American Congress.*

5. Some business and residential addresses for JPW were 68 Camp, Orange near Camp, and 82 Camp; CAW to Mrs. Powers, June 13, 1852; obituary, New Orleans *Daily Picayune,* Mar. 13, 1861.

6. The obituary for James Wilkinson Wilde is in New Orleans *Daily Picayune,* Apr. 30, 1857.

7. Some business and residential addresses for WCW were 50 Camp, 182 Bienville, Nayades near Josephine, St. Charles near Josephine, 199 Canal, 196 Camp, 384 Constance, and 48 Euterpe.

8. M. W. Mount, *Some Notable Artists of New Orleans* (New Orleans, 1896), p. 26; JPW to William Gilmore Simms, Mar. 20, 1855; WCW to Powers, May 26, 1858; WCW to Sumner, May 11, 1852.

9. M. L. Rutherford, *The South in History and Literature* (Athens, 1906), p. 125.

10. CAW to Mrs. Powers, June 13, 1852; his addresses were 283 Magazine for 1878 and 199 Canal Street for 1880. Bearing the return address of Box 692, New Orleans, one of his manuscripts entitled "A Bit of a Cherub" was received on Sept. 28, 1876, by Roberts Brothers but was rejected. Mount in *Some Notable Artists* refers to him on p. 26.

11. Material on Jenny Wilde can be found in the following sources: *Daily Picayune,* Mar. 6, 1892; T. P. Thompson, *Louisiana Writers and Artists* (New Orleans, 1904), pp. 61, 64; Grace King, *Memories of a Southern Woman of Letters* (New York, 1932), pp. 352-353; Mount, pp. 26-28.

12. Addresses for Emily Wilde were 2220 St. Charles and 158 Howard. The addresses given in these notes came from city directories.

13. Information on the Giraud family has been furnished me by J. I. Giraud of San Antonio, Texas.

PART TWO: SELECTED POEMS

I. INTRODUCTION

1. *Conjectures and Researches,* I, 13; *The Italian Lyric Poets,* I, 216-218; *Hesperia,* Canto I, Stanza X.

2. The quoted passage is from: "Dear George, tho' no more in the morn of our youth." See also "Dear record of departed years." RHW to Ann C. Wilde, July 13, 1836: "I leave Florence with infinite regret. It is now the only spot of Earth I shall long after except one—six feet in length and almost as deep."

[273]

3. The first line of this poem is "Another of my wasted years is gone."

4. RHW to editor of the Augusta *State Rights Sentinel*, Dec. 31, 1834; *Address Delivered November 17, 1898, upon the Presentation to the City of Augusta of the Monument erected by the Hayne Circle to the Memory of Richard Henry Wilde* (Augusta, 1898), p. 15; Augusta *Chronicle*, Sept. 21, 1833, and Sept. 3, 1842.

5. John Forsyth to RHW, Apr. 21, 1819; RHW to John Patterson, May 22, 1827. In a letter to JPW, May 6, 1846, RHW said that JPW's melancholy was not unconquerable: "I know it to be otherwise, having often struggled against & overcome it under circumstances tenfold more dark and desperate than your's."

6. RHW in the "Dedication" to *Hesperia*, p. v, speaks of his "own want of invention". *Conjectures and Researches*, I, 13; I, 59; I, 74; I, 67. *The Italian Lyric Poets*, I, 219.

7. *Address Delivered Nov. 17, 1898*, p. 16; Francis Lieber to Charles Sumner, Dec. 16, 1843.

8. (New Orleans, 1907), XIII, 5791-5792. The criticism of RHW in this series seems much more satisfactory than that of most of the other Southern authors treated.

9. RHW to Griswold, Mar. 7, 1845.

10. RHW to Verplanck, Nov. 15, 1834.

11. RHW to Griswold, Mar. 7, 1845; RHW to a lady in New York, Feb. 14, 1846; RHW to Griswold, Feb. 6, 1843; RHW to Powers, Mar. 15, 1846.

II. "THE LAMENT OF THE CAPTIVE"

1. The material in this section is based mainly on an unpublished article by A. H. Starke entitled "The Date and Text of Richard Henry Wilde's 'Summer Rose.'" Other sources are the following: Anthony Barclay, *Wilde's Summer Rose; or The Lament of the Captive* (Savannah, 1871); and James Wood Davidson, "The Authorship of 'My Life is Like the Summer Rose,'" *Southern Literary Messenger*, XXIII (Oct., 1856), 249-251, reprinted from the Columbia, South Carolina, *Examiner*.

2. New-York *Mirror*, Feb. 28, 1835, reprinted in Barclay, pp. 29-51. Note in Barclay for the Secretary of State: "Mr. Forsyth."

3. Barclay, p. 36. Further information on the expedition is in Volume III, Chapter XVII of Garcilasso de la Vega's *Historia de la Florida;* see also Sidney Lanier's *Florida* (Philadelphia, 1875), pp. 181-182.

4. Davidson, "Authorship," p. 251.

5. Augusta *Chronicle*, Apr. 21, 1819.

6. According to a letter to Dr. R. D. Arnold, published in the Savannah *Georgian*, Dec. 27, 1834 (reprinted in Barclay, pp. 64-69).

7. Davidson, p. 251; Mackenzie to WCW, July 2, 1856 (reprinted in Davidson, p. 250).

8. *New York Weekly Register and Catholic Diary*, II (Aug. 9, 1834), 302 (reprinted in Barclay, pp. 40-42).

9. Barclay, pp. 22-23.

10. *Ibid.*, pp. 24-25, 27.

11. RHW to editor of Augusta *State Rights Sentinel*, Dec. 31, 1834, reprinted in the *Southern Literary Messenger*, I (Jan., 1835), 252; RHW to Barclay, Jan. 7, 1835; Barclay to RHW, Jan. 24, 1835.

12. Basil Hall believed that the Countess Purgstall, the original of Scott's Diana Vernon in *Rob Roy*, was the author. See *Skimmings* (Edinburgh, 1836), Chapter X. An article in the Charleston *Observer* stated an Irishman named La Ruse had written the lines (Davidson, p. 251).

13. The following are musical settings:

Music by Charles Thibault (manuscripts in Library of Congress and New York Public Library). The latter dates it as 1822.

Music by Sidney Lanier (no manuscript available). See A. H. Starke, "Sidney Lanier as Musician," *Musical Quarterly*, XX (Oct., 1934), 388, 398.

Music by Stephen Foster, entitled "None Shall Weep a Tear for Me," consisting of the first two stanzas (copy at Brown University), published 1860.

Music by Fred Buckley (Balmer & Weber, St. Louis, 1857).

Music by Robert Schumann. Adapted to his "The Jolly Farmer" for mixed voices (Volume 7 of *Franklin Square Song Collection*, Harper and Brothers, 1891).

Music by S. Seiler (Oakland, California, 1904).

Music by Alonzo Stone (setting unlocated). See A. H. Starke, "Richard Henry Wilde: Some Notes and a Check-List," *American Book Collector*, V (Jan., 1934), 7-10.

The following are imitations or parodies:

Mrs. Eliza Sloan Buckler, "The Answer of a Lady of Baltimore," beginning "The dews of night may fall from Heaven," Richmond (Virginia) *Enquirer*, Aug. 22, 1823.

Robert Emmett Hooe, "My Life is Like the Shattered Wreck," *Knickerbocker*, XXX (Dec., 1847), 562.

Anonymous, "My life is like a wreath of smoke," Augusta *Chronicle*, Oct. 4, 1841, as copied from the New York *Sunday Mercury*.

"Taurus," "My life is like a sickly pear," Athens, Georgia, *Southern Banner*, July 22, 1842, as copied from the Philadelphia *Inquirer and Gazette*.

Professor Thomas O. Mabbott has long believed that Longfellow's "Psalm of Life" is to some extent an answer (perhaps a *conscious* one) to the poem (letter to Edward L. Tucker, Mar. 18, 1957).

There is a translation by N. C. Brooks beginning "Esta vita similis rosae" in the *Southern Quarterly Review*, II (July, 1842); also there is a translation by Piero Marconcelli in the appendix to his work entitled *My Prisons: Memoirs of Silvio Pellico*. The latter, beginning "Estiva rosa somiglia mia vita," is in Chandler Beall, "Un Tassista Americano di Cent' Anni Fa," *Bergamum*, XVII (June, 1939), 92.

14. *Graham's Magazine* (Dec., 1841). (John G. Palfrey, 1796-1881).

15. Whittier to C. C. Jones, Nov. 10, 1885.

16. *Lectures on the English Language* (New York, 1850); Hayne to Jones, Sept. 29, 1885.

17. Miller, *Bench and Bar of Georgia*, II, 342.

18. The version used appeared in the New York *Mirror*, Feb. 28, 1835.

19. Note in *Mirror*: "Afterwards published anonymously in the Portfolio." III (Feb., 1814), 200.

20. Note in *Mirror*: "The language of this stanza derives some interest from being, almost *verbatim*, the exclamation of that gallant soldier, then lieutenant, and afterward Colonel Appling, at the close of a hard day's march. He also was a partaker in the dangers and hardships of Colonel Williams's expedition."

21. Note in *Mirror*: "The daily or Florida rose, opens, fades, and perishes during the summer in less than twelve hours."

22. Note in *Mirror*: "Not Tempe, as frequently, though most absurdly written and printed; but TAMPA, the Indian name of that bay, called by the Spaniards ESPIRITU SANTO."

III. *Hesperia*

1. O. H. Prince to RHW, Jan. 13, 1827.
2. RHW to JWW, Aug. 17, 1830. Wilde knew both Washington Irving and Fitz-Greene Halleck.
3. Canto II, Stanzas LV-LVII; WCW to Powers, June 21, 1860.
4. Notes, p. 257.
5. RHW to Catherine and Ann Wilde, Dec. 1, 1828.
6. Canto IV, Stanza CXVIII.
7. "The Dedication of Richard Henry Wilde's *Hesperia*," *American Book-Collector*, VI (May and June, 1935), 204-209; Canto I, Stanzas LXXVII-LXXXI; Canto IV, Stanza XC.
8. Greene to RHW, May 28, 1840.
9. RHW's note to this stanza, p. 231: "Civilized men, the inhabitants of countries made classic by a thousand memories, tired of the eternal presence of their kind, and satiated with all common emotions, may long for the wilderness, and suppose savage Nature the true and only source of the sublime. But let them try to embody their feelings and ideas so as to impart pleasure to others; let them attempt to extract poetry from inanimate or irrational objects apart from man, and see how soon monotony produces weariness."
10. These last seven stanzas were rearranged as a poem entitled "The Poet's Lament," the first line being "As evening's dews to sun-parched summer flowers." This poem was published in the *Louisiana Book*, ed. Thomas McCaleb (New Orleans, 1894), p. 492.

IV. *Poems: Fugitive and Occasional.*

1. RHW to Mrs. Benham, March 12, 1844, on the subject of "The Lament of the Captive": "Having long since laid aside the cap & bells of rhyme, not being able any longer to indulge 'small vices,' you may well imagine I value these trifles very differently from my friends, the proof of which is, that I have destroyed hundreds of compositions, which so far as my judgment goes, were much better than the fugitive 'Versicles' that escaped to the Public by accident, and have found as many claimants as 'the child of thirty six fathers.' "
RHW to Ann C. Wilde, July 13, 1836: "I have furnished poor Liverati [the father of the Carlo Liverati who painted Wilde's portrait] with a parcel of songs and he has set music to them and they will be published in America for his benefit—and you shall sing them to me over the waters."
2. Wilde did not identify the *Iole* to whom he dedicated his collection. Iole in mythology was wooed unsuccessfully by Hercules; she indirectly caused his death. Frequently, as a part of his playful nature, Wilde took the pose of the scorned lover. The name *Iole* appears also in *Hesperia*, Canto I, Stanza XVII:
"And thou, sweet *Iole!* my earliest friend,
Of all beloved the loveliest and most true,
My heart, that breaks, yet knows not how to bend,
Trembles a moment as I think of you!
What teeming thoughts of fond devotion blend
As all thy charms arise to Fancy's view,

Thou sweet, calm, cold Madonna, all divine,
The Virgin of St. Luke at Padua's shrine!"
Elsewhere Wilde calls Mrs. Julia Cumming, an old friend, "Madonna" (see note, Part Two, IV, 8). The *Iole* is, therefore, probably Mrs. Cumming.

3. This poem was printed in the New York *Mirror*, XII (December 27, 1834), 206. When RHW allowed Verplanck to submit the poem, he made a condition: the date of composition (June, 1825) had to be included to show that it was an early poem (RHW to Verplanck, Dec. 12, 1834).

The New York *Mirror* has a missing line: "A vision of ethereal flame" (line 4 in stanza 10).

The story in *Arabian Nights* is generally called "The Tale of the Fisherman and the Jinni." *Sacar* is often spelled *Sakhr*.

4. This poem, printed in *Orion*, II (Jan., 1843), 127, illustrates Wilde's interest in Florence and also his favorite theme of parting.

5. This poem is discussed in detail in Part Two, Section II, of this book. The Crockett manuscript has two pages missing at the very beginning of the poem. Apparently they contained some more of the introductory sections.

6. A manuscript of this poem signed "RHW, 7 Apr. 1827," is in the autograph album of Mrs. Valeria Georgia Berrien Burroughs at the University of Georgia Library. There is another in the Library of Congress.

7. A manuscript of this poem, dated Dec. 3, 1829, is in the Library of Congress.

8. A manuscript of this poem at Duke is dated Nov., 1829. It was enclosed in an envelope addressed to Mrs. Julia Anne Bryan Cumming, who married Henry H. Cumming, the great-grandfather of Joseph Cumming of Augusta. The poem was probably written to Anne Eliza Cumming (1805-1883), a sister-in-law of Mrs. Julia A. B. Cumming. The following note precedes the poem: "Madonna Mia! Be my intercessor with St. Ann. I am taken with one of my fits of depression, and could not say 'Good bye' to her, if any thing less than Paradise—Christian or Moslem—were depending. I do not forget or love her less however—the word will not startle her pure and gentle—spirit—since it is St. John's, and as some little proof, I have found her, not without some trouble, and copied with a melancholy pleasure, the slight memorial of long by gone years—fraught with more sweet and bitter fancies, than Earth can ever reproduce—for me—"

9. An undated manuscript of this poem, written at Augusta, Georgia, exists in the autograph album of RHW's sister, Mrs. Ann Wilde Anthony.

10. A manuscript of this poem, dated Jan. 2, 1835, is in the Library of Congress.

11. This poem was printed in the *Southern Literary Messenger*, I (Nov., 1834), 99, with the following introductory note: "We do not remember where or when the following *Sonnet to Lord Byron* was published. All we know is that it has been in print before, and has been ascribed to the pen of the Hon. R. H. Wilde, of Georgia." The poem illustrates Wilde's interest in Byron; there are various references in *Hesperia* to Byron's poetry, especially *Childe Harold's Pilgrimage*.

12. Luis Vaz de Camoens (1524?-80).

13. Carlo Roncalli Parolino (1732-1811).

14. One of Wilde's first works to be published, this poem appeared in *Magnolia*, IV (Jan., 1842), 57, with the date of composition as Feb. 3, 1819, and with the following introduction: "From a Volume of Mss. Poems, by Richard Henry Wilde. On the device of a seal; Minerva taking

the bandage from the eyes of Cupid and presenting him wings, with the legend—'Se vedesse fuggirebbe.' "

15. A manuscript of this poem is in the Library of Congress.

16. A manuscript of this poem is in the Library of Congress.

17. A manuscript of this poem is owned by the Historical Society of Pennsylvania; another manuscript is in the Library of Congress.

18. This poem was printed in the Augusta *Chronicle* of Aug. 1, 1882, with the following introductory note: "From the Port Folio. The following lines belong to, the Port Folio, if they are worthy of such ownership. They were suggested by a little French Ode, entitled 'La Gloire et le Repos' and printed in that paper some years since: but the fancy of the author, who too much loves what he praises, led him to change the plan of his poem, 'til it scarcely retains a trace of the original, and has lost in beauty as much as in resemblance." There is a manuscript of the poem in the Library of Congress.

19. Niccolò di Bernardo Machiavelli (1469-1527). A manuscript of this poem is in the Library of Congress.

20. A manuscript of this poem in the Library of Congress is dated March 10, 1835.

21. Sonnet XLIII. This poem appeared in the Augusta *Chronicle*, Nov. 12, 1821, with the pseudonym *Surrey*. It was printed in the *Southern Literary Messenger*, I (Dec., 1834), 186, with RHW's name attached.

22. A manuscript of this poem, dated Mar. 3, 1828, is in the Library of Congress.

23. This poem, published in *Southern Literary Messenger*, VIII (Nov., 1842), 11, was taken from an album. The last three stanzas of it also appear in the manuscript journal of Mrs. Octavia Walton Levert (1811-1877), now in the possession of a descendant in Augusta. Freeman Walker, for whom Wilde wrote a tombstone inscription, was her uncle.

24. There is a manuscript of this poem, beginning "He who that burning eye has seen," in the Library of Congress.

25. A manuscript of this poem, with the title "To Ann," written July 23, 1830, is in the autograph album of Mrs. Ann Wilde Anthony. The work illustrates several conventions Wilde used frequently: his present sense of melancholy, his sadness because of the loss of loved ones and the joys of youth, and his longing for the grave.

26. The second stanza of this poem appeared in *Southern Literary Messenger*, I (Oct. 15, 1834), 53. The *Opal* (1844), p. 31, has the entire poem with the title "Ruth and Naomi."

27. A manuscript of this poem is in the Library of Congress.

28. This translation from the French is in an undated newspaper clipping in Anne Wilde's album, which states: "The following translation of the 128th Fable of La Fontaine is understood to have been made as long ago as 1806." The date must be erroneous. Jean de La Fontaine (1621-1695).

29. This poem dated 1823 was published in the *Southern Literary Messenger*, I (Jan., 1835), 231. With the title changed to "Twilight Reflections" and certain of the stanzas changed, it appeared in *Knickerbocker*, XIX (March, 1842), 287.

30. A manuscript of this poem, with an additional stanza, is in the Library of Congress.

31. RHW dated this poem "Florence, 4 Oct. 1836" in a letter to JWW, Oct. 15, 1836, and added that the Marquis Bocella, who offered

RHW an apartment in his villa, "was the *Platonic* lover of my fair friend the Princess Galitzin and wrote for her some years ago the Barcarola or boat song of which I send you an imitation."

32. A manuscript of this poem dated Feb. 1, 1835, is in the Library of Congress.

33. A manuscript of this poem, beginning "Oh! let us part while yet we may," is in the Library of Congress.

34. Other titles for this sonnet are "To Virginia" and "The Natural Bridge." It was printed in the *Southern Literary Messenger*, I (Dec., 1834), 187. A manuscript dated 1820 is in the *Hesperia* manuscript owned by Mrs. Crockett and another is in the manuscript owned by the Library of Congress. The poem is printed in *Hesperia*, pp. 268-269.

35. A manuscript of this poem is in the Library of Congress, dated Washington, Dec. 1, 1815. If considered autobiographical, it contrasts Dublin and Augusta.

36. A manuscript of this poem, with five additional stanzas, is in the Library of Congress.

37. Samuel Rogers (1763-1855), "Ginevra."

38. This poem, entitled "A Farewell to America," was printed in the Richmond (Virginia) *Enquirer*, June 30, 1835, with the following introductory note: "(From the National *Gazette*) The following lines by the Hon. Mr. Wilde, of Georgia, were probably not designed for publication; but, the feeling and taste which pervade them can scarcely fail to be admired, and permission has therefore been obtained of the lady to whom they were enclosed, to hand them over to you for that purpose." This printing further gives the time of composition as "Ship Westminster, at sea off the highlands of Neversink, June 1, 1835." In various other printings the poem has been called "Lines at Sea" and "At Sea." In March, 1842, RHW sent an autographed copy of the last two stanzas to Rufus Griswold, and this copy is now in the Boston Public Library. Karl Theodore Körner (1791-1813).

39. A manuscript of this poem, dated June 5, 1829, is in the Library of Congress.

40. This poem, with the title "Lines Written for Viscountess _____'s Album," was printed in the Columbus *Enquirer*, Sept. 15, 1841.

41. This poem, written to Mrs. Rebecca Tiernan Somerville (1795-1863) of Baltimore, was printed in *The Tiernan Family in Maryland* (Baltimore, 1898), pp. 63-65, with the following notation about Wilde: "He addressed a number of poems to her, and the following is one of the several, which are preserved in his own handwriting." John Pendleton Kennedy was a good friend of both Wilde and Mrs. Somerville, and it has been suggested that Edward Coote Pinkney addressed her in his poem "A Health."

42. A copy of this poem is enclosed in a letter from RHW to Carolina Stanford, Aug. 28, 1845.

43. This poem illustrating Wilde's humor was published in *Magnolia*, I (Sept., 1842), 146-147. A manuscript of the poem with many variations is in the Library of Congress. Antonio Guadagnoli (1798-1858).

44. A manuscript of this poem, dated Sept. 15, 1842, is in the Library of Congress.

45. Gemma Donati married Dante c. 1292.

46. The three stanzas of I and the third stanza of II are printed in the notes to *Hesperia*, pp. 317-318. The date of composition given is 1827. Madame de Staël (1766-1817).

V. The Italian Lyric Poets

1. The title as given by the Library of Congress is appropriate, for RHW in the preface to *The Life and Times of Dante* spoke of working on his "specimens of the Italian Lyric Poets." In a letter to Griswold, Feb. 6, 1843, RHW called it "Italian Lyrics." RHW also called it *Specimens of Italian Lyric Poetry* (to JWW, Aug. 11, 1837) and *Specimens of Italian Poetry* (to Greene, Nov. 4, 1837).

2. Theodore Koch, *Dante in America* (Boston, 1896), pp. 23-36.

3. New York *Times Book Magazine*, Feb. 13, 1921.

4. William Alexander Percy wrote a long poem entitled "Enzio's Kingdom" about this same historical figure.

5. RHW added the following note to this translation: "The terzets of the translation have been formed on the model of the original; that is to say the first line rhymes with the sixth, the second with the fifth, and the third with the fourth. This has been done with a view of exhibiting another of the legitimate varieties of the sonnet; but it may well be doubted whether terzets so constructed are at all adapted to English poetry; the rhyme for the most part is so long in recurring that the ear loses it."

6. This poem was published, with a slight rearrangement, in *Orion*, I (Mar., 1842), 24-25. A title added is "He reproves Florence with patriotic anger."

7. This poem was published, with slight editorial changes, in Koch, *Dante in America*, p. 25.

8. RHW wrote the following note to line 13: "'The Alps' was a term frequently used by the ancient Italian authors to designate any mountains covered with snow; and hence after applied to the Appenines."

9. This poem was published, with slight editorial changes, in Koch, *Dante in America*, p. 25.

10. RHW wrote the following note: "This is one of the sonnets written on the occasion of his mistress's annual visits to Baiae which . . . gave him uneasiness and jealousy. . . . In the original of the sonnet . . . the easy and natural flow of thought—the perfect truth in all the feelings and circumstances it embodies, from his hatred of the season to his involuntary and commanded absence, cannot be mistaken. The scene—the time—the man and his emotions all rise before us."

11. The poem and the Italian were published in *Magnolia*, new series II (Mar., 1843), 153.

12. The first part is a translation of "La notte, che tu vedi in si dolci alti."

13. The first line of the Italian is often written: "Dal ciel discese, e col mortal suo, poi." Longfellow's poem on Dante beginning "What should be said of him cannot be said" is a translation of an entirely different poem beginning "Quanto dirne si de'non si può dire."

14. The translations from Tasso and Guarini were printed in *Conjectures and Researches Concerning the Love, Madness, and Imprisonment of Torquato Tasso* (1842).

15. The title given in *Conjectures* is "To His Lady, the Spouse of Another."

16. The title given in *Conjectures* is "To the Duchess of Ferrara, Who Appeared Masked at a Fête."

17. The title given in *Conjectures* is "On Two Beautiful Ladies, One Gay and One Sad."

18. The title given in *Conjectures* is "To Lamberto, Against a Calumny."

19. The title given in *Conjectures* is "Al Signor Scipio Gonzaga, Sulla Sua Prigionia."

20. The manuscript has nine lines at the end which are not in the translation in *Conjectures*, and the second stanza in *Conjectures* is the third stanza in the manuscript.

21. RHW's note to the poem is as follows: "From the Falconieri MSS now in the possession of Count Alberti."

22. The title given in *Conjectures* is "To the Countess of Scandia."

23. The title given in *Conjectures* is "He Compares Himself to Ulysses."

24. The note to the poem by RHW states: "From the Falconieri MSS."

25. RHW's note to the poem is as follows: "From the Falconieri MSS first published by Rosini in his essay on the loves of Tasso." RHW's lack of accuracy can be seen in the first line. The translation of *Tormi potrei* is "I could deprive myself of life." "You . . . , mighty Lord" is *Tormi potrete*.

26. A rough draft of this poem beginning "Oh Sleep! quiet child of calm cool shadowy Night" in the Library of Congress is dated Mar. 28, 1833.

27. This dialogue, composed at Newport, Rhode Island, on Aug. 29, 1834, appeared in the *Southern Literary Messenger*, I (Feb., 1835), 318.

28. There are two manuscripts of this poem in the Library of Congress, one of them being dated Apr. 1, 1830.

29. There are two manuscripts of this poem in the Library of Congress, one of them being dated Mar. 27, 1833.

30. There are two manuscripts of this poem in the Library of Congress, one of them being dated Mar. 30, 1830.

31. There are two manuscripts of this poem in the Library of Congress, one of them being dated "R. Va. October 11, 1829."

32. A note by RHW states that *Nice* is "the abbreviation of Berenice."

33. This poem, copied from the wall of Petrarch's study, was translated in Florence, on Oct. 19, 1836.

34. This poem was printed in *Magnolia*, new series II (Feb., 1843), 117. RHW wrote a long note to the poem: "A sufficiently romantic origin is assigned to the stanzas here translated. According to the story, a young Bolognese was for a long time scorned and ill-treated by the object of his affections. His health sunk under the violence of his passion, the cruelty of his idol, long vigils and continual study. At length, one day in a moment of caprice or of weakness, moved by pity or overcome by importunity, she so far relaxed her rigor as to indulge him with a kiss and an embrace. He snatched at the moment some flowers from her bosom the fleeting momorials of his transient felicity. Joy however, only hastened the crisis that love, and grief had prepared. He had scarcely reached his chamber when the intensity of his emotions caused the rupture of a blood vessel, and before the morrow they told him, his hours were numbered. He took his cherished flowers, not yet quite faded, wrote the foregoing original lines, and expired directly afterwards. Copies are in circulation with several additional verses but besides being too numerous for the occasion, they are so inferior in spirit, simplicity, and nature, as to diminish the apparent truth and deep pathos of the others. In short they are diffuse and a dying man is apt to be laconic."

35. This poem was printed in *Graham's* XXII (Apr., 1843), 235. When it was reprinted in the New York *Daily Tribune*, it was called "Love Song—from the Italian."

VI. OTHER POEMS

1. The Library of Congress manuscript, used here, is dated Oct. 5, 1829. Another copy is in the autograph album of Mrs. Ann Wilde Anthony. The poem was published in the Boston *Museum,* Oct. 12, 1850 (from the New York *Mirror*).

2. This poem, dated "Florence, February 15th, 1837," was printed in *Magnolia,* III (Feb., 1841), 95, which is the version used here. A manuscript copy is at Duke.

3. This sonnet was composed in New Orleans on March 29, 1846, by RHW and sent to his friend, John Kenyon. Kenyon in turn presented it to his second cousin, Elizabeth Barrett Barrett. She referred to it twice in her letters to Robert Browning, and in one letter called it "trash," saying of it: "The sonnet was purely manuscript, and for the good of the world should remain so." Eventually the sonnet came into the possession of Robert Browning, who was interested in Elizabeth Barrett's transatlantic fame and who had reviewed RHW's work on Tasso. In 1940 the sonnet was sold by Henry Sotheran, Ltd., in a group of letters to Browning.

The source of the above information and the poem is Louise Greer, "Richard Henry Wilde to Elizabeth Barrett Barrett: an Unpublished Sonnet" in *English Studies in Honor of James Southall Wilson* (Charlottesville, Va., 1951), pp. 73-79, ed. Fredson Bowers. The manuscript is on deposit in the University of Virginia Library.

4. No manuscript copy of this translation is available. Horatio Greenough, the sculptor, and RHW, who were warm friends, made the translations of an epitaph beginning "Qui giace un Cardinale." They were printed in the *Literary World,* XIII (Sept. 3, 1853), 90-91, in an essay by "Friar Lubin" (i.e., John Bigelow) entitled "The Sculptor Greenough." This essay was reprinted from the New York *Evening Post.* Greenough's translation is as follows:

"Here lies a cardinal who wrought
  Both good and evil in his time,
  The good he did was good for naught;
  Not so the evil: that was prime."

5. This translation, for which a manuscript copy is not available, appeared in *Knickerbocker,* XVII (Mar., 1841), 258. The "Editor's Table," in humorous tones, stated that RHW had returned from Europe after a long absence with trunks the contents of which were unknown. During a fire in the neighborhood where they were stored, it was found that they contained "miscellaneous papers, labelled, it would seem, with the names of their former owners, such as Dante or Durante Alleghieri, Francisco Petrarca, Torquato Tasso, Ludovico Ariosto, Victor Alfieri, and others, all believed to be foreigners, since none of them were known by any of our most vigilant police men. As nobody has appeared, to claim the goods, it is thought the theft, if they were stolen, may have been committed in Europe, and the effects brought to this counrty to escape detection." In order that the owners might identify the papers, one poem by Meléndez Valdés was left at the office of the *Knickerbocker.*

6. The manuscript of this undated poem is in the Library of Congress. The poem illustrates the fascination of Chatterton for other poets.

7. The manuscript of this poem, written Jan. 5, 1835, is in the Henry E. Huntington Library. RHW wrote of the work: "The first stanza was suggested by the beautiful passage of Dante commencing 'Era gia l'ore &c' *Purgatorio* C VIII, the second by an account I have somewhere seen of the death of Rousseau."

8. The manuscript of this poem is in the Library of Congress. Written in 1807, it is one of the two earliest poems that definitely can be dated.

9. The sculptor Horatio Greenough, who lived in Florence, Italy, became one of RHW's close friends. RHW wrote this poem about Greenough's statue of Washington, which originally was commissioned for the Rotunda of the Capitol by the United States Congress in 1832. RHW dated the poem as "Florence March 1839." Greenough wrote RHW on Mar. 6, 1839, that he appreciated "the beauty and pregnant meaning" of the lines and "the feeling which dictated them." He also liked the sound of "a voice that stirs my blood like the sound of a trumpet and that by assuring me I have not labored all in vain, bids me hope for a fair result to my future toils."

The manuscript of the poem is in an album of Mrs. Greenough's owned by Mr. David Richardson of Washington, D. C. The source for all the information in this note and the poem itself is Nathalia Wright, "Richard Henry Wilde on Greenough's Washington," *American Literature,* XXVII (Jan., 1956), 556-557.

10. The manuscript of this translation is in the Library of Congress. Dated Sept. 26, 1842, it is probably one of RHW's last translations.

11. The manuscript of this poem, dated 1807, is in the Library of Congress.

12. The version used here was printed in the Richmond (Virginia) *Enquirer,* Oct. 25, 1836, with the following introductory note: "The following incomparable lines we preserve from an early number of the New Monthly Magazine, when under Campbell's superintendence. The editor professed himself ignorant of their authorship, which he surmised had a transatlantic origin: what American will dare claim them?—*Ed. Lou. Adv.*" The poem was not signed. One manuscript of the poem is owned by the Historical Society of Pennslyvania Library, another by the Library of Congress in its *Hesperia* notes, and a third by Mrs. Crockett in the *Hesperia* manuscript. The poem was printed in *Hesperia,* pp. 235-236.

Additional Poems by Wilde

The poems listed below are not included in this book. The following information (if available) is given about each poem: the first line, the title. the number of lines in the poem, the date and location of the manuscript. and the first record of publication. LC is the Library of Congress; VGC is Mrs. Virginia Giraud Crockett.

"After a thousand years" (AFTER A THOUSAND YEARS); 70 lines: mss., 1846, Mrs. Kathleen Wilde Viscarra and Duke; pub. *Banner of the South*, Vol. II (Dec. 18, 1869).

"Alas the thirst of Power and alas"; 16 lines; ms., 1829, LC.

"All hail, thou mightiest, monstrous Power!" (OCEAN. A NAVAL ODE); 271 lines; pub. *Port Folio*, II (Nov., 1813), 541. The Augusta *Chronicle*, Apr. 21, 1819, called this a "prize poem."

"And art thou gone ungrateful maid" (TO _____); 12 lines; ms., LC.

"And thou my friend—since unavailing woe"; with the obituary for James Wilde; 18 lines; ms., VGC.

"As evening's dews to sun-parched summer flowers" (THE POET'S LAMENT); 28 lines; pub. *Louisiana Book* (New Orleans, 1894), 492. (A re-arrangement of certain lines from *Hesperia*, Canto IV, Stanzas CVII-CXIII).

"At length the long long horrid night has past"; 4 lines; ms., LC.

"Beauteous and sincere thou art" (FROM THE ITALIAN OF BARTOLI); 8 lines; ms., 1821, Mrs. Kathleen Wilde Viscarra.

"Beneath thy friendly roof dear F_____w" (EPISTLE III TO I. A. F., ESQR.); 126 lines; two mss., one dated 1809, LC. Addressed to Ignatius Alphonso Few (1789-1845).

"Blessings be on thee!—multiplied and more"; 16 lines; ms., LC.

"Bright be the morning's dawn on you Boy!" (TO MY SON JOHN ON HIS BIRTH-DAY); 16 lines; ms., RHW to JWW, Sept. 24, 1837; VGC.

"Can I refuse when ladies fair demand"; 4 lines; pub. *Southern Literary Messenger*, VIII (Nov., 1842), 11.

"Closed are the labours of the day!—tis night"; 16 lines; ms., 1828, LC.

"Come! Come to us J. . . . ! thou art weary and worn" (EPISTLE I TO J. C. ESQR.); 24 lines; ms., LC. Addressed to John Cormick (died 1826).

"Dear Erato farewell! we shall wander no more" (TO MY MUSE); 38 lines; ms., LC.

"Dear George, tho' no more in the morn of our youth" (EPISTLE IV TO G.W.C. ESQR.); 52 lines; ms., LC.

"Dear scroll! which breathes the soul of love" (TO A BILLET); 17 lines; ms., 1828, LC.

"Forgive and pity me! no mortal on earth"; 32 lines; ms., 1834, LC.

"From love, from joy and friendship far" (TO THE EVENING STAR); 32 lines; ms., LC.

"Give me that faded rose sweet girl!" (TO _____); 28 lines; ms., LC.

"Go! blessings be with thee! tis time we should part" (TO MRS _____); 28 lines; ms., LC.

"Go! then, and since it costs thy heart" (TO _____); 36 lines; ms., LC.

"Good Law me! what's this? 'An Album.' oh! how queer!" (AN ALBUM); 40 lines; ms., LC.

"Here Lies! (no brazen colum marks the spot)" (A BRACE OF EPITAPHS); 8 lines; ms., LC.

"His life was but an humble stream" (LINES ON THE AU-THOR); 28 lines; two mss., one dated "1810 or 11," LC.

"How cold how weak the story marble tells"; 10 lines; ms., LC.

"How dared my name be seen upon such pages" (MRS. BUSS-ES'S ALBUM); 6 lines; ms., LC.

"How long the hours of absence seem"; 20 lines; ms., 1830, LC.

"*I* make you wicked!—no indeed!" (EPIGRAM TO A LADY WHO TOLD ME I ALWAYS MADE HER WICKED); 4 lines; ms., RHW to JWW, Sept. 28, 1832; VGC.

"I see thee sought caressed admired of all"; 12 lines; ms., 1828, LC.

"If fate by whose command we sever"; 8 lines; ms., LC.

"If I've profaned thy vestal shrine" (TO _____); 16 lines; ms., LC.

"I'm single—double—chips—a spell" (A RIDDLE); 16 lines; ms., University of Georgia.

"Image of Her! the lovely—the unnamed"; 20 lines; ms., 1830, LC.

"In a lone wood, one sultry day" (TO ....); 36 lines; ms., LC.

"In early youth I own tis true" (THE PICTURE OR INCONSTANCY EXCUSED); 56 lines; ms., LC.

"In Heaven Hell and Earth" (A RIDDLE); 24 lines; ms., LC.

"In thy life's spring—so sweet so gay" (TO MARIA); 12 lines; ms., 1827, LC.

"It is Herself—save motion in the eyes" (ON A PORTRAIT); 14 lines; ms., 1833, LC.

"It was Capponi's palace—an old name" (PALAZZO CAPPONI); 88 lines; ms., RHW to Mrs. Isabella M. Pleasants, Dec. 24, 1835; VGC.

"Italia mia! benchè de'tuoi non nato" (MY ITALY); 14 lines; ms., LC; pub. *Hesperia* (1867), 311-312.

"A leaf that glows and breathes like thee"; 32 lines; ms., 1817, LC.

"Memory to Love in absence taught the art"; 6 lines; ms., LC.

"My joys depart" (WRITTEN IN THE DIARY OF AN ENNUYÉE); 15 lines; ms., University of Georgia.

"My task of life is almost ended—thine"; 16 lines; ms., LC.

"Need I remind thee how we met?"; 16 lines; ms., 1828, LC.

"Need I to tell with rhyming art" (EPISTLE II TO JWW ESQR); 118 lines; ms., LC.

"No vain remorse for fancied guilt"; 16 lines; ms., 1828, LC.

"O had I met thee not too late"; 20 lines; ms., LC.

"O! heard ye the war-note that summoned us all" (WAR-SONG); 40 lines; ms., LC.

"O were I in my woodland home"; 20 lines; ms., 1833, LC.

"Of life's enchanted cup he did but sip" (CONSECRATED TO THE MEMORY OF WILLIAM DAVIS BERRIEN); 4 lines; ms., VGC.

"Oh no! I never could love—"; 12 or 15 lines; ms., LC.

"On his high throne King William sate"; 8 lines; ms., LC.

"Since first we met and parted gloomy years"; 16 lines; ms., 1828, LC.

"Since first we met the world can claim"; 16 lines; ms., 1828, LC.

"Spirits of the illustrious dead"; 12 lines; ms., LC.

"St. Mary at thy shrine I bow"; 24 lines; ms., 1833, LC.

"This is your birth day Will! . . . tho' on the sea" (TO WILL); 16 lines; ms., June 6, 1835; VGC.

"Tho far away my footsteps roam" (TO ....); 20 lines; ms., LC.

"Tis a pity I've said to myself with a sigh"; 12 lines; ms., LC.

"'Tis Night! . . . the lovely night of cloudless climes" (TO

SAINT AUGUSTINE); 14 lines; ms., 1829, LC; pub. *Hesperia*, 243-244.

"To curse the present to lament the past"; 8 lines; ms., 1828, LC.

"Upon my life's most marked, eventful day"; 16 lines; ms., 1835, LC.

"Valeria! if a friend, more gray than sage"; 8 lines; ms., 1827, University of Georgia.

"What a Highway-man-woman to stop and demand"; 4 lines; ms., RHW to JWW, Mar. 7, 1842, VGC.

"What wonder if thy pulses thrill"; 20 lines; ms., 1828, LC.

"When all that you cherished and prized and carest" (TO –––––––); 24 lines; ms., LC.

"When Charles ruled the British isles"; 20 lines; ms., LC; pub. Ralph Graber, "New Light on the Dedication of Richard Henry Wilde's *Hesperia*," *Georgia Historical Quarterly*, XLIV (Mar., 1960), 97-99.

"When life & love & hope were young" (TO ANN); 28 lines; ms., 1827, LC.

"When we long have been used to the glance and the sigh"; 8 lines; ms., LC.

"Whene'er I see those smiling eyes" (LINES); 16 lines; pub. Milledgeville, Georgia, *Journal*, Mar. 14, 1820.

"Who sees thee tho' but once, must hope, or fear"; 16 lines; ms., LC.

"Why should the bower where Love and Joy" (TO A LADY'S WATCH. WORN IN HER BOSOM); 8 lines; ms., 1811 or 1812, LC.

"Words are exhausted—fainting utterance sinks"; 16 lines; ms., 1828, LC.

"Years ages—an eternity of bliss"; 16 lines; ms., 1829, LC.

"You may say what you please there's a charm to names"; 12 lines; ms., LC.

"You say you're Wicked—yet your eyes"; 12 lines; ms., RHW to JWW, Aug. 25, 1830, VGC.

Selected Bibliography

LETTERS

The manuscript letters cited in this volume are owned by the following:

Boston Public Library: to Griswold, Feb. 6, 1843, and Mar. 7, 1845.

Duke: to ? , Nov. 24, 1814; to Mary Pasley, Mar. 27, 1816; to CAW and Ann Wilde, Dec. 1, 1828; to John Nicholson, May 5, 1843; J. M. Berrien to RHW, Dec. 10, 1826; J. H. Hammond to RHW, Dec. 17, 1843; J. L. Petigru to RHW, Dec. 20, 1843; P. H. Hayne to C. C. Jones, Sept. 29, 1885; J. G. Whittier to Jones, Nov. 10, 1885.

Harvard: to A. W. McGill, Jan. 8, 1818; to Sumner, Sept. 15 and Nov. 24, 1839, and Aug. 4, 1841; Longfellow to G. W. Greene, Jan. 6. 1838; WCW to Sumner, May 11, 1852; Edward Everett to WCW, June 3, 1852; Horace Binney to WCW, June 11, 1852.

Huntington: to Francis Lieber, 1847; Forsyth to RHW, Apr. 21, 1819.

Historical Society of Pennsylvania: to Bank of U. S., May 18, 1818; to Simms, Dec. 21, 1844; George Cary to RHW, Nov. 27, 1831.

New York Historical Society: all the letters to G. C. Verplanck.

New York Public Library: to JWW, Apr. 19, 1816; to Simms, Nov. 1 and Dec. 4, 1852; JPW to Simms, Mar. 20 and Apr. 4, 1855.

New York State Library: to Harmanus Bleecker, Oct. 19, 1840; Bleecker to RHW, Mar. 8, 1841.

University of Georgia: to JWW, Apr. 26, 1816; to Governor of Georgia, Oct. 23, 1836; to William Mann, Mar. 31, 1840.

University of North Carolina: to J. M. Berrien, c. Feb., and May 22, 1827.

Miss Nannie Rice: to Maria Hopkins Walker, c. Mar., 1846, and Apr. 9, 1847.

A. H. Starke: to JWW, Apr. 18, 1816; to John Patterson, May 22, 1827; Sumner to RHW, July 28, 1841.

Miss Nathalia Wright: all the letters to Hiram and Mrs. Powers. See Nathalia Wright, ed., "The Letters of Richard Henry Wilde to Hiram Powers," *Georgia Historical Quarterly*, XLVI (Sept. and Dec., 1962), 296-316, 417-437.

Mrs. Virginia G. Crockett: all the other manuscript letters mentioned in this work.

PROSE WORKS BY WILDE

A. Long Prose Works

Conjectures and Researches Concerning the Love, Madness and Imprisonment of Torquato Tasso. New York, 1842. Two volumes.

Life and Times of Dante, with Sketches of the State of Florence, and of his Friends and Enemies. Unpublished manuscript in the Library of Congress.

Biographical introductions to the poets in *The Italian Lyric Poets.* Unpublished manuscript in the Library of Congress.

B. Some Speeches

Substance of the Arguments on the Unconstitutionality of the Alleviating Act. Augusta, 1814.

Speech in the criminal case of Calvin, Jones, and Howel. Augusta *Chronicle*, Apr. 1, 1822.

Speech delivered July 4 on the 50th anniversary of the Declaration of Independence. Augusta *Chronicle*, July 8, 1826.

Speeches of Mr. Wilde, of Georgia, on Internal Improvements. Washington, 1828.

Speech of Mr. Wilde, of Georgia, on the Bill for Removing the Indians from the East to the West Side of the Mississippi. Washington, 1830.

Substance of an Argument in the Supreme Court of the United States in the cases of Colin Mitchell and F. M. Arredondo. By Joseph M. White and Richard Henry Wilde. Washington, 1831.

Speech of Mr. Wilde, of Georgia, on the Currency. Washington, 1832.

Speech of Mr. Wilde, of Georgia, on the Bill to Alter and Amend the Several Acts Imposing Duties on Imports. Washington, 1832.

Speech at a Columbia dinner in honor of those Georgia delegates who voted against the Force Bill. Augusta *Chronicle*, Oct. 12, 1833.

Speech of Mr. Wilde, on the Reasons of the Secretary of the

[289]

Treasury for the Removal of the Deposites. Washington, 1834.

Speech at the Whig Convention at Milledgeville nominating Henry Clay. Augusta *Chronicle*, June 23, 1842.

Most of the above speeches are printed also in the *Debates and Proceedings in the Congress of the United States* (Washington: Gales and Seaton). In addition, that series, especially for the years 1828-1835, has a number of other speeches and remarks made by Wilde in the House of Representatives.

C. OTHER PROSE WORKS

"The Involuntary Story Teller," *Magnolia*, new series II (May, 1843), 320-326.

"Narrator" essays written when about sixteen years old with George Cary. RHW to Griswold, Mar. 7, 1845.

"Review of Campbell's *Life of Petrarch*," *Southern Quarterly Review,* 1843. This is a portion of his essay on Petrarch in *The Italian Lyric Poets.*

State Banks, Abstracts, Returns and Estimate of the Condition of the Several State Banks. Washington, 1834. Wilde collected material for this work.

Freeman Walker epitaph in L. L. Knight, *Georgia Landmarks, Memorials and Legends* (Atlanta, 1913), 998.

"Wilde, John W." Biographical sketch. The manuscript is in the Boston Public Library.

"John W. Walker" in Alfred J. Pickett, *A History of Alabama, and Incidentally of Georgia and Mississippi from the Earliest Period* (Charleston, 1851), II, 402-406.

J. G. Schwarz to RHW, Feb. 5, 1837: RHW wrote a "short and able" report "as to the condition of the Catholics in Georgia."

PORTRAITS OF WILDE

A portrait by Cook made a few months before the death of Wilde is mentioned by JPW in a letter to Stephen Miller, *Bench and Bar*, II, 342-343. RHW to JWW, Apr. 22, 1844: Cook was getting up "a Southern Gallery of Painting."

A bust of Wilde by Greenough is mentioned in a letter from Mrs. Greenough to Hiram Powers, Apr. 4, 1863 or 1864. This is apparently the same bust referred to in Frances Appleton's journal, May 15, 1836. RHW to JWW, Nov. 5, 1835: "Today is one of the days I shall meet him [Greenough], & I'll make him set about my bust forth with for fear of my recall." Greenough to RHW, c. Sept. 1840: "I hope to soon find time to call on you to arrange with you about your portrait."

[290]

J. Eastman Johnson's crayon portrait of Wilde, reproduced as an engraving by J. Sartain in Griswold, *Prose Writers of America* (1847), opposite p. 258. Wilde stated in a letter to Rufus Griswold, Mar. 7, 1845: "No good portrait has ever been taken of me if I may believe others. I find that in crayons by a young artist J. E. Johnson now in Philadelphia, who has it with him, very exact."

Portrait by Cavalier Ernesto Liverati. Frances Appleton's journal, May 23, 1836: "Liverati the painter we found fortunately at home. . . . The picture of Mr. Wilde is doleful—looks as sick as a cat a very painful expression." RHW to his sons, Jan. 21, 1837: "Liverati's picture of me has been lithographed, that is engraved on stone, & I have the first copy as a keepsake."

Painting made in 1819 by Mr. Parker of New York. Presented by Mrs. Emily P. White to the Augusta Public Library.

Powers' bas relief portrait of Wilde. In *Appleton's Encyclopedia of American Biography* (New York, 1900), VI, 505.

Painting by Miss Clara Wilde made just after Wilde's return from Europe. Presented by Mrs. Emily P. Wilde to the Augusta Public Library.

Portrait by an unknown artist. Augusta Museum.

Portrait by an unknown artist. Mrs. Virginia G. Crockett.

SELECTED LIST
Works Containing Information on Wilde

Barclay, Anthony. *Wilde's Summer Rose: or the Lament of the Captive. An authentic account of the origin, mystery, and explanation of Hon. R. H. Wilde's alleged plagiarism.* Savannah, 1871.

Baxter, Edgeworth B. *Address Delivered November 17, 1898, upon the Presentation to the City of Augusta of the Monument erected by the Hayne Circle to the Memory of Richard Henry Wilde.* Augusta, 1898.

Beall, Chandler B. "Un Tassista Americano di Cent'Anni Fa, R. H. Wilde," *Bergamum*, XVII (July, 1939), 91-99. This was reprinted as *Un Italofilo Americano* (Bergamo, Italy, 1939), some of Wilde's translations being added.

Duyckinck, Evert A. and George L. *Cyclopedia of American Literature.* New York, 1856. II, 106-108.

Graber, Ralph S. *The Fugitive Poems of Richard Henry Wilde with an Introduction.* University of Pennsylvania dissertation, 1959.

Graber, Ralph S. "New Light on the Dedication of Richard

Henry Wilde's *Hesperia*," *Georgia Historical Quarterly*, XLIV (March, 1960), 97-99. Professor Graber agrees, on the basis of a poem in the LC, that the Marchesa is Mrs. Ellen White-Beatty.

Greer, Louise. "Richard Henry Wilde to Elizabeth Barrett Barrett: An Unpublished Sonnet," in *English Studies in Honor of James Southall Wilson*, edited by Fredson Bowers. Charlottesville, 1951.

Griswold, Rufus Wilmot. *The Poets and Poetry of America*. Philadelphia, 1842. Pp. 75-79; has a biographical sketch and the following poems: "Ode to Ease," "Solomon and the Genius," "A Farewell to America," "Napoleon's Grave," "Stanzas," "To Lord Byron," and "To the Mocking-Bird."

Griswold, Rufus Wilmot. *The Prose Writers of America*. Philadelphia, 1847. Pp. 258-262; has the following items: a biographical sketch, a portrait drawn by J. E. Johnson and engraved by J. Sartain; a portion of Wilde's speech on the tariff entitled "Stars of the XIV Congress"; and a portion of his work on Petrarch.

Irving, Washington. "American Researches in Italy; Life of Tasso; Recovery of a Lost Portrait of Dante," *Knickerbocker*, XVIII (Oct., 1841), 319-322.

Jones, Charles C., Jr. *The Life, Literary Labors and Neglected Grave of Richard Henry Wilde*. Augusta, c. 1885. A reprint from the Augusta *Chronicle*, Sept. 27, 1885. Duke has Jones's copy of the work plus letters sent to Jones commenting on the book and on Wilde.

Jones, Charles C., Jr., and Salem Dutcher. *Memorial History of Augusta, Georgia*. Syracuse, New York, 1890. Pp. 235-238, 250, 291.

Kettell, Samuel, ed. *Specimens of American Poetry*. Boston, 1829. III, 363-365; has earliest printing, up to now discovered, of certain portions of the "Epic Fragments."

Koch, Theodore W. *Dante in America*. Boston, 1896. Pp. 23-36; has an account of Wilde's Italian studies, a discussion of the fresco of Dante, portions from the preface to the *Life and Times of Dante*, and two translations, one from a poem by Boccaccio and one from a poem by Dante.

(Longfellow), Frances Appleton. *Journal*. Manuscript in Craigie House, Cambridge. I, 72—II, 49, *passim*.

Longfellow, Henry Wadsworth. *The Poets and Poetry of Europe*. New York, 1857. This book contains seventeen of the translations from Tasso.

The Louisiana Book. Edited by Thomas McCaleb. New Orleans,

1894. Pp. 244-245; has a brief sketch of Wilde and his essay on "Petrarch and Laura." Pp. 491-493; has "The Lament of the Captive," "To the Mocking-Bird," and "The Poet's Lament."

Lyell, Sir Charles. *A Second Visit to the United States of North America*. London, 1850. II, 121-129, 165.

Miller, Stephen F. *The Bench and Bar of Georgia*. Philadelphia, 1858. II, 342-368.

Parks, Edd W. "Richard Henry Wilde on the Making of Poetry," *Tennessee Studies in Literature*, III (1958), 73-81. Reprinted in Parks, *Ante-Bellum Southern Literary Critics* (Athens, 1962).

Sketch of the Life of Richard Henry Wilde. Prepared at the request of Congress for use in revising the biographies of Congressmen. Prepared by Miss Martha Wilde Pournelle, Principal, Davidson School, Augusta.

Starke, Aubrey H. "The Dedication of Richard Henry Wilde's *Hesperia*," *American Book Collector*, VI (May and June, 1935), 204-209.

Starke, Aubrey H. "Richard Henry Wilde in New Orleans and the Establishment of the University of Louisiana," *Louisiana Historical Quarterly*, XVII (October, 1934), 605-624.

Starke, Aubrey H. "Richard Henry Wilde: Some Notes and a Check-List," *American Book Collector*, IV (November, 1933), 226-232; IV (December, 1933), 285-288; and V (January, 1934), 7-10.

Wright, Nathalia. "The Death of Richard Henry Wilde: A Letter," *Georgia Historical Quarterly*, XLI (December, 1957), 431-434.

Wright, Nathalia. "The Italian Son of Richard Henry Wilde," *Georgia Historical Quarterly*, XLIII (December, 1959), 419-427.

Wright, Nathalia. "Richard Henry Wilde on Greenough's Washington," *American Literature*, XXVII (January, 1956), 556-557.

Wright, Nathalia. "Richard Henry Wilde's Italian Order of Nobility," *Georgia Historical Quarterly*, XLIII (June, 1959), 211-213.

[293]

Index

[294]

[295]

Index